Moral Realities

An essay in philosophical psychology

Mark de Bretton Platts

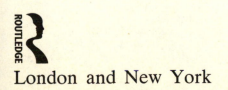

London and New York

First published 1991
by Routledge
11 New Fetter Lane, London EC4P 4EE

Simultaneously published in the USA and Canada
by Routledge
a division of Routledge, Chapman and Hall, Inc.
29 West 35th Street, New York, NY 10001

© 1991 Mark de Bretton Platts

Typeset in 10/12 pt Times by
Input Typesetting Ltd, London
Printed in Great Britain by
T.J. Press (Padstow) Ltd, Padstow, Cornwall

British Library Cataloguing in Publication Data
De Bretton Platts, Mark
  Moral realities: an essay in philosophical psychology.
  1. Philosophical psychology
  I. Title
  128.2

Library of Congress Cataloging in Publication Data
Platts, Mark de Bretton
    Moral realities : an essay in philosophical psychology / Mark de
  Bretton Platts
      p. cm.
    Includes bibliographical references and index.
    1. Ethics. 2. Desire (Philosophy) 3. Values. I. Title.
  BJ1012.P633 1991
  170—dc20   90–44550

  ISBN 0–415–05892–9

To the memory of Juan Manuel Romo Santos

Contents

Preface

Thomas Love Peacock reported an old friend's opinion that to publish a book without a preface is like entering a drawing-room without making a bow; Michael Dummett thinks that finding a book to have no preface is like arriving at someone's house for dinner and being conducted straight into the dining-room. So this is my brief bow along with an invitation to the reader to help himself to a (stiff) drink (the dinner may prove indigestible).

In writing this essay I have drawn upon various publications of mine (although in every case I have either developed or modified the views there expressed). I am therefore grateful to the editors and publishers concerned for permission to include material from the following articles:

1 'La moralidad, la personalidad, y el sentido de la vida', *Diálogos* 117, 1984.
2 'The object of desire', *Crítica* XVII, 1985.
3 'Desire and action', *Noûs* XX, 1986.
4 'Hume and morality as a matter of fact', *Mind* XCVII, 1988.
5 '¿Tiene algún porvenir la filosofía moral?', *Revista Latinoamericana de Filosofía* XIV, 1988.
6 'Introducción' and 'Hume: La moralidad y la acción', in Mark Platts (ed.), *La Ética A Través De Su Historia*, Mexico 1988.
7 'The metaphysics of morals', forthcoming in a volume on the philosophy of P. F. Strawson to be edited by Roop Rekha Verma and Pranab Kumar Sen for the Indian Council of Philosophical Research.

I am also greatly indebted to Martha Sasía for the patience and skill with which she converted an illegible, but presumably English, draft into a legible typescript, and to Mexico's Sistema Nacional de Investigadores for support that has made it possible for me to stay in this country. But my most substantial debts are to John McDowell and to Paul Snowdon for their comments upon the penultimate version of this essay: they have stopped me from saying many mistaken things which I would otherwise have said here and have made many helpful suggestions for improvements.

As with my first book – once pleasingly enough referred to in print in Mexico as *Waste of Meaning* – I consider the ideas of others only to the extent to which that consideration helps with the understanding of the ideas preferred here. I should have liked to echo Collingwood's thought that others are mentioned here only *honoris causa*, but that might have been thought to add injury to insult. So I have tried to keep such references to a minimum. (I had even thought of including a second bibliography of works which though not referred to in the main text have, I am sure, influenced me; but the risk of sinning by *double* omission made me drop the idea.) Doubtless the reader will recognize certain unmentioned influences; I just hope nobody feels offended.

A quite distinct kind of omission is any consideration of 'first-order' moral questions, of 'practical ethics'. Since it is just possible that that will be a disappointment to some, I should perhaps say at this point that they should rather count themselves lucky. My view of the world is a bleak one, and my opinion of the efficacy of discussion of 'first-order' matters somewhat far from optimistic; where human beings are concerned my natural tendency is to assume that the light at the end of the tunnel is an oncoming train. Still, I happily recognize that I have been privileged: I came to know someone who quite unconsciously opened others' eyes to the seemingly small things of value in this world and so made their journey through it something to be lived and shared, not just endured – and certainly not rejected through meaningless, muddled ideas. He was neither famous nor a saint: but all who knew him had their lives immeasurably enriched. This book is for him.

M. de B. P.
Instituto de Investigaciones Filosóficas,
Universidad Nacional Autónoma de México,
México, DF

Introduction

> Sir, if I fall into a river, an unsophisticated man will jump in and
> bring me out; but a philosopher will look on with the utmost
> calmness, and consider me in the light of a projectile, and, making
> a calculation of the degree of force with which I have impinged
> the surface, the resistance of the fluid, the velocity of the current,
> and the depth of the water in that particular place, he will
> ascertain with the greatest nicety in what part of the mud at the
> bottom I may probably be found, at any given distance of time
> from the moment of my first immersion.
>
> (Thomas Love Peacock)

Karl Kraus held morality to be a venereal disease, its primary phase
being virtue, its secondary boredom and its final phase syphilis.
Little thought is needed to realize that Kraus was thinking of the
prevailing orthodoxies as to 'sexual morality' in his time and place
and also of the hypocrisy involved in their very status as orthodoxies.
It is also clear that he was providing a fiercely *moral* criticism of the
content of those orthodoxies and of that hypocrisy. Nor is there
much difficulty involved in finding examples of more wide-ranging
yet still moral criticisms of moral orthodoxies within specific cultures
or societies. Indeed, it is even relatively easy to identify cases of
criticisms of morality in its totality, of *all* moralities, grounded upon
certain non-moral values subscribed to by the critics. The theme of
the defectiveness of morality seems always to have been its near
companion. And so it would in itself scarcely be surprising to come
across now the suggestion that morality is in a state of grave disorder,
is in a mess.

Nor need it be surprising if that suggestion is found to be
accompanied by another: namely, that the *philosophy* of morality is
in a mess too. Suppose that morality is, in some way or other,

radically and irreparably defective. Suppose further that, having realized that, we come to accept that we ought if it is humanly possible to abandon it completely. Suppose even – although this is not essential for the point here – that we do in fact so abandon it. We might then still continue with philosophical study of the deserted institution of morality – just as, say, we might continue with the philosophical study of witchcraft or of religion. Such continuing philosophical study might seem at best a somewhat feeble matter. None the less, it is important to recognize that in such a context the philosophical study of morality would be far more like that of religion than like that of witchcraft. In the case of religion there remains, for example, a task which is in part philosophical and of undeniable interest: that of identifying the needs, desires and interests which the institution of religion at least supposedly met and reference to which could thus in large part serve to explain the persistence of that institution. And there would then be the subsequent task of considering and evaluating the alternative options which might be directed to meeting those needs, desires and interests. Just the same tasks would arise after the hypothesized total abandonment of the institution of morality: they would correspond in part to the subject-matter of the then future moral philosophy, in part to the subject-matter of its descendants.

So if morality were indeed in a radically and irreparably defective state, that would have serious and problematic consequences for the practice of moral philosophy. But there is another putative analogy between morality and religion of far more importance for our present purposes. In the case of the defective states both of religion and of the philosophy of religion many have believed there to be a connection in the other direction: that is to say, many have believed that the defective state of religion is owing precisely to the failures of philosophers of religion to provide coherent philosophical foundations for religious beliefs and practices. And many have held a similar belief about morality: they have held the belief that morality is in an essentially philosophical mess. But I think the belief concerned to be one of great complexity; and that I shall now try to show.

When faced with any human institution, with any human practice, the problem immediately arises of *identifying* that institution, that practice. Consider the case of the institution of science. As an initial characterization – rough but ready – we might say that this institution consists of at least the following activities: empirical scientific investigations such as laboratory experiments; the invention of scientific explanations; the postulation of scientific laws and theories; the publication of scientific articles and books; participation in scientific conferences; the teaching of science; the administration of grants for scientific research; etc., etc., etc. . . .

Once considering an institution of this kind, we can imagine, in general terms, two distinct types of theories about the institution. A theory is *internal* to the institution, to the practice, if the claim is that those who participate in the practice do what they do because they believe, albeit perhaps tacitly, in the theory concerned. A theory is *external* to the institution if that condition is not satisfied. But just what is the real content of that condition and so of that distinction? One initial suggestion might be that at least part of that content can be captured like this: one who proffers an internal theory holds in effect that if the participants in the institution concerned were to come to reject that theory, then *ceteris paribus* they would cease their practice, they would abandon the institution.

Two points must be noted before continuing. First, in the example given, the initial characterization of the institution of science might seem rough and unready: and that might seem so because of the fact that the expression 'scientific' is repeatedly used within that characterization. And second, the phrase '*ceteris paribus*' used in the attempt to explain at least part of the content of the distinction between internal and external theories might seem to render that explanation useless. The idea behind the use of the phrase is clear: even after coming to reject the theory internal to some institution, the participants might remain within it, might continue with the same practice, for any of an indefinite number of reasons – lack of imagination, habit, continuing economic security, etc., etc., etc. . . . It is impossible to give a priori a complete list of the motivations in virtue of which human beings might enter into, or might continue within, a given activity. But it therefore seems that for all that has been said so far the distinction between internal and external theories is a distinction without an empirical difference.

But let us suppose that those anxieties can in some reasonable way be calmed. And let us also now suppose that the theory internal to the institution of science is, at least in part, a philosophical theory. Then under these circumstances the failures of philosophers to find some philosophical grounding for that theory might make manifest the critical state of science itself: science might be in an essentially philosophical mess. Under these circumstances it would not be that philosophers had wandered into a terrain where they had no right to be; it would rather be that they find themselves where they are anyway needed. But under these circumstances they are unable to meet the need.

Back now to the institution of morality. This consists of at least the following: our moral thoughts and judgements (specific moral evaluations of a variety of kinds of item, general moral evaluations of those same items, practical moral judgements directed towards possible actions); our moral practices like punishing and rewarding; our moral emotions like gratitude and guilt. Faced with that institution we might contemplate the possibility of there being a theory internal to this institution which is, at least in part, philosophical; and then we might contemplate the further possibility that that theory proves to be philosophically indefensible. Contemplating these possibilities, we find ourselves contemplating a situation in which the labours of moral philosophers might make manifest the mess in which morality finds itself. In such circumstances morality needs some philosophical grounding; but *ex hypothesi* morality in such circumstances does not have what it needs.

One of these circumstances is this: that the theory internal to morality prove to be philosophically indefensible. Now, if that is so it might be so just because of the inadequacies of then current moral philosophers: it might just be that these philosophers are incapable of defending the theory – or that these philosophers have a mistaken view of what a successful defence of the theory would be. Thus it need not be a *philosophical* problem that there are hard moral problems, that moral discourse is often used for non-moral ends, that there is no unanimity in moral matters or that there is much immorality around; rather, the general idea needed here is that there is some goal or condition which morality should meet if it is to be defensible and which it does not meet. But then the possibility must be considered that the problem is with the goal or condition imposed by philosophers upon a successful defence of morality. So it might just be that moral philosophers themselves are in a state of grave disorder. But suppose that that is not so; and now, finally, suppose that current moral philosophers have found some convincing philosophical proof that the theory internal to the institution of morality is indeed indefensible – is false or incoherent or senseless or groundless. Then in these circumstances *philosophical* scepticism about morality is in place. In these circumstances morality is, and can reasonably be believed to be, in an essentially philosophical mess – a mess which philosophers can distinctively appreciate. But the circumstances concerned are indeed complex.

Such philosophical scepticisms about morality have taken many forms, but two are especially instructive. One takes its lead from the long, messy history which has issued in our present moral thought and practice. This thought and practice is the outcome of diverse historical influences or inputs which are by no means obviously compatible: from notions of classical Greek origin and the distinctive ideas of Christianity through the preoccupations of the Enlightenment to at least the contributions in the nineteenth century of liberalism, utilitarianism, socialism and marxism (cf. MacIntyre 1981: 6–11). Reflection upon that history can easily seem to suggest that our present moral thought and practice is no better than a hodge-podge of very doubtful rationality. The second kind of philosophical scepticism about morality concerns itself with various elements seemingly distinctive of moral thought and practice and which it finds to be of at best very doubtful coherence: the idea, for example, of free will, or the thought that moral reasons for acting are reasons which agents have regardless of their desires and beliefs – are 'external reasons' for acting (cf. Williams 1981a; 1985: ch. 10).

There are of course important differences between the resultant forms of philosophical scepticism about morality. They are likely, for example, to return quite different answers to the following questions: has morality always been in a mess or is its supposedly defective state of more recent origin? And is there any alternative to the complete abandonment of the institution of morality, can anything be saved from the present ruins? None the less, there is also something common to these forms of philosophical scepticism about morality: each presumes it to be (relatively) easy to identify the theory internal to our institution of morality. But that identification, I wish to insist, is far indeed from being easy.

One example from the recent history of moral philosophy will serve to indicate the difficulty here. Some years back Philippa Foot tried, and very successfully, to call into question the coherence of the idea of a 'categorical imperative' as that has been used by philosophers within the Kantian tradition (Foot 1972a); and more recently Bernard Williams has undertaken a similar task in relation to what he calls the idea of an 'external reason' for acting (Williams 1981a). There were of course subtle differences between the targets and methods of these philosophers; notwithstanding that, the broad similarity in at least their target ideas was clear. The interesting point for present purposes is that, roughly speaking, while Mrs Foot seems to have taken herself to be criticizing a misconception on the part of moral philosophers of the nature of morality, Williams seems to have taken himself to be criticizing an error within moral thought itself. The one has a mere philosophers' thesis as her target, the other an element of the institution of morality itself. The question as to which of these philosophers had the more veridical appreciation of the character of their common target turns upon the issue of which theory can truly be claimed to be internal to our moral thought and practice: the elusiveness of that issue is testified to by the as yet unresolved difference between the philosophers concerned.

The general difficulty so indicated might have a surprisingly close bearing upon the seemingly quite distinct issue of the identification of the institution of morality. One reasonably attractive thought is that all that should be attempted in the way of resolution of that issue is the contrasting of *specific* elements of our moral thought and practice with other *specific* things: the focusing, that is, upon doubly specific contrasts. But another possibility might also be considered: this is to claim that the identity of the institution of morality is in the most general terms determined by the matter of the theory which can truly be claimed to be internal to it. And then the further claim might be entered that the worry which prompted the inclusion of the problematic *ceteris paribus* clause was a spurious one: for even if agents seem to continue to behave as if they were participants within the institution after coming to reject the theory internal to it, that rejection shows that they cannot be continuing participants within the *same* institution as before. If the protest now presents itself that the issue of, so to say, the 'external' identification of the institution has not been addressed, the proper response might very well be to claim that there is no reason to presume in general that there is any such issue to be addressed. The terms within which the theory internal to the institution of morality is characterized must of course be such as to lend themselves to empirical application; but there is no reason to believe that that condition of empirical applicability should be construed either in terms of some behaviourist conception of the external manifestations of that theory or even just in terms which preclude the use of moral notions themselves within descriptions of possible external manifestations. No reductivist construal of the idea of an internal theory need be in play here: so if the demand that the issue of the external identification of the institution be addressed is the demand for such a construal, we have every right to reject that demand.

If it can truly be said that there is an at least partially philosophical theory internal to the institution of morality, that theory would be the subject of a *descriptive metaphysics of morality* in something like Strawson's sense of 'descriptive metaphysics' (cf. Strawson 1959;

1985). The construction of such a metaphysics would be an attempt to describe the most general structures and features presumed within our moral thought and practice: an attempt to lay bare the most general conceptual connections and priorities enmeshed within that thought and practice. The construction of such a metaphysics of morality would be in one way a more modest task than that of the construction of certain other descriptive metaphysics: for once the distinctiveness of the institution of morality is appreciated, it seems unlikely that the resultant metaphysics will illuminate much 'the contrast between that which is *unavoidable* in the structure of human thought and that which is contingent and changeable' (Hampshire 1959: 9, emphasis added). Still, that touch of modesty might seem deceptive as to the general character of the enterprise of constructing a descriptive metaphysics of morality: for all that has been said so far it seems that we still have little or no idea as to how to set about that enterprise. Indeed, certain further considerations serve to heighten uncertainty on this point.

No help will be forthcoming for the enterprise from an examination of what people say *about* morality. That is so not just because any theory internal to morality might be accepted by moral agents only tacitly, nor just because the opinions given voice to are likely to be merely 'first-order' moral opinions; it is also so because too many extraneous factors can come into play in determining what people say about morality – politeness, provocativeness, self-deception, half-baked philosophical-cum-cultural ideas, etc., etc., etc. Perhaps more worrying is the fact that it is very far from obvious that much help will be forthcoming for the descriptive metaphysician of morality from examination of people's *usage* of moral vocabulary. J. L. Mackie seemed to think it more or less evident that our moral thought and talk purport to be objective (Mackie 1977: ch. 1); but against that Simon Blackburn has tried to show that any feature of our usage of moral language which is supposed to be the defining mark of such a purportedly objective stance can be reproduced within his usage of moral language by an out-and-out subjectivist of a broadly Humean kind (Blackburn 1984: ch. 6). So, for example, neither talk of moral beliefs, truths and facts nor attachment to some principle of bivalence serves to distinguish the objectivist from the subjectivist. Any general conclusion along Blackburn's lines is of course vulnerable to an overlooked possibility; none the less, the tentative moral I wish to draw from the present state of this debate is that examination of facts about our usage of moral vocabulary is likely to have but a relatively indirect role within the enterprise of identifying the theory internal to our institution of morality. But how, then, should we set about that enterprise?

Within the long and tortuous history of the metaphysics of morals a distinctive answer to that question can at times be detected: this, in the most schematic of terms, is the suggestion that the best approach to the identification of the theory which can truly be said to be internal to our moral thought and practice is through philosophical investigation of our moral psychology. In terms of strategy, that is to say, moral philosophy is best seen as a part of philosophical psychology. But it is essential to distinguish that strategic recommendation from the results putatively arrived at through its adoption at the hands of particular philosophers. The greatest of those philosophers, Hume, thought that deployment of that strategy would lead us to subjectivist results according to which the seemingly objective metaphysical materials of morality are *reduced* to mere psychological realities. One can however favour the strategic recommendation while doubting those results: for one can suspect that, within the terms of the strategic recommendation, a veridical description of the psychological realities concerned will support, in descriptive terms, a metaphysics of morality diametrically opposed to Hume's (and so one can suspect that the psychological realities as so described lack the conceptual independence of the pertinent objective metaphysical materials of morality requisite for the *reductive* endeavour).

This essay is a partial exploration of that possibility – Humean strategy without Humean results – an exploration which I hope at least serves to place some flesh upon the skeletal description just now given of that possibility. When, thinking on that possibility, I began to take moral philosophy seriously, I ran across one great stumbling-block: the concept of desire. That concept occupies a central place, not just in philosophical discussion of morality, but in philosophical discussion of a remarkably wide range of topics: so much so that any hope for a rigorous 'analysis' of the concept seems fated to frustration. But that does not preclude the possibility of, nor reduce the need for, less formal speculation designed to issue in something at least approximating to some plausible conception of what desire is. Misunderstanding of so central a concept can but wreak havoc in our understanding of our thought about the mind's place within the world.

The first part of this essay is, predominantly, the outcome of my attempts to become a little clearer upon that concept. The first chapter leans upon one of the rare cases in which a great philosopher has given an explicit statement of his conception of desire; the chapter does that so as to eliminate certain widespread, almost natural, misunderstandings of the nature of desire. The second, more constructive, chapter is a consequent attempt to present some more plausible view of what desire is and of its place within human mental and active life; that attempt is made within a perspective determined by some most important distinctions between kinds of desires. Then finally, in the third chapter, the results of that more constructive discussion are deployed for the purposes of presenting what might, in somewhat archaic and grandiose terms, be called *A General Theory of Value* – a general and systematic descriptive metaphysics of value. By that point the general outlines of the ways in which I wish to divorce the Humean strategy from Humean subjectivist results should have become clear.

In the second part of the essay that descriptive metaphysics of value receives some further refinement in the process of trying to deploy it as part of the enterprise of constructing a partial descriptive metaphysics of morality. This second part of the essay is, in general, much less constructive than the first. In the attempt to illuminate the theory internal to the institution of morality, I approach that institution from a number of different angles: from a consideration of the views of that institution held by the greatest of the philosophers to have opposed the views I myself wish to defend (Chapter 4); from an examination of one of the problems, that of moral relativism, presumed to arise in relation to that institution and to have received most attention in recent philosophical writings (Chapter 5); and from reflection upon the views of certain philosophers who have, or who at least have been deemed to have, criticized that institution (Chapter 6). The outcome is, at most, a *partial* descriptive metaphysics of morality, and in more than one way: only certain features of moral thought and practice receive direct, sustained attention; little or nothing is said about the further filling that would be needed if comprehensiveness were to be pursued; and little or nothing is explicitly said about what would make such a filling a correct filling out, descriptively speaking. Whether or not the outcome is also partial in the pejorative sense of that expression is of course for the reader to decide.

There is one charge, however, that I should wish to reject at the outset. I no more see my concern with *descriptive* matters as the manifestation of some merely temperamental conservative preference than I see it as the manifestation of a calm passion for calculation of the ways in which morality has us stuck in the mud. Perhaps the theory which can truly be claimed to be internal to moral thought and practice is in one way or another defective; perhaps that theory is defective in some distinctively philosophical way; perhaps we should now re-evaluate all our moral concepts and practices and call into question the whole institution within which those concepts and practices have their place. Perhaps, perhaps, perhaps. . . . But such critical claims and such revisionary or revolutionary projects will have pellucid contents and transparent motivations only when the theory which can truly be claimed to be internal to moral thought and practice has indeed been identified.

Part One

There is no prejudice more natural to man, than to conceive of the mind as having some similitude to body in its operations.

(Reid)

Although each person in a large circle of people can be sitting upon the knees of the person behind him, this is not a feat which only two or three people can manage.

(Gareth Evans)

1 Misconceptions of desire

'Entre le désir et l'action, monsieur, il y a place pour le respect'.
La phrase était drôle, bien que peu claire.

Maupassant

The one basic rule for experts on females: confine yourself absolutely to explaining why she did what she has already done because that will save the trouble of explaining why she didn't do what you said she would.

Rex Stout

A RUSSELLIAN CONCEPTION OF DESIRE

In *The Analysis of Mind* (1921) Russell presented a most characteristic discussion of desire: concise, witty, honest and almost perversely imaginative. Among many other claims – some of which were perhaps of more concern to him – he maintained the following:

1 The common-sense view of desire is radically mistaken.
2 The common-sense view of desire sees it in part as a specific feeling towards some image.
3 The common-sense view of desire sees it in part as an attraction from the future rather than as an impulse away from the actual – as a pull not a push.
4 The study of non-human animals is in many ways the best preparation for the analysis of desire.
5 The prime mover in action upon desire is a sensation of discomfort.
6 Desire is a causal law of our actions: an impulse or tendency to action, a power of influencing actions.

Similar ideas are to be found, I think, within many philosophers' tacit conceptions of what desire is; it is a virtue on Russell's part to have made his conception explicit. None the less, adapting a phrase of his: desire is a subject upon which, if I am not mistaken, true views can only be arrived at by an almost complete reversal of the ordinary unreflecting *philosophical* opinion (and of Russell's reflective opinion).

But first a word of caution. My discussion here is not meant to correspond in any simple way to the details of the usage of the specific expression 'to desire' and its cognates, nor even to such details of usage for the humbler 'to want' and its cognates. Some aspects of the relationship between my discussion and those facts of usage will be clarified during the discussion; but as an initial indication, the theme of this discussion is anchored by the following thought: whenever an agent intentionally ø's, he desires (or wants) to ø.

So understood (or misunderstood), some of the Russellian claims can quickly be dismissed. Perhaps the most obvious victim is number 5, the universal claim that the prime mover in action upon desire is a sensation of discomfort. For in ever so many mundane cases of intentional action, it is clear that there is no sensation of discomfort present to move the agent to act: normal cases of crossing the street, opening a newspaper, shutting the door, talking. And unless common sense be remarkably blind to that fact, a similar error is found in number 2, the claim that the common-sense view of desire sees it in part as a specific feeling towards some image. Why should common sense deny to itself either the phenomenological variety manifested in cases of desiring or the commonplace phenomenological void that occurs in many mundane cases of intentional action upon desire? Why cannot common sense recognize both the distinctions within cases of desiring and the evident fact, for example, that the incidence of *felt* desire depends in large part upon the extent to which action upon the desire is obstructed by psychological or physical difficulties?

Continuing with a minimum of charity towards common sense, a further error occurs in claim 2: for in many mundane cases of intentional action, it is again clear that the agent need have no image of the future action or of some future resultant state of affairs. In some cases of planning and deliberation images of the future may have some role to play; and the incidence of such images may be greater in cases of obstruction and difficulty. But the universal claim attributed in number 2 to common sense is so clearly false that it is difficult to see how common sense could fall into such error.

The error attributed by Russell to common sense in claim 3 – the view of desire as a pull from the future rather than as a push from the actual – is of a quite different nature. For involved here is no mere phenomenological falsification of the experiences of desire and of action upon desire but instead a bizarre metaphysics of causation: a metaphysics in which the not yet existing now causes something. But Russell's attribution of such a metaphysics to common sense is undermined by a far more plausible account of the common-sense view of this matter. On this account, that view of the matter is that the 'prime mover' in action upon desire is something *now* existing – namely, the desire itself! – together with the thought that a full specification of that thing involves the specification of its distinctive *propositional content*. That content will, at least generally, be a description of some possible future action or state of affairs; but its specification will not *require* the attribution to the desirer of an image of that future action or state of affairs. My desire is that I cross the street, and so I do it; but the cause of my doing so is not some not yet existing item, nor is it of necessity my now having some image of such an item, but rather is merely the desire I now have with the specified propositional content. Doubtless there are philosophical obscurities within that view of the matter which must be clarified; and maybe that, *the* common-sense view of desire, is mistaken. But if that is so, it is owing neither to some obvious falsification of the phenomenology of desire nor to some obscure metaphysics of causation.

Fortunately, there are more instructive errors within Russell's discussion of desire; some of them connect with the more superficial errors so far mentioned.

ON DESIRE AS AN ACTIVE POWER

Russell held (as in claim 6) that desire is a causal law of our actions: an impulse or tendency to action, a power of influencing actions. By holding this, Russell placed himself within an almost universal philosophical tradition: a tradition, unsurprisingly, within which subtle differences of opinion and of emphasis can be detected. I now want to examine some principal members of the family of conceptions of desire which make up that tradition. Some members have obvious inadequacies but all, I think, are flawed. If that claim can be made systematically good, the result will be established that it is simply a misconception to think of desire as being essentially an active power of the mind: that is, roughly, to think of desire as being essentially a disposition or tendency to act so as to try to bring about the desired state of affairs.

Desires are ascribed to agents as part of making some of their doings intelligible to ourselves. More specifically, desire ascriptions are key components within rationalizations of intentional actions. For example, in what might seem the simplest of cases the action concerned is seen through the rationalization to be such as 'directly' to bring about the desired state of affairs; but there are of course countless more complex ways in which a desire can be seen as being acted upon.

One who focuses exclusively upon that range of employment of the concept of desire might naturally be led to embrace a conception of desire given sharp expression by the creator of Don Quijote: 'whenever the desire for something ignites in our hearts, we are moved to pursue it and seek it and, seeking and pursuing it, we are led to a thousand unruly ends' (*La Galatea*, bk IV).

Error enters here with the focus. Ascriptions of desires to agents are not made only as part of producing rationalizing descriptions of their intentional actions such that the agents are thereby seen to be acting upon the desires so ascribed. Even if all desire ascriptions have to be 'grounded' in aspects of the agent's conduct, still there are many ways in which his desires can be made manifest in that conduct other than by his acting upon them. So not all desires need to be acted upon. Nor are they, since the agent concerned may have no idea as to how to seek and pursue the object of desire; that is, he may have no beliefs as to which courses of action open to him would make it more likely that the desired state of affairs come about. Indeed, not all desires could be acted upon. A set of desires had by an agent can, in virtue of their contents, be such that he rightly believes it impossible that they all be reasonably acted upon in the special sense of being acted upon with some reasonable hope that all the desired states of affairs come about. Perhaps more common are sets of desires whose members are rightly believed to be rendered in this sense incompatible by some further contingent circumstance: an interesting example is the shortness of life in relation to any considerable stock of desires. For most people most of the time it is impossible that their desires all conform to the Cervantine conception.

The more familiar ways of trying to amend that conception in the face of these evident failings make recourse, among other things, both to some idea of an agent's beliefs as to what it is in his power to bring about and to some notion of the comparative strength of his desires. So whether a desire in fact gives rise to any action at all depends upon the agent's beliefs and upon the natures and strength of his other desires. That thought can be developed in a number of different ways; in considering those ways, matters are simplified by focusing attention more narrowly upon the notion of an agent's wanting to do something or desiring that he do it. Thus for example are side-stepped, what any comprehensive theory of desire must of course handle, the problems arising from Quine's wanting a sloop and Prufrock's desire for love.

Donald Davidson has recently defended the following principle about the notion of an agent's wanting to do something:

> P1. If an agent wants to do x more than he wants to do y and he believes himself free to do either x or y, then he will intentionally do x if he does either x or y intentionally.
>
> (Davidson 1969: 23)

One common objection to that principle is illustrated by the following kind of apparent counter-example. I want to visit Jack more than I want to visit Tom, and I correctly believe myself free to visit either; but Tom lives nearby, whereas Jack lives far out in the sticks, so I visit Tom, not Jack, intentionally. There is nothing even minimally puzzling about such an outcome; but, the general thought behind the objection is, there is for Davidson simply because his principle P1 mistakenly focuses exclusively upon, so to say, the expected benefits of contemplated action thereby neglecting the matter of the expected costs of action in terms of time and effort required, discomfort incurred and so forth.

That objection is as readily countered as it is encountered. Any theorist will need to distinguish wanting to do x more than to do y in abstraction from consideration of costs from wanting to do x more than to do y taking into account the expected costs of doing either. I can want more to visit Jack than to visit Tom in the former, cost abstracted, terms while wanting more to visit Tom than Jack once expected costs are taken into account. Davidson's principle P1 is thus readily shielded from the posited kind of apparent counter-example – and is indeed most naturally construed – by taking the agent's expectations as to the costs of the contemplated actions to be reflected in, to be internal to, the comparative strengths of his desires. Likewise, different degrees of confidence on the agent's part as to the benefits and costs of the actions can be understood to be internal to the strength of his desires. And for one who dislikes my importation of pseudo-economic jargon into the description of that case, there are a number of more or less natural ways of describing it and other similar cases. Consider as a further example the following dialogue (which I believe is owed to Philippa Foot):

A: I want to leave you now.
B: I thought you liked me. How can you *want* to leave me?

By 'want' person A means, roughly, *wanting all things considered*; person B means, roughly, *wanting for or in itself*. My initial anchoring of my theme – whenever an agent intentionally ø's, he desires (or wants) to ø – makes clear that my general concern here is with the former kind of usage. One can intentionally do something even though one does not want to do it *for or in itself* – maybe it is the least disagreeable of the options open to one.

What would seem to require substantial modification in the formulation of Davidson's principle P1, as opposed just to clarification of its interpretation, is the wish that, in the interest of comprehensiveness, it apply to cases in which the agent's degree of confidence in his ability to execute the contemplated actions differs as between those actions. That consideration is often critical in cases where the temporal dimension is involved; understanding of many such cases also requires that account be taken of any belief the agent has, and of the strength of any such belief, as to the possibility of his executing more than one of the contemplated actions. Both considerations, along with the agent's degrees of expectation as regards benefits and costs, are of especial importance for realistic understanding of an agent's contemplations directed, not towards isolated actions, but towards plans of action extending well into the future. But for present purposes attention can be restricted to the simpler kind of case.

I now want more to buy a porcelain hippopotamus tomorrow morning than to buy now a bottle of champagne. I believe myself free to do either, but I also believe that if I do the latter I shall then be unable to do the former. Yet I now buy a bottle of champagne, doing so intentionally, thus apparently frustrating, and believing myself to frustrate, my stronger want. How can my action be accounted for?

Given the earlier stipulation about the internalization of the expec-

tation, and of the degree of expectation, of costs to the strength of
the agent's desires, no help is now to be had from that quarter. The
most natural way of understanding many cases of this type is by
seeing the agent's belief in the incompatibility of the two contemplated actions as being less than full-blooded conviction: we see him
as believing or hoping, however unreasonably, that 'something will
turn up' which will enable him still rationally to act upon his stronger
desire when the time for such action comes. Another (potentially
connected) possibility, significant too when the temporal dimension
is not important, is to hold the degree of the agent's belief in his
capacity to execute the action to be appreciably different for the
contemplated actions. Such a difference might be the result of some
belief on the agent's part as to the non-temporal characters of the
actions and of himself; alternatively, it could be the result specifically
of their presumed temporal differences reflecting, say, the agent's
general beliefs as to the uncertainty of the future (or of his future).
Yet another, again potentially connected, possibility is that the agent
discounts somewhat his (otherwise) stronger, more distant future
directed, desire through some degree of doubt as to whether he will
still have that desire, or at least still have it with its strength
unmodified, when the time for action comes.

That last kind of consideration can reasonably be taken to be
internal to the present strength of the agent's desires. It is a nice
question whether the other, belief-invoking, possibilities of explanation mentioned admit of treatment in terms of a comparable
internalization. Passing that nicety by, however, we might contemplate the seeming possibility of cases of the type exemplified in
which we are led to dismiss all the kinds of possible explanation
just sketched. At least one further possibility of explanation would
remain: this would be that, even when the other considerations have
been taken into account, the agent is yet further influenced by the
temporal dimension. This too could naturally be accommodated in
terms of internalization. Even when account has been taken of all
other considerations, the desire which the agent believes he can
presently act upon is, in virtue of that fact, stronger than the desire
which the agent believes he can only more distantly act upon. That
might be true just of the particular desires now under consideration;
or it might be true of all the agent's desires at the present time; or
it might be true of all the agent's desires through time. Independently
of the other considerations mentioned, an agent can have a propensity, persisting or otherwise and of stable strength or otherwise, to

discount his current, more distant future directed desires because of their more distant future directedness.

That cases of the type exemplified can be explained does not mean that in such cases agent's actions are beyond reproach. Each possibility of explanation mentioned brings with it a distinct possibility for criticism of the agent's conduct. And each corresponds to a distinct kind of proto-practical deliberation.

Important as those considerations are for understanding, and perhaps amending, Davidson's principle P1, they do not seem to necessitate substantial modification of Davidson's conception of wanting to do something. Appreciation of the more substantially contentious comes, I think, when we ask why it is that Davidson appends the clause 'if he does either x or y intentionally' to his principle. One obvious reason, prompted by the level of generality at which Davidson conducts his discussion, is the need to accommodate the possibility that the agent has some yet stronger desire which he believes himself able to act upon. A second reason of comparable obviousness is the need to allow for cases in which the agent's belief in his ability to do that which he more wants to do is false. And a third, apparently distinct, reason for the appendage arises from cases in which an agent, while correctly believing himself able to do that which is what he more wants to do, fails none the less upon this occasion to exercise correctly that ability: he attempts the appropriate action but upon this occasion his execution is faulty.

If that exhausts the main considerations determining Davidson's appending of the clause concerned, then I think his principle simply implausible. Useful here is reflection upon what might be called 'apparent one desire cases'. I am sitting at my desk, staring aimlessly out of the window. My room is full of smoke, my eyes are smarting and with each passing moment my discomfort is the greater. So I want to open the window. I believe it within my present powers to do so. And yet I remain seated, gazing morosely at the window. Such a scenario is not uncommon, in my life at least. But does it follow that I do not really want to open the window? Or is that consequence averted only either by holding that my belief that I am able to open the window is false or by holding me to have, all appearances to the contrary, some other, stronger, desire upon which I am then at least attempting to act? Surely not: it may just be that the only desire pertinent in my present situation, and so my strongest pertinent desire, does not move me to action nor moves me to attempt action nor even issues in an appropriate intention to act. The desire fails, one might say, to engage my will.

In considering the description of such cases it is important to bear in mind a doctrine of long philosophical standing which Davidson himself tells us 'has an air of self-evidence': namely, 'that, in so far as a person acts intentionally he acts, as Aquinas puts it, in the light of some imagined good' (Davidson 1969: 22). Now, in many apparent one desire cases we can account for the agent's inaction by reference to some passing feature of his mood, emotional state, or more generally, mental life at the time when action is possible; on other occasions the account may be in terms of some more persistent trait of the agent's personality. I shall say that these accounts give, respectively, mental and personal explanations of the agent's inaction, without thereby wanting to suggest that there is any sharp distinction here between kinds of explanation. Of the accounts we can give some may, at least tacitly, introduce reference to other desires of the agent; and of those accounts, some may reveal his inaction to be intentional, to be the result of the appropriate influence of some other, supposed stronger, desire. But must every acceptable account of an agent's inaction in an apparent one desire case do that? The difficulty is obvious: in many cases there simply is no plausible specification of an 'imagined good' in the light of which the agent would remain intentionally inactive. More simply, there is often no plausible specification of a (stronger) desire upon which the agent is intentionally acting. Even within the context of an agent's correct belief in his appropriate abilities, principle P1, as here understood, incorporates an excessively simplified view of when his strongest desire will issue in a corresponding intention to act, let alone in action itself.

DESIRE AND CAUSAL THEORIES OF ACTION

The argument thus far can be reconciled with a conception of desire as essentially an active power of mind, with the claim, for example, that to attribute a want for something to someone is to say that he is disposed to try to get it. For all that have been uncovered are some potential ambiguities in, and some complexities of, any plausible specification of the circumstances under which that power is exercised, the disposition actualized. But the following claim remains unassailed:

P1* If an agent believes himself able to do that which he most wants to do, then normally he will intend to do it.

The claim is not devoid of content, for the force of the *normally* is to express commitment to the availability of some mental or personal explanation in any case in which an agent does not have the corresponding intention. Nor does it matter that we may have only schematic and anecdotal ideas as to how to fill in the details of the full range of explanations gestured at: for just the same is true for many of our ordinary dispositional concepts.

But why in every such case *must* there be some mental or personal explanation of the failure of the agent's strongest desire to engage his will? Perhaps the 'primitive sign' of wanting is 'trying to get' (Anscombe 1963: section 36). But a sign, albeit primitive, is just that: it is not some inevitable concomitant, nor even some normal concomitant, of that of which it is a sign. And it is difficult to believe that the admission, against P1*, of the possibility of some 'no explanation' cases – that is, cases where there is no explanation in terms of other features of the agent's mental life or personality of his lack of intention – could reduce ascriptions of desires to agents to senselessness. Of course, whenever an agent lacks the appropriate intention one can talk of his 'inertia' if one wishes: but such talk does not provide even the schema of an explanation of any kind.

A perhaps more plausible defence of some principle like P1* comes by trying to connect such a principle with the current orthodoxy of the causal theory of reasons for action. For present purposes that orthodoxy, or at least the here pertinent part of it, can be understood as follows: if an agent successfully acts upon some reason he has for so acting, then (a) that reason consists of some combination of desires and beliefs such that, in virtue of the propositional contents of those mental states, his action is thereby *rationalized*, made at least minimally reasonable; and (b) that reason is the *cause* of his action. (Condition (a) was tacitly relied upon at the beginning of this discussion of desire and action.) Now suppose a philosopher is convinced by the familiar arguments in favour of this causal theory of reasons for action, and suppose also that the philosopher accepts some connecting argument purporting to show that rejection of all active power conceptions of desire requires rejection of the causal theory of reasons for action. Then obviously the philosopher concerned will be led to reject the rejection of all active power conceptions of desire.

One such connecting argument might be this. Any true singular causal statement entails the existence of a covering causal law. So if we accept, simplifying somewhat, that an agent's intentional action is the effect of some desire of his, we shall be committed to the existence of a corresponding covering causal law. But the rejection of the active power conception of desire, the acceptance of 'no explanation' cases, is precisely the rejection of the claim that there must be any such law connecting desires of that kind with intention, let alone action. The point of that rejection, to repeat, is not that we have only the most schematic of ideas as to how to articulate the mental and personal conditions under which intention and action will occur; it is rather that that rejection denies that there must be any such set of conditions to be articulated.

It is unnecessary to pause over the assumption of the deterministic nature of causal laws, tendentious as that might be, for Davidson has equipped us with a more direct rejoinder to the connecting argument. The correct statement of the relation between singular causal statements and 'covering' causal laws is this:

> if '*a* caused *b*' is true, then there are descriptions of *a* and *b* such that the result of substituting them for '*a*' and '*b*' in '*a* caused *b*' is entailed by [a law together with a statement that there occurred a unique event of some specified kind of which *a* is an exemplar]; and the converse holds if suitable restrictions are put on the descriptions.

(Davidson 1967: 159–60)

So that a desire is the cause of some action does not entail that there is some law cast in terms of desires of that kind. Comparably, then, principle P1* gains no support from the consideration that when an agent does indeed intend to do that which is what he most wants to do, his intention is the effect of his desire. Due appreciation of the (presumed requisite) nomological grounding of such a causal relation may require a radical shift in our terms of reference. The need to locate desire that results in action or even just intention within the causal nexus does not necessitate acceptance of desire in general as an active power.

Consider two agents with identical personalities who up until now have enjoyed identical mental lives. Imagine even that the 'physical realizations' of their mental lives and personality traits have always been and still are identical. But now one comes to have the intention to do that which is what he most wants to do and so does it, while the other does not. Then, assuming causal determinism at the physical level, there must have been some prior physical difference between the two agents. But why *must* that physical difference be the realization either of some unnoticed difference between their mental or personal lives or of some difference in their abilities? Why cannot it be just a physical difference? And dropping the supposition of the identity of the physical realizations of the mental and the personal reveals the defensive manœuvres available to the active power theorist to be yet more clearly the expression of nothing but dogma.

DESIRE AND INTENTION

It should be stressed that the defence just given of the rejection of active power conceptions of desire is a maximally concessive one. Both the assumption of the deterministic nature of causal laws and the need for a backing to a singular causal statement of some covering causal law have been conceded for the sake of argument. Perhaps more importantly, the same is true of the current orthodoxy of the causal theory of reasons for action. I wish now briefly to emphasize the inconclusive nature of one of the now familiar arguments in favour of the causal theory; for that inconclusiveness connects with an important point just now touched upon.

The argument concerned might seem to amount to a direct defence of some principle similar to P1*. This argument begins from the fact that people often know, or have reasonable beliefs about, what they are going to do before they do it: they have knowledge or reasonable beliefs about the future as regards their own actions. That may sometimes be straightforwardly inductive knowledge: knowing that every day for the last few years I have taken a neat whisky at 11 o'clock at night, *ceteris paribus* I am justified in believing that I shall do so tonight. Such knowledge or reasonable belief about my future actions is at least in principle equally accessible to another. But suppose, irked by my just noticed predictability, I come to have a strong desire to change tonight to a tequila sunrise: then I can know, or reasonably believe, that I shall drink a tequila sunrise at 11 o'clock tonight. But *how* can I know, or reasonably believe, that? One suggestion (cf. Pears 1964) is that, on pain of countenancing some mysterious act of precognition, it has to be the case that (i) I know something about the present, and (ii) I know, or reasonably believe, that the object of that present knowledge is the kind of thing that causes future drinkings of tequila sunrise. That is, the suggestion continues: I know my present desire, and I know that

that desire is the kind of thing that causes future drinkings of tequila sunrise. Clearly, in a given case I might prove to be mistaken: I might later change my mind, there might be no tequila to be had, I might die before the happy hour. Still, the suggestion is, unless I know my present desire together with some rough-and-ready causal generalization similar to P1* which connects desires of that kind with kinds of future action, my knowledge or reasonable belief as to what I shall do would be utterly mysterious.

That argument merits a more patient treatment than that which it is to receive here. The obvious rejoinder to it takes the form of an alternative account of our knowledge of our future actions (cf. O'Shaughnessy 1980). Most schematically, one such account has the following structure: first, some notion of *knowledge without observation* is introduced within the context of one's knowledge of one's present actions – practical knowledge of what one is now intentionally doing (cf. Anscombe 1963: section 8). Clearly one can be mistaken about what one is now intentionally doing: but if so the fault lies, so to say, in the action not in the belief. And second, that same notion of practical knowledge is extended to apply to future actions: as I know now what I am intentionally doing, so I know now what I shall intentionally do in the future. Of course, any such knowledge claim about future actions requires some *ceteris paribus* clause; and of course, even if things do stay the same, there might be some practical error in my future action upon the intention. But in the latter case the fault again rests in the action, not in the belief.

That alternative account has indeed been presented most schematically; but its form of presentation serves to draw attention to a further defect in the argument given for the causal theory – a defect which makes it unnecessary for present purposes to leave the schematic level so as to adjudicate in fine detail between the accounts of one's knowledge of one's future actions. The alternative account given began from our practical knowledge of what we are now intentionally doing, and attempted to extend that notion to our present knowledge of what we shall in the future intentionally do. The point now is an obvious one: in this argument in favour of the causal theory, a move was made from the general structure of the account of future knowledge of action – the elements (i) and (ii) – to the claim that desire is the appropriate factor in the more concrete realization of that structure. But it is most unclear that desire is the appropriate factor: far more plausible candidates, within the terms of that account, would be decision or intention. Once again, it seems that a theorist is blurring the crucial distinction between desire, on the one hand, and intention, say, on the other. It might be that a detailed adjudication between accounts of knowledge of future action would reveal the need for some rough-and-ready causal generalizations linking present intentions or decisions with future actions; but that would leave the matter of desire untouched.

EXPLANATION OF ACTION

In search of arguments in favour of some principle like P1* let us leave causation for the distinct though related matter of explanation. Rejection of principle P1* is acceptance of the possibility that the totality of other mental and personal truths about an agent is as compatible with his not having the intention to do that which he most wants to do as it is with his having that intention and acting accordingly. But if that were possible, how could it be that reference to that totality of other mental and personal truths, let alone to some favoured part of it, can serve to *explain* the agent's intention and action in cases where they occur?

The presumption that the worth of explanations which make reference to the mental and personal lives of agents depends upon the truth of general principles of the form of P1* is fed by many sources. All I wish to do here is to make one brief diagnostic remark designed to expose one of those sources, one pertinent prejudice natural to man. If one starts with the thought that the mental and personal life of another is of necessity outside one's perceptual grasp – if, that is, one assumes that any defensible ascription of mentality or personality to another has to be the result of inference – one will naturally be led to think of defensible ascriptions of mental states and personality traits to others in terms of the hypothetico-deductive model of explanatory inference to the unperceived (because unperceivable). Then once convinced of the rightness of that model, the need for general principles of the form of P1 and P1* to underwrite our speculations about the hypothesized mechanisms will seem simply obvious.

Perhaps the starting-point of those reflections is completely natural to us. But the natural is neither always unavoidable nor always correct. That starting-point, with its Cartesian conception of mentality and personality as the fugitive inner, can be rejected without it thereby being necessary to embrace as all some behaviourist conception of the outer. This dual rejection is opened to us by our taking literally the thought that, say, we can see the seducer's desire in his face. His desire is not reduced to a nothing by rejection of the thought that it is a mere something whose presence and nature is only inferentially accessible to others: it can be *that thing* which others *see* (cf. Wittgenstein 1953: section 304). By being equipped with the language of the mind, we are not placed to entertain a new range of explanatory hypotheses about the perceptually inaccessible, nor even are we initiated into a new theory which we can then bring to bear in inferential interpretation of the perceptually accessible: rather, we have brought within our immediate, non-inferential perceptual reach a new realm of facts. And this perspective upon knowledge of others' mental and personal lives is no more undermined by the facts of occasional error and occasional inference than is the comparable perspective upon our knowledge of the external world.

DESIRABILITY CHARACTERIZATIONS

Giving voice to 'the ordinary unreflecting opinion', Russell wrote:

> We think of the content of the desire as being just like the content of a belief, while the attitude taken up towards the content is different. According to this theory, when we say: 'I hope it will rain,' or 'I expect it will rain,' we express, in the first case, a desire, and in the second, a belief, with an identical content, namely, the image of rain. It would be easy to say that, just as belief is one kind of feeling in relation to this content, so desire is another kind.
>
> (Russell 1921: 58)

A doubt has already been expressed about Russell's attribution to the common-sense view of desire of any such universal role for images and feelings: rather, it was suggested, that view is that desire is a propositional attitude directed towards some specific propositional content. Even so it anyway seems clear that Russell would have rejected this last view.

Such a rejection would place Russell in sharp opposition, not just to the view that desire is a propositional attitude, but also towards another, somewhat elusive, view about desire which has occasionally accompanied the propositional attitude view. We have already (p. 21) encountered Aquinas's doctrine that, in so far as a person acts intentionally, he acts in the light of some imagined good. That doctrine about the nature of intentional action invites another about the form of understanding intentional actions as intentional actions: namely, that the rationalization of some given intentional action should reveal the imagined good in the light of which the agent concerned performed that action. Simplifying away from some very important but here irrelevant complexities, and relying upon contemporary orthodoxy about the general structure of such rationalizations, we might take that requirement to be met by some suitable specification of the content of whichever desire is invoked within a fully articulated rationalization of the intentional action concerned.

Not all desires are acted upon, nor are all desire ascriptions made as part of producing rationalizations of intentional actions. None the less, it is difficult to deny that the suitability of desire ascriptions for the outlined role within rationalizations of intentional actions is essential to the point of the concept of desire. That being so, the preceding suggests adoption of the following general condition upon desire ascriptions: an explicitly acceptable ascription of some specific desire to an agent is one which, in virtue of the specification of the content of the desire, serves to reveal the imagined good in the light of which the agent would act were he indeed to act upon that desire.

What would it be 'to reveal the imagined good' through the specification of the content of a given desire? G. E. M. Anscombe once claimed that it would be 'fair nonsense' to say: 'Philosophers have taught that anything can be an object of desire: so there can be no need for me to characterize these objects as somehow desirable; it merely so happens that I want them' (Anscombe 1963: section 37). That might invite the following rephrasing of the condition upon explicitly acceptable desire ascription which was extracted from Aquinas's doctrine: a necessary condition of the acceptability of an ascription of some specific desire to an agent is that the ascriber should have 'reached and made intelligible' some 'desirability characterization' of the (potential) state of affairs there specified. That desirability characterization will directly reveal what the imagined good is in the light of which the agent acts if he does in fact act upon that desire. So either the propositional content specified in the desire ascription must be a desirability characterization, or, so to say, it must be backed up by some such characterization. Clearly, one who, like Russell, denies the propositional attitude status of desires will be able to make no sense of this further thought purporting to connect the notion of desire with that of a desirability characterization.

That further thought will later need both considerable elucidation and qualification. For the moment it may suffice to add the following: a desirability characterization of the object of desire has been achieved when the questioning of why the agent wants that object is brought to an agreed end. The desirability characterization is one adequate to the communication of the object's desirability: once given, or having achieved, that characterization, the imagined good has been revealed to our eyes.

'ANIMAL DESIRES'

We can now appreciate, I think, some of the complexity of Russell's claim 4, that the study of non-human animals is in many ways the best preparation for the analysis of desire. Let us start, however, with a seemingly almost human case.

> Sisyphus, it will be remembered, betrayed divine secrets to mortals, and for this he was condemned by the gods to roll a stone to the top of the hill, the stone then immediately to roll back down, again to be pushed to the top by Sisyphus, to roll down once more, and so on again and again, *forever*.
>
> (Taylor 1984: 256–7)

That, according to Richard Taylor, is 'a clear image of meaningless existence'. He goes on to present his favoured account of how that meaninglessness can be eliminated by the following example:

> [Suppose that the gods,] as an afterthought, waxed perversely merciful by implanting in [Sisyphus] a strange and irrational impulse . . . to roll stones. . . . [T]o make this more graphic, suppose they accomplish this by implanting in him some substance that has this effect on his character and drives . . . . [T]hey have by this device managed to give Sisyphus precisely what he wants – by making him want precisely what they inflict on him.
>
> (ibid.: 259)

More generally, Taylor concludes that we can

> reintroduce what has been . . . resolutely pushed aside in an effort to view our lives and human existence with objectivity; namely, our own wills, our deep interest in what we find ourselves doing.
>
> (ibid.: 266)

The meaning of life is from within us, it is not bestowed from without, and it far exceeds in both its beauty and permanence any heaven of which men have ever dreamed or yearned for.

(ibid.: 268)

It is clear that Taylor takes himself to have described a case in which the gods do indeed induce a desire 'within' Sisyphus to roll stones. And his accompanying talk of 'a strange and irrational impulse' and of 'drives' suggests why Taylor takes himself to have done just that. For that talk, like his general conclusions, suggests that Taylor tacitly subscribes to a conception of desire as an active power, as a mere disposition to act, to the complete neglect of the considerations consequent upon acceptance of Aquinas's doctrine. If a disposition to roll stones has been induced in Sisyphus, then he unproblematically has a *desire* to roll stones.

What on earth, or elsewhere, does Taylor's Sisyphus want to roll stones for? What does he see in it? The case would be different if Sisyphus were concerned to appease the fury of the gods in the hope of avoiding further punishment or of ending his present one. It would be even more interestingly different if he were concerned with, and convinced of, the justice of their punishment. (Perhaps he excuses the form of the punishment because of the gods' limited financial resources.) Both would be cases where we could understand what is 'within' Sisyphus in terms of his perception of what is 'without'. But in the case described by Taylor the only way in which we can understand the supposed desire 'within' Sisyphus is in terms of something literally within him, the substance implanted there by the gods; and that gives us no idea at all of any imagined good in the light of which Sisyphus supposedly acts.

Doubtless it is possible to induce impulses and drives of the strangest kinds in human beings – and in parrots, rats and sea slugs. But we should not be too quick to help ourselves to the notions of desire and intentional action in describing the outcomes of such machinations. Compare Taylor's Sisyphus with the imagined case in which Sisyphus is concerned to appease the fury of the gods in the hope of avoiding further punishment or of ending his present one. The analogy which invites extension of the talk of desire to Taylor's Sisyphus is clear: in both cases the 'behaviour' of Sisyphus is the same. But there are crucial differences too. The Sisyphus of my case may well come by his desire to roll stones, or may well be led to modify its strength, by what I earlier (p. 20) called 'proto-practical deliberation' aimed at answering the question 'What do I most want to do?'. His desire, and its strength, may be consequent upon other beliefs, desires and conceptions of the world that he has. Moreover, the desire of Sisyphus in my case is no mere disposition to 'behave' in some routine way: it can give rise to limitlessly various patterns of action depending upon the other desires and beliefs which Sisyphus has. If the Sisyphus of my case believes that other actions too will appease the fury of the gods, we may well find him attempting some of them; if the Sisyphus of my case comes to believe that the gods are dead, he will presumably cease his stone-rolling activity; if the Sisyphus of my case begins to doubt, and so wishes to test, his belief that his activity is appeasing the gods' fury, he may pause for a while in his labours; if the Sisyphus of my case becomes utterly exhausted and wishes to rest a while, he may arrange 'accidentally' to break a wrist. In understanding any such cases of alternative actions it will prove necessary to make reference to the general desirability characterization acceptance of which first led my Sisyphus to particular stone-rolling actions: namely, the avoidance of further punishment or the termination of the present one. And that will require the attribution to Sisyphus of possession of the relevant *concepts*, as of course would the account of any proto-practical deliberation in which my Sisyphus might have engaged in coming by his desire. Whereas for Taylor's Sisyphus, or for a simple drive soaked sea slug, no such conceptual ascription is required. Taylor's Sisyphus need have no conception at all of his 'activity'; he therefore need have no desirability conception of it. There is a contemporary echo here of the historical coincidence of attachment to active power conceptions of desire and the tacit denial of the propositional attitude status of desires: a coincidence which in consistency necessitates abandonment of the employment of the concept of intentional action.

In *Ulysses and the Sirens* (1984) Jon Elster expresses interesting ideas about both 'the characteristic feature of man' and the point at which '*mind* enters the evolutionary arena'. Man is capable both of *waiting* and of using *indirect strategies*: that is, man is capable both of forgoing a favourable possibility now in order to have a yet more favourable one later on, and of embracing an unfavourable possibility now in order later on to obtain a very favourable one. These two capabilities are constitutive of the capacity for what Elster calls *global maximization* (ibid.: 15–17). This capacity is found in some non-human animals too; but in such animals, 'globally maximizing behaviour . . . is found in highly specific and stereotyped situations'. Whereas, Elster claims, 'the characteristic feature of man is . . . a *generalized capacity for global maximization* that applies even to qualitatively new situations'. Further, in cases of situation specific global maximization, 'there is no need to appeal to intentional or mental structures'; but 'the use of globally maximizing strategies in novel situations must imply an analysis of the context, a scanning of several possible moves and finally a deliberate choice between them'. Thus the generalized capacity for global maximization requires the ability to relate to the future and the merely possible; and Elster suggests that 'with this generalized capacity *mind* enters the evolutionary arena'.

The Sisyphus of my case, with his desire to roll stones being comprehensible in terms of his recognition of the desirability of the avoidance of further punishment or the termination of the present one, could well come to exemplify *in this particular but novel situation* his generalized capacity for global maximization. Faced with novelty, he might for example decline an offer of help in his labours since he can envisage that such aid, by increasing the gods' fury, might reduce his future possibilities of freedom (waiting). Or he might now elect the disagreeable option of rolling a heavier stone since he can envisage the possibility that, by appeasing the gods' fury, he thus increases his future possibilities of freedom (indirect strategies). Whereas for Taylor's Sisyphus, *as described*, there seems no intelligible way in which such possible diversity could be generated.

Perhaps the strangest thing about Richard Taylor's conception of desire, like any conception which disregards the insights consequent upon Aquinas's doctrine, is that an adherent to it must simply have overlooked the different degrees to which, and different ways in which, we can understand the objects of many desires. In a discussion of Taylor's views David Wiggins gave some good examples:

> there is . . . a difference, which as participants we insist upon, between the life of a man who contributes something to a society with a continuing history and a life lived on the plan of a southern pig breeder who . . . buys more land to grow more corn to feed more hogs to buy more land . . .
>
> (Wiggins 1976: 100–1)

And again:

> To the participant it may seem that it is far harder to explain what is so good about buying more land to grow more corn to feed more hogs to buy more land . . . than it is to explain what

is good about digging a ditch with a man whom one likes, or helping the same man to talk or drink the sun down the sky.

(ibid.)

If all that human desires ever amounted to were strange and irrational impulses, mere drives, it would be quite unintelligible that there be such clear, agreed and important differences between the activities of these two men. The only way in which a desire could be puzzling would be through being statistically unusual; in that way, I fear, it is not the southern pig breeder who would now occasion puzzlement.

We might finally note that genuine animal desires – not the 'animal drives' of Taylor's Sisyphus and of sea slugs – are not mere unintelligible drives: Taylor's Sisyphus is just as bad a general model for understanding animal desires as it is for understanding our desires. Part of the trouble with Russell's claim 4, that the study of non-human animals is in many ways the best preparation for the analysis of desire, is that, in combination with the other claims about desire made by Russell, it invites an account of animal desires precisely along Taylor's lines.

Most of the elements of Russell's conception of desire which have been here targeted for criticism are to be found, I think, within most other philosophers' tacit conceptions of desire. Perhaps the denial of the propositional attitude status of desire is now comparatively rare, and perhaps the exaggeration of the role of feeling is also now less frequent; but a dispositional misconception is still widespread, whether accompanied or not by attachment to a causal view of that supposed disposition. And more than one contemporary philosopher has persisted with the thought that non-human animals constitute a key starting-point for reflection upon the nature of desire. Russell's errors were no individual eccentricities.

An almost universal reaction to the treatment here accorded to Russell's conception is likely to be this: if desire is not something like that, then what is it? It remains to be seen whether some of the ideas invoked within this criticism of Russell's conception can be made to lend themselves to some more plausible conception of what desire is, or at the very least to some more adequate view of the place of desire within human mental and active life.

2 The distinctions of desire

Men nearly always follow the tracks made by others and proceed in their affairs by imitation, even though they cannot entirely keep to the tracks of others or emulate the prowess of their models. So a prudent man should always follow in the footsteps of great men and imitate those who have been outstanding. If his own prowess fails to compare with theirs, at least it has an air of greatness about it.

(Machiavelli)

There is no more unfortunate creature under the sun than a fetishist who yearns for a woman's shoe and has to settle for the whole woman.

(Karl Kraus)

NEEDS, WANTS, DESIRES

According to the classical misconception, a desire is an 'introspective something' (a feeling) which constitutes a disposition or tendency to do something (a force that moves us), and which contains no representation of any state of affairs, be that state real or merely imaginable. But however natural that conception of desire might be we have seen reason to think it completely mistaken. Yet, while avoiding the falsifications of 'feelings' and the vacuities of 'dispositions', can a more veridical conception of what desire is be found?

A more instructive, albeit finally mistaken, answer to that question can be arrived at (see pp. 40–8) through a consideration of the distinct notions of *needs* and *wants*. The most general notion of a need for something applies when that something is necessary for, is needed for, the realization of some state of affairs (cf. Wiggins 1985). The term 'needcessity' in usage in the south of the United

States of America until at least the end of the last century is as pleasing in its resurrection of this Aristotelian thought as its embodiment of that thought is ugly. A less jarring idiom capturing the same idea of a necessity arising from the facts of the case is 'it is needful that'. There is some reason for thinking that most general notion of a need to be derivative from a somewhat narrower notion: namely, that of a basic need which applies when the something needed is necessary for the flourishing and well-being of the subject of the attribution of the need. For we ought surely to be impressed by the fact that ascriptions of needs with that more specific, but perhaps unstated, relativization are in general independently intelligible, whereas ascriptions relying upon the completely general notion of a need require for their intelligibility specific contextual guidance as to what the appropriate relativization is.

The distinctive notion of a want is grasped by those duly appreciative of the first line of Psalm 23: 'The Lord's my shepherd, I'll not want.' Among other places, that version is found in *Scottish Metrical Psalms* of 1650; the 1662 *Prayer Book* spells things out, albeit at a heavy poetic price: 'The Lord is my shepherd: therefore I can lack nothing.' A want is a lack: my want now is intelligence, yours is probably patience. (Dr Johnson's *Dictionary* defines a *wantwit* as a fool or an idiot.) Unsurprisingly there is a corresponding distinctive verb form, although the common neglect of prepositions as parts of verbs can lead to a confusion of that form with the verb most naturally used in talk of desires: thus I want for intelligence, you for patience. Alexander Pope was trading upon the potential confusion when he wrote:

'With ev'ry pleasing, ev'ry prudent part,
Say, what can Cloe want?' – She wants a heart.

Not just any absent item, any gap, constitutes a want or lack. I no more lack, say, malnutrition than I need it. Indeed, that suggests a tidy formula as to when an absence amounts to a want: when and only when that which is absent is needed. (Thus the acuteness in the rewriting of Psalm 23 in *Private Eye* (11 November 1988): 'The Lady is my shepherdess, I shall not be deprived of any necessary amenity.') Entertaining that suggestion we shall be struck by the parallelism obtaining between ascriptions of wants or lacks and ascriptions of needs in terms of the varying roles of specific contextual considerations, including particular relativizations, in the rendering intelligible of those ascriptions. So, for example, those considerations appreciation of which would be necessary in some particular case to make sense of the thought that I need a cold would also have to be invoked in making similarly intelligible in that same situation the idea that I want for a cold. The difference between the concept of a need and that of a want might then seem to turn upon the anodyne point that while I can need what I in fact have yet I cannot want for it.

Ascriptions of needs and wants can intelligibly be made to things lacking the capability of intentional action, and even to things lacking a mental life altogether. Even when the subject of such ascriptions is a normal human being, the ascription need imply nothing whatever about the mental life of the subject. Cloe's want of a heart says much about her mental life, whether or not she herself recognizes the truth of what is said; but that is so just because this is a case in which the lack concerned is a spiritual one. Simply eliminate the metaphorical aspect, arrange for the blood to be pumped through her body in some other, efficient way, and then nothing follows about Cloe's state of mind from the fact of her heartlessness.

That serves to call into doubt any thought that self-ascriptions of wants and needs are in general grounded upon some distinctive 'epistemological relation' in which each subject is deemed to stand to his own mental states. Instead, the thought is invited that the capacity for such self-ascription may merely reflect the subject's sensitivity to the relations obtaining between his present circumstances and his (potential or actual) well-being. The grounds of self-ascriptions of wants or needs may be no different from those of comparable other-ascriptions. Thus the possibility is left open that others may be better placed to adjudicate the subject's needs and wants than he is himself.

Consider self-ascriptions of specifically mental wants or lacks. Involved in such cases is, in part, putative recognition of some mental absence, some gap in the mental life. It would be evidently wrong-headed to hold that such absences must be self-intimating. No recourse is needed to the paraphernalia of self-deception, the sub-conscious, and so on, in order to understand the possibility of Cloe's remaining unaware of a central truth about her mental life, her heartlessness. Moreover, even if Cloe, after much introspective rummaging, ascribes heartlessness to herself, there is no general reason to think her claim incorrigible. Soul searching need not issue in an exhaustive inventory of the soul's contents.

An agent's recognition, or misrecognition, of some need or want of his can give rise to a corresponding desire. And any puzzlement we might feel about some particular desire of an agent can be eliminated by our coming to see that desire as arising from the agent's recognition, or misrecognition, of some corresponding need or want.

Two disclaimers must immediately be entered. I am not maintaining that needs or wants only give rise to desires through the agent's recognition of those needs and wants. There seems nothing impossible, for example, about an agent's being led to appreciate some need or want of his through reflection upon some desire he has which arose from that need or want. Nor am I maintaining that all desires can be understood as arising from agent's needs or wants. Such a view can seem defensible only through a disregard of the varieties of human desire or a wilfully *ad hoc* postulation of human needs and wants.

Many needs and wants arise only consequently upon particular desires had by agents, which desires may have to be cited in elucidation of the claim that the agents have those needs and wants. But basic needs and wants, those necessary for the flourishing and well-being of the subject, are not thus consequent upon the subject's desires. That is why such needs and wants can intelligibly be ascribed to things lacking a mental life altogether.

Although the question of quite what a given individual's basic needs and wants are may be a tendentious one in many areas, it none the less remains true that claims in answer to that question purport to be objective in character. This is not because such questions are the domain of some supposedly value-free scientific investigation. Doubtless, consideration of the *kind* of thing exemplified by a given individual – plant, human being, Bengal tiger – can reveal some of that individual's basic needs and wants through appropriate scientific investigations. But there can be formidable disputes about what exactly constitutes, say, an individual human being's flourishing and well-being; and it is the worst kind of blinkered scientism to insist that all such disputes are only properly resolved through further value-free scientific investigation. Any such total account of the matter will indeed be valueless – although not in the sense favoured by proponents of such accounts. Rather, once we move beyond consideration of conditions for mere survival, we shall be immediately immersed in matters of value, matters resolvable only by employment of distinctive resources like imagination and empathy. In considering questions such as what it would be to live a life like *that*, we may learn considerably more from, say, the products of a novelist than from the outpourings of a natural scientist. Yet with all the difficulties and complexities thereby introduced, objectivity is by no means immediately banished; for none of those difficulties and complexities should blind us to the considerable agreement upon these matters even for beings as complex as ourselves, nor to the considerable agreed resources and procedures available to those engaged in disputes about these matters.

Indeed, were the introduction of questions of value to herald the banishment of objectivity, not even the basic survival needs and wants uncovered by scientific investigations could avoid the stigma of subjectivity. For that uncovering trades crucially upon ideas of explanatory power, goodness of fit with the data, coherence, comprehensiveness, functional simplicity, degree of testability, fit with other accepted theories and instrumental efficacy which are themselves value-notions (cf. Nozick 1981: 483; Putnam 1981: 127–37). They guide the practice of scientists, they figure in the accounts scientists themselves give of their reasons for acting as they do – and they are, moreover, matters of as tendentious dispute as are those involved once we move beyond consideration of mere survival basic needs and wants. It is not just that a value-free scientific account of basic needs and wants would fall short of comprehensiveness; rather, there is no such account available to us.

DESIRABILITY CHARACTERIZATIONS AND DESIRABILITY PERCEPTIONS

In the first chapter (pp. 27–9) I introduced the notion of a desirability characterization in the following terms: a desirability characterization of the object of a desire is one adequate to the communication of that object's desirability. Now, one paradigm of a desirability characterization is a specification of the object of desire in terms which reveal that object to be suitable to meeting some need or want which the agent recognizes himself to have. Such a specification brings to an end the questioning of why the agent has that desire: we are in agreement in such cases that the question has been answered. This kind of characterization of the object of desire is indeed one adequate to the communication of that object's desirability; once given that characterization the imagined good has been revealed to our eyes.

Those features of a desirability characterization cast in terms of an agent's recognition of some need or want of his are, I think, quite general features of desirability characterizations. But let me add that such a desirability characterization may be something that can be reached and made intelligible only by considerable effort. It is no part of my view that another must be treated as 'a dull babbling loon' simply because we cannot immediately understand his desires in terms of our own antecedently accepted desirability characterizations. The genuine effort to attain understanding of others might as surely extend the range of desirability characterizations we ourselves accept as it might deepen our understanding of those desirability characterizations we anyway accepted. We might be led, for example, to recognize some human need or want which we had previously overlooked, or we might be led to a deeper appreciation of some antecedently recognized need or want. Indeed, nothing can rule out a priori the possibility that the effort to understand the desires of others and their reciprocal efforts to understand our own lead to our recognizing that at least some of our antecedently accepted desirability characterizations served to distinguish *merely* imagined goods.

In the first chapter (p. 28) I attributed to Miss Anscombe the following condition upon desire ascriptions: a necessary condition of the acceptability of an ascription of some specific desire to an agent is that the ascriber have 'reached and made intelligible' some 'desirability characterization' of the (potential) state of affairs specified by the content of the desire so ascribed. The elucidation of that condition has so far been cast in terms of ascriptions of desires to others; now we need to consider self-ascriptions of desires.

Consider the case of an outsider engaged in the project of trying to come by an understanding of the desires of the people within some alien culture. After entering into their practices, he might reach the point of being himself moved, independently of his adopted project, to engage in some ritual activity – the gnawing of the bones of the dead, the polishing of the car of a Sunday morning – without yet being able to produce any characterization of that activity which seems to him adequate to revealing, to capturing, its desirability. He sees the ritual activity 'as somehow desirable'; he has, so to say, been infected with the desires of those in the, now not so alien, community; yet those perceptions of desirability, those desires, predate attainment of forms of expression adequate to the communication of those perceptions as specific desirability perceptions of the objects of those desires. (Talk of being 'infected with' some desire might prompt the question of how these cases differ from Taylor's

Sisyphus (Chapter 1, pp. 29–33); the question is shortly answered below (pp. 44–5).

Admittedly, such a position will represent a halfway house in the enquirer's pursuit of understanding. Yet it does not seem to me 'fair nonsense' to think that some level of understanding has been achieved. Our enquirer will now be as puzzled by himself as he is by those around him; but that puzzlement will be of a quite different character from that which he experienced upon first encountering the alien community's activities, and quite different again from that felt upon confrontation with an individual who claims simply to 'want' a saucer of mud. While individual eccentricities with utterly opaque contents can perhaps on occasion be dismissed, transmissible communal practices with clear contents cannot; and reception of a transmissible desire constitutes a challenge to shape some communicable expression of the perception of desirability in the object of that desire.

ANOTHER MISCONCEPTION?

We can now appreciate the instructive suggestion mentioned at the beginning of the chapter (p. 34) as regards what desire is. This suggestion takes the central case of an agent's desiring something as being constituted by his having a desirability characterization of the object of desire, with one derivative case being constituted by his having merely a desirability perception of that object. That is, in the central kind of case an agent's desiring something is his having a characterization of the object of desire which serves by his lights to bring to an agreed end the questioning of why he wants that object: a characterization of the object of desire which serves by his lights to communicate the desirability of that object. The insertion of the phrase 'by his lights' marks no relativization within the notion of a desirability characterization itself but simply serves to record recognition of the possibility of error. In these central cases, so the suggestion goes, to desire is to have a putative desirability characterization *period*.

The obvious rejoinder is that the tendentious classical misconception of what desire is has been replaced by a clearly erroneous one: for ordinary discourse is surely cluttered with observations of the form 'I see that doing such-and-such is desirable but I don't want to do it.' That can no more plausibly be denied than can the claim that the same discourse is punctuated by observations of the form 'I didn't want to do it but I did it.' But does this latter phenomenon reveal current orthodoxy about reasons for acting to be mistaken? Not in any straightforward way: for one who subscribes to that orthodoxy will attempt to explain away the problematic significance of the phenomenon through an account of the different things speakers might mean when they say what they do say. Just the same strategy is open to a defender of the conception of desire here at issue.

I shall begin by mentioning some of the obvious possible diagnoses of what is going on when someone says 'I see that doing such-and-such is desirable but I don't want to do it.' In such a remark the speaker may be making manifest his attachment to some quasi-philosophical idea about the possible objects of human desires, some restriction upon those possible objects in terms, say, of pleasure or self-interest: 'There's nothing in it for me, so desirable as it is I *cannot* want to do it.' (Such a restriction is closely related to a doctrine which plays a large role in Kant's moral philosophy.) Or again, the kind of remark at issue may be the manifestation of some general misconception on the part of the speaker as to the nature of desire itself, some general identification of desire with, say, 'felt impulse': 'I don't feel anything for it, so desirable as it is it is not the case that I want to do it.' A more complex possibility is that the speaker's talk of what is desirable should be understood in terms of mere 'grading' or 'classifying' in accordance with some scheme of values which he does not in fact subscribe to – be they the values of bourgeois society, of The School, or of the Ministry of Agriculture and Fisheries (cf. Urmson 1946). In such a case precision of expression would *require* an explicit relativization of the 'desirability' claim. And finally there are the cases in which what is in play is some general contrast between moral considerations and others: the claim to which voice is being given in such cases amounting to the idea that the desires which arise from non-moral considerations outweigh those which arise from moral ones.

Aside from those more obvious possibilities, a remark of the form 'I see that doing such-and-such is desirable, but I don't want to do it' might be the manifestation of a view, perhaps held only tacitly, which I shall call that of *the atomistic character of desirability perception*: this is, loosely speaking, the view that having once seen what appears to be a desirable feature of, say, some action, consideration of other, undesirable features of that action can never eliminate that initial perception of desirability. Further consideration of the action could issue in recognition of undesirable features of the action which are deemed to count for more than the originally perceived desirability; but the original desirability perception lives on. Things could only be otherwise, on this view, if the recognition of the undesirable features serves to blind the agent to the desirable feature.

What a battlefield the human mind would be if this atomistic view were correct! Once thus thinking atomistically, it will seem plausible to say of any action whatsoever: 'There is something to be said for, and something to be said against, doing it – and also for and against not doing it' (Davidson 1969: 35). And any action, except those arising from a blinding focus, will be seen as the outcome of a battle waged between conflicting desires – a battle in which usually many troops will be found upon either side of the front.

It is instructive to compare two different kinds of case which count against this atomistic view of desirability perception. One such kind of case stems from the thought, familiar since the time of Aristotle, that the boundaries between any given virtue and its flanking vices are vague and that there are no directly applicable rules elucidating the content of the virtue which serve to resolve all disputable cases. The difference between a brave action and a foolhardy one need not come readily to even the open eye and the clear mind. In many such disputable cases an agent can be led to revise his initial judgement that some particular action would truly be an instance of, say, bravery by his coming to see through consideration of other aspects of the contemplated action that to perform it would be to neglect the requirements of, say, justice. Convinced that *in this case* the dictates of justice and bravery do not conflict, he is led to retract the initially proffered desirability characterization of the action: he accepts that it would not be brave to do it. But in the other kind of case there is a sense in which the agent is not led literally to retract his initial 'desirability characterization' of the contemplated action: it is rather that, in the light of his consideration of further aspects of the contemplated action, the agent no longer sees that characterization as constituting a *desirability* characterization of the action. By thinking atomistically he could still accept that there is some 'desirability characterization' of the contemplated action; by considering the action in its totality, so to say, he can see nothing desirable in *it*. (Compare – and contrast – McDowell 1978: 26.)

So, *pace* the atomistic view of desirability perception, one can seem to see some feature of an action as desirable while attending only to that feature and yet come to see it as having no desirability at all within the specific context of the action as a whole. Now, when someone says something of the form 'I see that doing such-and-such is desirable, but I don't want to do it', it might be the case that the first part of his judgement arises from an adopted atomistic view-point, whereas the second part of the judgement issues from his contemplation of the action as a whole. The speaker is partially under the influence of the atomistic view: but only partially since otherwise, on the conception of desire here being examined, he would have the appropriate desire, albeit an outweighed desire.

Doubtless there are other possibilities open to one who wishes to explain away the putative force of observations of the form 'I see that doing such-and-such is desirable, but I don't want to do it'; but enough has already been said to cast doubt upon this *kind* of objection to the conception of desire at issue.

Another objection to that conception is this: the equation, roughly, of desiring with thinking desirable ignores the distinction between desires and mere wishes. Perhaps the having of some desirability characterization captures at least the central cases of wishing that such-and-such be the case; but desire requires the occurrence of some further element, be it of feeling, of tendency or of some combination of those elements. Or so runs the objection.

It cannot be denied that in English there are clearly distinct verb-forms 'to desire' and 'to wish'. But it does not follow either that there are two distinct kinds of mental states, desires and wishes, or that desiring is wishing *plus* something else. Very roughly – at the level of 'folk semantics' – the situation seems to be this: the English verb 'to wish' is used as the expression of desire under certain specific circumstances, of which the most central is that in which the agent believes it beyond his capacities to realize the object of his desire. (Think, for example, of past-directed desires.) That is only the most central of cases: for the phenomenon to be accounted for is a messy one. But one who wishes to trade upon that mess as an objection to the contemplated conception of desiring also has some accounting to do: perhaps most notably, for the fact that the very same considerations which undermine in a given context a speaker's claim to sincerity in the expression of his 'desires' also serve within that same context to undermine the speaker's claim to sincerity in the expression of his 'wishes'. It matters not whether I say 'I wish that window were open' or 'I want that window open': if you offer to open it, and I react by rejecting your offer, the same thing is afoot.

That is at the level of folk semantics; things are not that different when theory is allowed to enter the scene. Maybe for some theoretical purposes a vivid distinction between desires and wishes is useful. So let us consider one such case. In his William James lectures, Richard Wollheim said:

> I wish for something rather than merely desire it, when I desire it: and because I desire it I tend to imagine (in the appropriate mode) my desire satisfied: and when I imagine my desire satisfied, it is for me as if that desire were satisfied.
>
> (Wollheim 1984: 90)

Despite Wollheim's subsequent caution upon the point, the conceptual dependence of this notion of wishing upon that of desire seems clear: the objection which treats desiring as wishing *plus* conceptually places the cart right before the horse.

DEEPLY OBSCURE OBJECTS OF DESIRE

Earlier we were led to recognize the existence of a halfway house in an enquirer's pursuit of understanding: one in which the enquirer has come to see an activity 'as somehow desirable', and to act accordingly, while not yet having attained any desirability characterization of the activity concerned. That halfway house blocked any identification *simpliciter* of desiring with having a desirability characterization. But the objection now arises that that talk of seeing an activity 'as somehow desirable' amounts to no more than the registering of the fact that the person acts accordingly – i.e. has the pertinent desire! The conception of desire under examination threatens to collapse into vacuity. And that being so, the objection might continue, we now have no reason at all to call into question the status as desires of the 'desires' that the gods induced in Richard Taylor's Sisyphus by implanting some substance in his veins (Chapter 1, pp. 29–33). Moreover, one engaged for example in some ritual activity because of some desirability perception but who yet lacks any desirability characterization of that activity has been conceded here to have a desire (p. 39); but that 'infectious' desire seems to be just as isolated from interaction with the subject's other desires and beliefs as is the supposed desire attributed to Sisyphus by Taylor.

The worries here cannot be immediately dismissed by reference to our knowledge of how Sisyphus's supposed desire was induced. Rather, the following points should be stressed. We lack any reason to believe that an enquiring outsider joining Sisyphus in his activity will come, independently of his project of enquiry, to share Sisyphus's supposed desire. We lack any reason to believe that there is a desirability perception with a masked desirability characterization which connects with other actions performed by Sisyphus. And we lack any reason to believe that there is a desirability perception with a masked desirability characterization which were Sisyphus to discover it could lead, depending upon his other desires and beliefs, to any of a limitless variety of actions or to any form of proto-practical deliberation. Think how different the case would be were the implanted substance to work by heightening Sisyphus's unarticulated concern for his physical development. His desire would then be transmissible (to some at least); it would be likely to show itself in other actions of his; and even if it did not, it would be likely to do so were he to come to recognize that that was indeed what had moved him to engage in his stone-rolling. Moreover, were he to come by that recognition he would then be placed to engage in some proto-practical deliberation which could issue in a changed appreciation of that desire's place within his scheme of things, a changed appreciation which might have innumerable ramifications within his conduct. Just so for our enquirer into the alien culture when lodged in the halfway house. He has come to see the ritual activity 'as somehow desirable'; the desire has been transmitted to him even though he lacks any desirability characterization of the ritual activity. But that novel desirability perception is likely to manifest itself in new, or modified, forms of behaviour on his part. And even if it does not so manifest itself, it is likely that it would do so were he to come to recognize the masked desirability characterization of that activity. And such a recognition would permit proto-practical deliberation directed towards appreciation of that desire's due place within the enquirer's scheme of things. The point here is not just that Taylor's characterization of the case of Sisyphus is silent upon all these further considerations which might begin to ground employment for that case of the concept of desire; rather what matters for present purposes is that appreciation of those further considerations frees the conception of desire under consideration of the appearance of vacuity.

None the less I think there to be a more formidable difficulty facing this conception of desire. Desirability perceptions were introduced to take account of the existence of the halfway house: of cases where an agent has some desire yet lacks any adequate desirability characterization of the object (pp. 39–40). A simple illustration of such cases would be one in which some unrecognized need or want gives rise directly to a desire. In many such cases little reflection is needed upon the agent's part for him to recognize the issuing need or want, and so to come by an adequate desirability characterization. But whether much reflection is needed or not the discussion of the last objection has made it clear that the content of talk of desirability perceptions comes to rest upon its connection with talk of *available* desirability characterizations. Yet in an important group of cases it is far from clear that there is any such connection: for we find in such cases *deeply* obscure objects of desire.

Consider what might be called *substitution activities*. These range from the lonely husband who, away from home, kisses a photo of his wife before sleeping, through the case where, when alone, one continues the violent argument which has just driven one from the company of another, to at least the case of compulsive hand-washing. Russell gave a characteristic example in *The Analysis of Mind*:

> Suppose you have been jilted in a way that wounds your vanity. Your natural impulsive desire will be of the sort expressed in Donne's poem:
>
>   When by thy scorn, O Murderess, I am dead,
>
> in which he explains how he will haunt the poor lady as a ghost, and prevent her from enjoying a moment's peace. But two things stand in the way of your expressing yourself so naturally: on the one hand, your vanity, which will not acknowledge how hard you are hit; on the other hand, your conviction that you are a civilized and humane person who could not possibly indulge so crude a desire as revenge. You will therefore experience a restlessness which will at first seem quite aimless, but will finally resolve itself in a conscious desire to change your profession, or go around the world, or conceal your identity and live in Putney. . . . [However], you will find travel disappointing, and the East less fascinating than you had hoped – unless some day, you hear that the wicked one has in turn been jilted.
>
> (Russell 1921: 73)

A perhaps more exotic example is found in Genet's *Our Lady of the Flowers*:

> Divine has introduced Our Lady to her. Some days later, showed

her, decent girl that she was, a little 'photomatic' photo of the murderer.

Mimosa takes the photo, puts it on her outstretched tongue, and swallows it.

'I simply adore that Our Lady of yours. I'm communioning her.'

(New York 1963: 204)

The examples are not so everyday; the general phenomenon is. In few of these cases is it easy to come up with a plausible desirability characterization of the activity; and even when that seems easy, it is correspondingly difficult to make much sense of the belief consequently attributed to the agent in the rationalization of his action.

It is important to be clear upon the distinctive difficulties posed by such cases. In some other, perfectly commonplace, cases of an agent's 'active error', the agent concerned has some straightforward adequate desirability characterization of a certain kind of action while also having an intelligibly mistaken belief about the character of the action he performs; in other cases, along with a correct belief about the character of the action he performs he also has some intelligibly mistaken putative desirability characterization of the kind of action exemplified. In both kinds of case the agent has some intelligible desirability characterization which makes itself manifest in a wide variety of behaviour within different circumstances. And even if there is a temporarily obscure object of desire – even if the agent for the time being merely has some desirability perception – we have seen how that perception, through its links with some available desirability characterization, might make itself manifest in a wide variety of behaviour within different circumstances (pp. 44–5). But substitution activities do not in general exemplify any such kind of case.

The difficulty here can be put in the form of a dilemma. Either we tie the notion of a desirability perception to that of an available desirability characterization, in which case at least some substitution activities represent cases of desire without desirability perception. Or we tie the notion of desirability perception to that of desire, shedding its ties *in these cases* to that of an available desirability characterization, thus using the notion of desirability perception merely to register the presence of desire. Then taking the conception of desire under consideration as an unrestrictedly general claim about the nature of desire, that conception is either false or vacuous.

I prefer to use the expression 'desirability perception' in accordance with the first horn of this dilemma, and am thereby led to reject as false the claim under consideration about what desire is. But this does not imply denial of the importance of the connections between the notion of desire, on the one hand, and the notions of desirability characterization and desirability perception on the other. Nor, therefore, does anything just said deny the importance of the progress made in extending the circle of concepts within which that of desire takes its place.

DESIRE ITSELF

In the first chapter reasons were given in favour of rejection of the classical conception of desire. So far in the present chapter reasons have been adduced against one alternative to that conception of what desire is (and further reasons against that alternative conception will later emerge). But what, then, is desire?

In *Ways of Meaning* I made the following remarks which I now think can serve as a gloss upon at least the distinction between desire, on the one hand, and desirability characterizations and perceptions (as here, now, understood) on the other:

> Miss Anscombe, in her work on intention, has drawn a broad distinction between two *kinds* of mental state, factual belief being the prime exemplar of one kind and desire a prime exemplar of the other (Anscombe, *Intention*, section 2). The distinction is in terms of the *direction of fit* of mental states with the world. Beliefs aim at the true, and their being true is their fitting the world; falsity is a decisive failing in a belief, and false beliefs should be discarded; beliefs should be changed to fit with the world, not vice versa. Desires aim at realization, and their realization is the world fitting with them; the fact that the indicative content of a desire is not realized in the world is not yet a failing *in the desire*, and not yet reason to discard the desire; the world, crudely, should be changed to fit with our desires, not vice versa.
>
> (Platts 1979: 256–7)

That is a metaphorical gloss; and I am doubtful about the likelihood of a more literal cashing out of the distinction so drawn. (I find it unsurprising that a recent attempt so to cash out that distinction rests upon a dispositional misconception of desire (Smith 1987).)

But the metaphorical character of this way of marking the distinction might threaten to render problematic any subsequent claims about the actual instantiation of the distinction. That is why I have preferred the more circuitous route of establishing a real distinction through consideration of the realities of substitution activities. The real distinction having thus been established, I then see no problem in its subsequent glossing in metaphorical terms.

The positive results so far of this enquiry into the nature of desire might seem somewhat thin. But why should it be presumed that in positive terms there is much to be said *at this level of abstraction* about so general, widely-used a concept?

What I now propose to do is to work towards a philosophical taxonomy of desire, a philosophical description of different general *kinds* of desire. Like any such description, this one will need to be both detailed and veridical; the more general philosophical interest of the descriptive details will then emerge in the following chapter.

SOME INITIAL DISTINCTIONS

In *The Possibility of Altruism* (1970: 29–32) Thomas Nagel distinguished motivated from unmotivated desires. The burden of his account of this exhaustive distinction was carried by his elucidation of motivated desires. In fact there seemed to be three distinct attempted elucidations. Initially the suggestion was that motivated desires 'are arrived at by decision and after deliberation', while the final suggestion seemed to be that motivated desires are ascribed in the same, derivative, way as beliefs in elementary principles of logic. But in between was a third suggestion which perhaps avoided the errors of the first, the elusiveness of the final and the marked appearance of tension between those two:

> if my desire is a motivated one, the explanation of it will be the same as the explanation of [the agent's pursuit of the goal], and it is by no means obvious that a desire must enter into this further explanation. Although it will no doubt be generally admitted that some desires are motivated, the issue is whether another desire always lies behind the motivated one, or whether sometimes the motivation of the initial desire involves no reference to another, unmotivated desire.
>
> (ibid.)

On that issue it was clear where Nagel stood:

If we bring these observations to bear on the question whether desires are always among the necessary conditions of *reasons* for action, it becomes obvious that there is no reason to believe that they are. Often the desires which an agent necessarily experiences in acting will be motivated exactly as the action is. If the act is motivated by reasons stemming from certain external factors, and the desire to perform it is motivated by those same factors, the desire obviously cannot be among the conditions for the presence of those reasons.

(ibid.)

Within the class of 'motivated desires', then, a subclass is first distinguished in something like the following terms: for any desire within this subclass a complete account of the presumed desirability of its object will logically make reference, not to the existence of the selfsame desire, but rather to the existence of some *other* desire had by the agent. Moreover, in any particular case of this kind, the agent may be able to support the claim that the account concerned serves to capture the object's desirability by reference both to the existence of his other desire and to the relevant facts about the role potentially played by the object in the project of satisfying that other desire. Two seemingly obvious examples of desires of this kind are, first, those in which the object of desire is a *means* to the object otherwise desired, and, secondly, those in which the object of desire is a *constitutive part* of the object otherwise desired. But, more problematically and more importantly, it is claimed that there is another subclass of motivated desires that are to be accounted for in terms which, shunning reference to other desires, refer only to 'reasons stemming from certain external factors'.

Nagel's main interest was indeed in the possibility of altruism; but a strategically crucial part of his argument aimed at establishing that possibility was dedicated to showing that at least some prudential desires are members of the problematic subclass of motivated desires just now mentioned. On that point Nagel was concerned to show how it is possible for an agent rationally to be motivated by the thought that he will in the future have a reason to promote a certain state of affairs independently of any present unmotivated desire. That possibility can be accounted for, Nagel claimed, by reference to a conception we have of time: that all times – past, present and future – are equally real. In the very briefest possible terms: for one fully possessed of that conception, his judgement that he will have a reason to promote a certain state of affairs commits him, independently of any present unmotivated desire, to the judgement that he now has a reason to promote that state of affairs; and acceptance of that latter judgement is, other things being equal, tantamount to being motivated to promote that state of affairs. Yet when motivation arises in that way, it remains true for Nagel that a corresponding present desire can be attributed to the agent: that the agent has the corresponding desire simply follows from the fact that the considerations motivate him. The desire so attributed is, then, a member of the problematic subclass of motivated desires.

Our present concern is not with the fine details of Nagel's account of prudence, but a word of caution is in place about the seeming widespread acceptance of that account. It is unclear to what degree later writers are committed to specific details of Nagel's account of prudential motivation. For example, Philippa Foot seemed to embrace Nagel's account when claiming that prudential reasons provide the most obvious counter-examples to the thesis that all reasons for action depend on the agent's desires. The desire rightly attributed to a prudentially motivated agent cannot, according to Foot, be the basis of the reasons for acting; rather,

> what we have here is a use of 'desire' which indicates a motivational direction and nothing more. One may compare it with the use of 'want' in 'I want to ø' where only intentionality is implied. Can *wanting* in this sense create the reason for acting? It seems that it cannot. For in the first place the desires of which we are now speaking are to be attributed to the agent only in case he is moved to action, or would be so moved in the absence of counteracting reasons or causes, and it is a mistake to set corresponding limits to the scope of reasons for acting. Moreover a false account is given even of the cases in which action occurs. For what happens there is that a man is moved to action by the recognition that he has reason to act. This would be impossible if there were not reasons to be recognized until the agent has been moved.
>
> (Foot 1972b: 149–50)

Yet in a later postscript to the paper in which she seemed to embrace Nagel's account, Mrs Foot expresses an inclination towards the view that all reasons for acting depend either on what is in the agent's interest or else on his desires (ibid.: p.156). But that suggests her distance from Nagel is great indeed: for in his account prudential reasons are reasons relating to any kind of provision for the future and have, in general, no particular connection with the future interests of the agent.

A more recent writer who seems closer to Nagel in his elucidation of the distinction between motivated and unmotivated desires and of the distinction within the class of motivated desires is John McDowell:

> A full specification of a reason . . . must contain enough to reveal the favourable light in which the agent saw his projected action. We tend to assume that this is effected, quite generally, by the inclusion of a desire. . . . However, it seems to be false that the motivating power of all reasons derives from their including desires. Suppose, for instance, that we explain a person's performance of a certain action by crediting him with awareness of some fact which makes it likely (in his view) that acting in that way will be conducive to his interest. Adverting to his view of the facts may suffice, on its own, to show us the favourable light in which his action appeared to him. No doubt we credit him with an appropriate desire, perhaps for his own future happiness. But the commitment to ascribe such a desire is simply consequential on our taking him to act as he does for the reason we cite. . . .
>
> (McDowell 1978: 14–15)

And in a later paper he writes:

> Explanations of actions in terms of reasons work by revealing the favourable light in which the agent saw what he did (or at least what he attempted). In ['Are moral requirements hypothetical imperatives?'] I distinguished between cases in which this is achieved only by citing, or taking for granted, a desire, and cases in which the mention of a cognitive state (the agent's conception of the situation) suffices to show the favourable light in which the agent saw his action.
>
> (McDowell 1982: 301)

So for McDowell, as for Nagel, the ascription of a member of the problematic subclass of motivated desires is simply consequential upon our taking the agent to act as he does for the reason we cite in explanation of his action; but the explanatory burden – explanatory both of the action and of the thus ascribed desire – is carried according to McDowell by the agent's 'view of the facts', by 'a cognitive state (the agent's conception of the situation)'. Thus Nagel's talk of 'reasons stemming from certain external factors' is glossed in terms of the agent's 'cognitive states', these latter perhaps being deemed to 'stem from' the facts of the matter (the external *fact*ors).

SOME INITIAL QUESTIONS

Two puzzles arise immediately. The cruder one is this. For both Nagel and McDowell (as also for Mrs Foot), desire never drops completely out of the picture of agency: even when the explanatory or motivational burden is carried, in McDowell's terms, by some cognitive state, by the agent's 'view of the facts', still a desire is to be attributed to the agent. The desire so ascribed is an 'appropriate' motivated desire, and its ascription is deemed 'simply consequential on our taking him to act as he does for the reason we cite'. The puzzle here is evident. The more familiar attempts to ground the part of contemporary orthodoxy to the effect that a complete specification of an agent's reason for acting must make reference to his desires (or 'pro-attitudes') as well as to his beliefs work by considering examples in which the agent's beliefs are supposed to be clearly neutral in motivational terms – a feature which is often secured by means of a lofty level of abstraction, through silence, in relation to the agent and his situation. If the examples are set up like this, then it will seem clear that what an agent will be led to do, to attempt to do, or seriously to consider doing will turn upon the nature of his so far unspecified desires. The specification of the contents of those desires will seem to be *the* means of revealing the imagined good in the light of which the agent acts or contemplates acting. But that result is secured only upon the assumption that the beliefs initially attributed to the agent are neutral in relation to motivational matters; and that is precisely what is not supposed to be so in the cases emphasized by Nagel and McDowell in their pursuit of establishing the existence of a distinct model of explanation of action. In the favoured cases of Nagel and McDowell the explanatory burden is to be carried by some 'cognitive state' of the agent: why, then, should they persist in the attribution of desire within those cases?

There is indeed a considerable distance between the views of Nagel and McDowell, on the one hand, and the full orthodoxy about reasons for acting attacked by them on the other. That orthodoxy does not merely claim that reasons for acting always include desires as well as beliefs; it also maintains that it is desires which in all cases carry the motivational-cum-explanatory burden. For this orthodoxy, that is, it is always desires that are the active powers involved in action upon a reason, it is always desires that motivate and move the agent to act. The rejection of that second element within the orthodoxy thus marks out some considerable distance. Still, the puzzle remains: exactly why should desire always be kept within the picture?

The other puzzle is less straightforward. At least at an intuitive level it seems that we can distinguish, for a given agent within a specific situation, three different *uses* of sentences in relation to his situation. (Not all of the uses can be distinguished by reference to the kinds of vocabulary occurring in the sentences used; perhaps none can.)

1 The self-ascription by the agent of a desire to do the action in fact performed under some specific description of that action.
2 The agent's giving of some desirability characterization of the action performed, which characterization is supposed by him adequate to the communication of the action's desirability in his eyes.
3 The agent's giving of some objective characterization of the action performed, which characterization, while not itself a desirability characterization, yet could serve as a reason in support of some desirability characterization.

Now, which if any of these uses is in play in the appropriate specification of the agent's 'conception of the situation', of his (motivating) 'cognitive state', which if any in play in an appropriate specification of his 'situation', of the 'facts', and what account if any can be given of the idea that the former 'stems from' the latter – an idea which is essential for the thought that the former is indeed a *cognitive* state?

REFINING THE INITIAL DISTINCTIONS

The first puzzle relates, then, to the persistence of Nagel and McDowell in the attribution of a desire to the agent even in cases in which the explanatory or motivational burden is carried by reference to some cognitive state, to the agent's 'view of the facts'. I suspect that the determining thoughts involved were along the following lines. First, there was an acceptance of the metaphorical account of desire in terms of its distinctive 'direction of fit' with the world. Then, within the scope of that acceptance, there was a further thought to the effect that, even when the motivational or explanatory burden is carried by a mental state with a belief-type 'direction of fit' with the world, yet action manifests the presence of a state of desire with *its* distinctive 'direction of fit' with the world. The argument for this further thought might, schematically, have been this: *any action (other than intentional omissions) is, and must be meant to be, a change in the world; but any such intended change requires the obtaining of a mental state with a 'direction of fit' of the kind distinctive of desire.* I presume that is also the line of argument behind Mrs Foot's talk of 'a motivational direction' (p. 51); I also presume that what is most likely to hide that line of argument is attachment to some active power conception of desire – a conception of desire as an atomistic quasi-mechanical phenomenon, as an inner shove free of propositional content. But it should anyway be clear that the line of argument concerned could scarcely be more different from the more usual arguments directed to establishing the same result which were earlier mentioned (p. 53); I also take it to be clear that this line of argument goes against the conception of desire which was rejected earlier on the more particular basis of the reality of substitution activities (pp. 47–8).

The other puzzle concerns three different possible uses of sentences by an agent: (1) to ascribe to himself a desire to do an action in fact performed; (2) to give a desirability characterization of the action; and (3) to give a characterization of the action in support of some other, desirability characterization of it.

On the view of desire now being relied upon here, the general distinction between the uses mentioned in (1) and (2) will be glossed anew in terms of their distinctive 'directions of fit' with the world. But in finer detail a difference which can often occur between the anyway distinct uses (1) and (2) is exemplified in cases where the *specification* of the action concerned within the content of the self-ascribed desire is different from that which constitutes the desirability characterization given of the action. That may simply be a matter of the desirability characterization's involving a greater, audience-directed, spelling out of detail; more interestingly, it may instead reflect the occurrence of a case in which the agent finds himself with a desire while initially having no adequate desirability characterization of the object of desire, thus searching for, and supposedly finding, such a characterization.

As regards use (3), I think the 'messiness' of the pragmatic phenomenon dictates that all that can be offered is a listing, perhaps inevitably incomplete, of the kinds of cases in which use (3), *as distinctively characterized*, occurs. (That emphasis is essential: many cases which might be confused with that usage amount to no more than a sharper degree of specification of the relevant desirability characterization.) In all such kinds of cases, what is said in the giving of the reason as well as quite how it is said will depend upon the nature of the particular audience to which the reason is directed; and the matter will be different in those cases in which the two 'agents' coexist within one and the same person. Still, in general terms, I suspect the most common such case to be something like this: two agents accept the same desirability characterizations but differ over the question of whether some given characterization applies to the case at hand because of some difference over a matter of fact. Perhaps the one thinks the recipient of the benefits of the action is a true and constant friend, the other thinking the recipient no better than a fair-weather companion. Diverse considerations might underlie the disagreement over that matter of fact; but only within a small subclass of such cases will that disagreement come to rest upon the phenomenon, much emphasized in general by McDowell, of a difference (in this case) in the agents' *conceptions* of what friendship is. (See, for example, his remarks about differing conceptions of what it is to be 'shy and sensitive' (McDowell 1978: 21–2.) Not every difference about beliefs cast in terms of friendship points to a difference of conception. Yet more important is the fact that that subclass of cases is distinct from those cases in which differing conceptions of what, say, friendship is issue in differences as to which *general* characterizations are indeed desirability characterizations, and quite distinct again from cases in which such differing conceptions issue in differences of *weighting* attached to agreed desirability characterizations. That is: the possible roles played by some 'difference of conception' constitute a notably heterogeneous bundle. And note, as a final word of caution, that none of the possibilities that have been mentioned need be in play in the case of some 'bare' disagreement over whether, say, a given action exemplifies generosity or extravagance: reasons can run out in such cases.

So, in what I think is the most common kind of case in which there occurs a distinctive reason-giving use of the kind (3), the reason therein adduced is directed towards showing the applicability of an agreed desirability characterization to some particular action through the resolution of some difference over a matter of fact. The profferer of the reason may think of the difference as having arisen only because of the other's having simply overlooked, or misperceived, some pertinent fact of the matter. But his adducing such a reason need not imply that his original application of the desirability characterization to the case at hand was the outcome of some inference.

Which if any of the uses distinguished is in play in the agent's specification of the content of his 'conception of the situation', which if any in play in an appropriate specification of the 'external factors', the 'facts', and what account if any can be given of the idea that the former 'stems from' the latter in such a way as indeed to reveal the former to be a cognitive state? I think the answers that should be given are, at least in large part, clear. In the distinctive kind of case at issue, within the problematic subclass of motivated desires, the motivational burden is carried by some cognitive state of the agent the full specification of which suffices to reveal the imagined good in the light of which he acted. In the more straightforward cases, the agent's specification therefore contains a desirability characterization of the action in fact performed. So cases of the agent's usage of kind (3), as distinctively characterized, cannot be cases of usage adequate for the full specification of that content. Rather, the agent's specification of that requires a usage of his of kind (2): his specification of the content of his cognitive state is achieved through the giving of a desirability characterization. Equally clearly, the thought that what has been specified is a cognitive state requires that an adequate specification of the 'facts' from which that state stems can be given by the use of the same desirability characterization: it requires, that is, the thought of such a characterization picking out 'external' desirability characteristics of the action concerned. Within the subclass of motivated desires, then, the agent thinks of the desirability of the action concerned as *independent* of his now having recognized that desirability.

What can be said of the relation between the state of desire reported by a use of kind (1) and the agent's having of some desirability characterization as reported by a use of kind (2)? Remaining within the problematic subclass of motivated desires, the best suggestion seems to me the following: in cases where appropriate intentional action ensues, the agent's having of a desirability characterization has *elicited*, has *given rise to*, has *reasonably issued in*, the desire made manifest in that action (cf. Platts 1980b: 76–8). The relation there being gestured at will be a recurring theme in much of what follows; still, some initial negative remarks may avert immediate misunderstanding. At the risk of assimilating quite distinct relations, consider first the relation between some appropriate belief-desire pair – regardless of the kind of desire involved – and a corresponding intention to act. If in a given case the former gives rise to the latter, the belief-desire pair rationalizes – makes at least minimally reasonable – the intention so formed. But it would be a desperate mistake to conclude from this that the intention so formed is intentionally formed. Likewise, to hold that an agent's having a desirability characterization can give rise to a corresponding desire is not to hold that the agent intentionally forms the desire. Next, consider the relation between some appropriate belief-desire pair – regardless of the kind of desire involved – and corresponding action. If action ensues, the belief-desire pair rationalizes the action so performed. But we have seen in the first chapter that such rationalizing explanation need not lend itself to a predictive project: if in a given case action does not ensue, there need be no explanation of that 'failure' cast in terms of the mental and personal life of the agent. Likewise, then, to hold that an agent's having a desirability characterization can give rise to a corresponding desire is not to hold, for example, that any difference of corresponding desires *must* reflect some difference of desirability characterizations had.

DESIRE AND DESIRABILITY

The views of John Stuart Mill provide an instructive contrast. He seemed to equate desiring an object and thinking it desirable, and notoriously sustained that 'the sole evidence it is possible to produce that anything is desirable, is that people do actually desire it' (Mill 1910: 32). Those claims are vague as to the kind of equivalence at issue, as to the connections if any between desirability and consensus of desires and as to the consequences for imaginable situations in which the desires of 'people' are different from what they 'actually' are. But at this point what matters most is, notwithstanding Mill's distaste for reflection on any 'point of Ontology', the clearly reductivist spirit in which his views are sustained: a spirit directed against mankind's predisposition 'to believe that any subjective feeling not otherwise accounted for, is a revelation of some objective reality' (ibid.: 39). Going along with that predisposition we shall think of all our desires as revelations of objective desirabilities; totally resisting it we shall think of the 'actual' desires of 'people' as the immediate and final source of all talk of desirability.

That something has gone wrong is testified to by the fact that nobody would indulge the presumed predisposition for *all* of his desires; and if it be granted that the predisposition comes most readily into play in the case of membership of the problematic subclass of motivated desires, some explanation should be given of this fact. Only with that explanation to hand will it be possible to determine the exact extent to which Mill's theory is revisionary. Still, freed of any such reductive spirit (without thereby falling into 'transcendentalism'), a similar looking claim to one made by Mill could be made in expression of the present view of desire and desirability in relation to the problematic subclass of motivated desires. Desiring is not here equated with 'thinking desirable' – with, say, the having of a desirability characterization – nor is the notion of desirability understood here in terms of what is 'actually' desired. Still, the following sounds right for these cases: the best evidence it is possible to produce that something is desirable is a desirability characterization of it, a specification of its external desirability characteristics; and the best evidence that that best evidence has been produced relates to the efficacy of that desirability characterization in eliciting desires.

DESIRE AND PLEASURE

Consider now the distinction drawn by Stephen Schiffer between what he calls 'reason-producing (r-p)' desires and 'reason-following (r-f)' desires. The latter, Schiffer tells us, are the same as Nagel's 'motivated' desires, so Schiffer's remarks upon 'reason-following' desires may help directly to elucidate the *general* class of motivated desires. Moreover, as we shall shortly see, his remarks upon 'reason-producing' desires may help with elucidation of one *sub*class of Nagel's 'unmotivated' desires. Schiffer writes:

> Should one's desire to ø be an r-f desire and should one in fact ø, then there will be a reason which is both the reason for which one desires to ø and the reason for which one ø's, and this reason will be entirely independent, logically, of the fact that one desires to ø. One thinks of one's ø-ing as being desirable in a certain way and it is because one's ø-ing is thought by one to be desirable in that way that one both desires to ø and ø's; it is not because one desires to ø that one finds one's ø-ing desirable; when one's desire is an r-f desire one believes that even if one did not have the desire one would have a reason to have it . . . the ultimacy lies, so to speak, not so much in the desire as in its object.

Matters are quite the reverse when we turn to r-p desires. When it is an r-p desire to ø that one acts on, the reason for which one ø's and, typically, the only reason one has to ø, is provided entirely by one's desire to ø. . . .

It is not because a thing is desirable in a certain way that one has an r-p desire for it; quite the contrary, it is desirable in that way precisely because one has the desire. . . .

. . . [W]hen one acts on an r-p desire one acts for the gain of pleasure and the relief of discomfort – usually both, always one or the other – that one's action affords. . . .

So with r-p desires generally: their *sine qua non* is that they are desires which, almost always, are both pleasurable to satisfy and discomforting to endure, always one or the other; in fact, the anticipated pleasure and relief of discomfort are nearly always inextricably related, in that what one anticipates is just the pleasurable relief of discomfort. . . .

(Schiffer 1976: 197–8)

If the desire, say, for the pleasure that eating will afford is a case of a 'reason-following' desire, then the pleasure is thought to be independent of the obtaining of that desire. That thought must seem senseless to one who, like Bishop Butler, holds that all pleasure depends upon desire reaching its appropriate object, that all pleasure stems from the fact that ø-ing satisfies the desire to ø. But this is false: imagine that with your mind elsewhere your smell is suddenly gratified with the fragrance of a rose (cf. Dent 1984:39). The example is Burke's, and it is perhaps better than the usually favoured one of eating since it is difficult to conceive a plausible possible case in which one *finds oneself* eating; moreover, it is easier to grasp the possibility in Burke's example that, the experience having once occurred, one comes to have a desire for the repetition of that pleasure in which the anticipated pleasure is still clearly independent of the obtaining of the desire. Doubtless the satisfaction of any of the majority of my desires gives me pleasure; but that may be merely an agreeable side-effect of the strict satisfaction of the desire. So in this extension of Burke's example, a chance encounter with some overlooked rose could afford the pleasure and satisfy the desire: but the person concerned should reasonably subscribe to the possibility that such an encounter would have produced such pleasure even if he had not had the desire which actually obtains.

Matters are different if the desire, say, for the pleasure that eating will afford is a pure case of a 'reason-producing' desire. The person wants to eat, say, because both of an uncomfortable feeling of hunger and of an anticipation of pleasure from so doing. In such a pure case, the anticipated pleasure is conditional upon the obtaining of the desire; thinking of a possible circumstance in which he does not have the desire which he actually has, the agent will be thinking of a possibility in which there would not be that anticipated pleasure produced by his eating.

Within our terms the most general difference between these two kinds of cases is simply put. If an agent acts upon a 'reason-producing' desire for pleasure, any complete specification of his desirability characterization of the action performed must make reference to the desire which he actually has: its desirability is consequent upon the obtaining of that desire. That is, such a desirability characterization will not be logically independent of an assertion of the obtaining of the desire. But no such condition upon complete specifications of desirability characterizations obtains in the cases of 'reason-following' desires: in harmless abbreviation, in such cases the desirability of the action performed is independent of the desire's actually obtaining (cf. Platts 1980b:77).

That account of the difference must be understood in the light of another. On contemplating a possibility in which he does not have the desire which he in fact actually has, the agent will in the case of that desire's being a 'reason-following' (i.e. motivated) desire still, here and now, think of the desirability of his performing an action of the kind which he in fact performs as untouched by the posited lack of desire on his part in the contemplated world; whereas in the case of his actual desire being a pure 'reason-producing' desire, he will think, here and now, of that desirability as having been eliminated within the envisaged circumstances. And finally, note that in cases of 'reason-producing' desires it would be obviously mistaken to try straightforwardly to apply talk of a desire's being a reasonable response to 'external' desirability characteristics of the action concerned: for there are no such characteristics in independence of the agent's actually having his desire.

JUST WANTING

So far we have distinguished three categories of desire. In Stephen Schiffer's terminology there is the category of 'reason-producing' desires. These have an essential phenomenological character, being either disagreeable in feeling when not satisfied, agreeable or pleasurable in feeling upon satisfaction or both. More theoretically, any such desire is logically self-referential in the sense that any full specification of the object of desire – any complete desirability characterization of its object – makes logical reference to the existence of the very desire itself. Moreover, the way in which that reference is there made serves to explain why it is that the 'desirability' of the object of desire does not 'transcend' the existence of that desire: on contemplating a possible world in which he does not have the desire concerned, the agent should see nothing desirable in the realization therein of what is his actual object of desire as specified by some *incomplete* desirability characterization of it.

Next, within the broader category of 'motivated' desires, of 'reason-following' desires, there is a subcategory characterized in the following terms: for any desire of this kind a complete desirability characterization of its object will logically make reference, not to the existence of the selfsame desire, but rather to the existence of some other desire had by the agent, whatever be the kind of this other desire. It is therefore obvious that, at least roughly speaking, while the putative desirability of the object of such a desire can 'transcend' the existence of that very desire, it will not 'transcend' the existence of the other desire had by the agent. Moreover, in any particular case of this kind, the agent can support the claim that the desirability characterization concerned serves to capture the object's desirability by reference both to the existence of the other desire of his and to the relevant facts about the role of the object so characterized in the project of satisfying that other desire.

And finally there is the remaining category of desire so far distinguished, the problematic subclass of 'motivated' desires focused upon in the discussions of both Nagel and McDowell. A desire of this kind neither has some essential phenomenological character nor need a complete desirability characterization of its object logically make reference to the existence of the desire itself. But nor need a complete desirability characterization of the object of a desire of this kind logically make reference to the existence of some other desire had by the agent. More positively, however, for any desire of this kind there is the possibility that the agent within some specific context produce some reason in support of the claim that the complete desirability characterization of its object is indeed one that serves to capture the desirability of that object: he is not fated to rest with the thought that he just wants it.

But there remains a final matter to complicate the picture. Schiffer tells us that Nagel's 'motivated' desires are the same as his own 'reason-following' desires whereas his own 'reason-producing' desires are only a proper subset of Nagel's 'unmotivated' desires (Schiffer 1976: 198–9, n. 4). Which desires, then, are 'unmotivated' and yet not, in Schiffer's terms, 'reason-producing'? The general characterization of desires of this remaining kind is essentially negative. The desires concerned lack the essential phenomenological character of 'reason-producing' desires, nor need a putative desirability characterization of the object of any such desire make logical reference to the existence of that desire (it thus being possible for the putative desirability of that object to 'transcend' the existence of the desire itself). But nor is it the case that for each desire of this kind a putative desirability characterization of its object must make logical reference to the existence of any other desire had by the agent. Nor, finally, is there any possibility in the case of a desire of this kind of the agent's producing some reason in support of any claim that the putative desirability characterization is indeed one that serves to capture the desirability of the object. Such desires are those which most invite the thought: *he just wants it.*

It is in these cases that we might most naturally follow Epictetus in talking of that which is desired being desired at random. Nagel mentioned some cases which we might think candidates here: my choosing to eat persimmon today, my wish that my ashes be scattered over the Potomac, my desire that there be parsley on the moon (Nagel 1970: 42–5). But there is no reason to restrict candidates to such choices, fancies and whims: why not include as candidates a desire for someone else's welfare or even the desire for the relief of suffering and the protection of the weak? This distinctive subcategory of unmotivated desires need not be limited to the fanciful, the funny and the flippant, nor need one who devotes his life to acting upon exemplars of this subcategory thereby become a character out of The Modern Novel (non-Californian, of course). But it must be stressed that the candidates mentioned are no more than that: very few everyday, pre-philosophical specifications of the content of a desire serve to determine the place of that desire within the taxonomy here presented. Nagel's examples seem good candidates for membership of this final kind of desire, especially that of persimmon with its suggestion of the common experience of choosing randomly from a menu; but whether a specific instantiation of any of those candidates will be elected will turn upon the question of whether that instantiation satisfies the characterization given of this remaining kind of desire.

Bernard Williams once considered a case with the following structure: the state of affairs S desired does not contain the desirer, nor does a specification of it essentially refer to him or imply his existence or imply any relation of his to anything or anybody in S; least of all does the specification of S, that which satisfies the desire, have to mention the desire itself. Of Nagel's examples, only that of parsley's being on the moon is likely to be of this kind; but desires for Mary's welfare or for the relief of suffering and protection of the weak might also be of this kind. Of his case Williams remarked:

> This being so, S could obtain without our man existing at all, and this our man should be able to reflect upon. We can invite him to consider two possibilities for a world without him, one in which S comes about and one in which it does not. . . .
>   It must follow from what we have already put in, that he prefers one of these possibilities to the other; the one, of course, that contains S.
>
> (Williams 1973: 264)

Now suppose that, within the terms of the present taxonomy, the case so described is an example of the final kind of desire just now distinguished. What this case then serves to show is that the 'transcendence' of the putative desirability of the object of desire *vis-à-vis* the existence of that very desire does not serve to mark the distinction between motivated and unmotivated desires. That 'transcendence' serves in general merely to mark off other desires from 'reason-producing' ones.

Suppose we have an agent in the actual world w with some stock of desires; and suppose that he is contemplating some imaginable world w' in which he has some distinct stock of desires. Then the following questions arise:

1   What does he, in the actual world w, want here and now to have come about in the world w'?
2   What, in the imaginary world w', would he there and then want to have come about in that world?
3   Given his actual stock of desires in w, what does he here and now say of his stock of desires in the imaginary world w', and so of the content of his answer in this world to (2)?

By his restriction to cases of worlds without the agent, Williams of course limits himself to the first of these questions: his answer to his question is clearly correct. But the question that matters for our purposes is the third.

Suppose that the relevant stock of desires had by the agent in the actual world are of the newly recognized kind: what can he say here of an imaginary world in which his desires differ on the relevant subject-matter? He is there drawn to red snapper, not persimmon; to garlic, not parsley; to the Thames, not the Potomac; to John, not Mary; to the development of some individual ideal, not to the relief of suffering and protection of the weak. He can say that his desires in that imaginary world are different from what they are in the actual world; and he can therefore say (in at least some imaginable circumstances) that the likelihood of what he here actually desires coming about in that imaginary world is lessened. But that need be no great criticism of the imaginary world, any more than it is a great criticism of the actual world that in it many of my desires are not realized. Nor would the case be substantively changed by the addition to his stock of actual desires of some 'higher-order' desire *of the same kind* to the effect that he have his (other) desires in all imaginable worlds. That multiplies the differences between the worlds and ensures that some of his actual desires will not, *ex hypothesi*, be realized in the imaginary world; yet that will not reveal the imaginary world to be in any other way worse off or less desirable.

Note how different matters would be were the relevant stock of desires in the actual world to be a stock of motivated desires. Such desires require the thought on the agent's part that the object of desire is desirable independently of *his, now*, having the desire; that in turn requires the thought that, *ceteris paribus*, it is desirable that he have, and continue in imaginary worlds to have, that desire. But *that* desirability need be no consequence merely of his having other desires of the finally recognized kind. Moreover, with motivated desires there is the possibility of the agent's producing reasons in support of the pertinent desirability characterization; and that brings with it in this case the possibility of substantive criticism within the agent's answer to question (3) of his part in the imaginary world.

The point is neither to deny the existence of nor to condemn desires of the finally recognized kind. Rather, it is to emphasize the distinctiveness of motivated desires, not in terms of 'transcendence' but in terms of the possibility of reason-invoking discussion and evaluation of those desires.

Schiffer's view that 'reason-producing' desires are self-referential is grounded upon a logical form proposal for sentences ascribing them. It would be a mistake to urge that proposal for all of the members of the finally recognized kind of desire; but at a less formal level there is a point to a similar view of those desires. Faced with any apparent case of desiring, we can try to determine some desirability characterization of its object had by, or available to, the desirer. But what can be offered in the case of a desire of this finally recognized kind? The desirer might say: 'That is just what I want'; or he might add: 'And you want it too'; or again he might add: 'And they want it too.' There is nothing further that might be said which would not be tantamount to 'shifting' the desire concerned either into the class of 'reason-producing' desires or into the class of motivated desires. So for the agent the question of *why* he wants the thing concerned will have to be answered in terms of *it is just what he wants* or of *it is just what we (he and his audience) want* or of *it is just what they (he and others) want*. There is nothing available to the agent but a 'pure reference' to some exemplars of the type of desire – including, so to say, his own exemplar. And that is why there is such a poverty of reasonable discussion available when contemplating possible variations of such desires.

It would perhaps make (my) philosophical life easier if it could reasonably be claimed that desires of this newly recognized kind are at best borderline cases of desire: if, that is, it could reasonably be claimed that *just* wanting is *only just* wanting. But it cannot, and it is of some further importance that it cannot. Earlier (pp. 28–9), fairly or unfairly, I attributed to Miss Anscombe the following condition upon desire ascriptions: a necessary condition of the acceptability of the ascription of some specific desire to an agent is that the ascriber have 'reached and made intelligible' some 'desirability characterization' of the (potential) state of affairs specified by the content of the desire so ascribed. And the notion of a desirability characterization therein invoked was explained in the following terms: such a characterization of the object of desire is one adequate to the communication of that object's desirability, is one that serves to bring to an agreed end the questioning of why the desirer desires that object by revealing the imagined good involved to the eyes of others. But it is clear that in cases of desires of this newly recognized kind there is no such desirability characterization available. Neither the requisite notion of *communication of desirability* (as contrasted with mere 'infection' by desire) nor the requisite notion of *agreement* (as contrasted with mere coincidence) has any application in these cases. But it is also clear that we can and do ascribe desires of this kind, that in such cases we can and do recognize *the object* of desire without thought of *its desirability*. We accept that other people can desire all sorts of things which we have not the slightest inclination to desire while also thinking that we can tell what those things are. Knowing of no reason to criticize that thought or those ascriptions, I conclude that desires of this newly recognized kind require us *either* to reject the universal condition attributed to Miss Anscombe upon desire ascriptions *or* to reinterpret that condition as invoking some weaker notion of a 'desirability characterization'. The second option threatening to make the condition concerned almost trivial – if the notion of a 'desirability characterization' is construed along the lines of, say, a characterization adequate to the communication of *the object* of desire – I prefer the first. But that does not require rejection of the regulative ideal that we should, at least in general, seek for desirability characterizations of the objects of desires, nor does it require denial of the importance for general understanding of the concept of desire of the notion of a desirability characterization.

Desires of the newly recognized kind are, then, cases of desires without (the possibility of) desirability characterizations. That necessitates a group of brief final comments. (a) That point was hinted at in the initial discussion of such desires on pp. 63–4 by repeated use of 'putative'; from now on it will be registered by talking of 'desirability* characterizations' when considering such cases, to be understood in terms of a characterization adequate to the communication just of *the object* of desire, and similarly for cognate expressions. (b) Given the stipulation on pp. 47–8 that the notion of a 'desirability perception' is to be understood as tied to that of an available desirability characterization, it follows that desires of this newly recognized kind are cases of desires without desirability perceptions. I think this a welcome consequence if the seriousness of the usage of the *perceptual* model for motivated desires is to be preserved. (c) At least those cases of substitution activities which really count against the contemplated identification of desiring with thinking desirable (pp. 46–8) will be cases in which the desires operative are desires of this newly recognized kind. (d) It is now clear that any attempt to identify desiring with 'thinking desirable' faces a difficulty in the way of elucidating that latter notion in such a way that the purported identification is neither obviously false nor utterly trivial (cf. pp. 40–4, 47–8). (e) It is in cases of the newly recognized kind of desire, including the desires made manifest in the pertinent substitution activities, that the connections between desiring and trying to get (or aiming) are conceptually the closest; connectedly, it is in cases of desires of this newly recognized kind, *not* in cases of motivated desires, that in a sense we find just a motivational direction *and nothing more* (cf. pp. 48–9, 51, 54–5). (f) Recourse to exemplars of this newly recognized kind of desire could serve in the construction of a new variation upon the Sisyphus case (pp. 29–33). But the non-applicability to such exemplars of the notions of desirability characterization and desirability perception, together with further considerations to be adduced within the next chapter, give reason enough to doubt the interest of such a case for the purposes of illuminating questions of meaning and value.

The first chapter having rejected the classical misconception of desire, the present chapter began with the articulation of an alternative: that which maintains, in brief, that desiring is to be equated with thinking desirable. The alternative so articulated faces three difficulties: the existence of what were called 'substitution activities' threatens to make that alternative false or trivial (pp. 47–8); the alternative fails to take account of the distinctive direction of fit of desires *vis-à-vis* the world (pp. 54–5); and cases of 'just wanting' broaden the threat to the substance of that conception anyway posed by the narrower class of substitution activities (pp. 67–8). None the less, the articulation of this alternative misconception served to introduce various ideas which were later to be of use; in this sense, the alternative is a more instructive misconception than the classical one.

An abstract conception of desire in terms of the distinctive direction of fit being *at best* somewhat thin, I was led to develop a detailed description of one possible taxonomy of desire. (In the terms of that taxonomy it is a plausible conjecture that adherents to the classical misconception have focused exclusively upon 'reason-producing' desires whereas adherents to the alternative misconception examined have focused primarily upon 'reason-following' or 'motivated' desires.) The result is indeed but one possible taxonomy of desire, and the exact description given of it but one of its possible descriptions. The worth of that description of that taxonomy must be assessed in the light of the results of its subsequent employment.

Spinoza held, in effect, that subjectivism about values is a consequence of an active power conception of desire; and there is indeed a striking historical coincidence between such subjectivism and such a conception. I have rejected that conception; but I have also suggested that it is unlikely that an abstract treatment of so general a concept as that of desire will lead to much in the way of a substantial conception. The substantial begins with the recognition of the diversity of kinds of desires; the next chapter is concerned with the consequences for the theory of value of recognition of that diversity.

3 Values

Troilus: What's aught but as 'tis valued?
Hector: But value dwells not in particular will,
         It holds his estimate and dignity
         As well where'in 'tis precious of itself
         As in the prizer. 'Tis mad idolatry
         To make the service greater than the god,
         And the will dotes that is attributive
         To what infectiously itself affects,
         Without some image of th'affected merit.

                                                    (Shakespeare)

As a university tutor I seek a neutral value-free academic environment in order to pursue academic analysis and objectivity. It is within the authority and discretion and academic freedom of a tutor to impose proper and reasonable conditions. A degree of authority is inherent in the tutor-student relationship. I impose certain conditions: decency; no smoking; no interruptions; no personal abuse; no racialist or anti-Semitic slogans; no pictures of politicians; no rosettes; no political badges, of any kind, left or right.

                        (Alec Samuels in a letter to the *Guardian*, 1983)

A CAREFUL SCEPTICISM

Philippa Foot once expressed a careful scepticism in the following terms:

I would suppose, for instance, that in some fundamental moral enquiries we might find ourselves appealing to the fact that human life is a value. But do we really understand this thought? Do we know what we mean by saying that *anything* has value, or even

that we value it, as opposed to wanting it or being prepared to
go to trouble to get it? I do not know of any philosopher living
or dead who has been able to explain this idea.

(Foot 1978: 165)

That scepticism is indeed careful since Mrs Foot clearly thinks that
there is work here to be done if we are to have much hope of
understanding quite what is going on in any real discussion of
divergent moralities:

> [W]e are able, for instance, to understand a man who says at the
> end of his life that he has wasted his time on 'things that don't
> matter'. But what are the things that 'matter' if they are not the
> trivial things on which we spend so much time? Clearly such
> questions are relevant to fundamental discussions of the moralities
> of other societies and our own. It is impossible to judge a society's
> morality if we cannot talk about its values, and we must be able
> to handle the thought of false values if we are to say what is
> wrong with a materialistic society such as ours. But what is it to
> have false values if it is not to think too highly of things that do
> not matter very much?

(ibid.: 166)

So the scepticism seems as important as it is careful.

A patient examination of the various forms in which our thoughts
of value are expressed – of the varieties of value-constructions we
employ and of the different contexts in which we naturally employ
them – would be neither uninteresting nor I suspect unfruitful. But
it might prove sufficient for present purposes to distinguish in a most
rough and ready way certain of those constructions and certain of
their natural contexts of use.

The most general context of use upon which I shall initially focus
is that in which value-constructions are deployed within the attempt
to explain intentional actions. And here a broad distinction needs
to be introduced. On the one hand we might say as part of a putative
explanation of some given action that the agent did what he did
because he values, say, honesty, or because he attaches value to
honest dealings, or because he prizes honesty, or because he thinks
honesty matters, or because he thinks honesty is of value or has
value. On the other hand, within the same context we might say
that the agent did what he did because he recognizes the value of
honesty, or because he recognizes that honesty matters, or because

he recognizes that honesty is of value or has value, or even because of the value of honesty, or because honesty matters, or because honesty is of value or has value. The ground of this broad distinction is obvious: while the first group of value-constructions are all strictly and literally neutral upon the question of the attitude taken towards honesty by a person who proffers the putative explanation, usage of any of the second group of value-constructions within this context requires at least that the person who proffers the explanation himself values honesty. A similar broad distinction can be detected within putative explanations of intentional actions in which reference is made to what might be called *comparative evaluations consequent upon valuings*: as, for example, when we say of some philosophy examiner that he ranks one student's work above that of another because he, the examiner, values clarity and prizes precision, or because he recognizes that clarity matters and that precision is of value. The 'value-commitment' of a person who proffers the explanation is clearly weaker when the explanation proffered is of the first kind. There is no need for present purposes to deny the seeming possibility that, say, some philosophy examiner who has long since ceased to care about clarity and precision might still be able to continue adequately to grade or rank the work of students in terms of clarity and precision. I shall none the less say, as a mere terminological stipulation, that such a possibility would not be one in which the ranking or grading is a manifestation of *evaluation*. In my usage here, evaluation is always consequential upon valuing.

FROM WANTING TO VALUING

Mrs Foot's careful scepticism was about what might be meant 'by saying that *anything* has value, or even that we value it, as opposed to wanting it or being prepared to go to trouble to get it'. But that scepticism about there being any theory of value and of valuing other than that which is grounded upon an *identification* of valuing with wanting or with being prepared to go to trouble to get is not yet careful enough. We have just now indicated certain intuitive, pre-theoretical distinctions within the ways we naturally talk of value and of valuing; if we now bring together those pre-theoretical distinctions and the distinctions made in the last chapter between four classes of desires we shall see certain difficulties in the way of the simple identification contemplated within Mrs Foot's scepticism.

(1) Within the class of Thomas Nagel's 'unmotivated desires' we distinguished a subclass which, following Stephen Schiffer, we called

'reason-producing desires'. Such desires have an essential phenomenological character, being either disagreeable in feeling when not
satisfied, agreeable or pleasurable in feeling upon satisfaction or
both. Yet more theoretically, any such desire is logically self-referential in the sense that any full specification of the object of desire –
any complete desirability characterization of its object – makes
logical reference to the existence of the very desire itself. Moreover,
the way in which that reference is there made serves to explain why
it is that this desirability of the object of desire does not 'transcend'
the existence of that desire: on contemplating a possible world in
which he does not have the desire concerned, the agent should see
no desirability of this kind in the realization therein of what is his
actual object of desire as specified by some incomplete desirability
characterization of it. The most familiar cases of desires of this kind
are the appetitive, but they by no means exhaust the exemplars of
the kind.

In cases of desires purely of this kind, it is surely worthy of note
that talk of value or of valuing has no natural direct place within
our consideration of them – and not even when the agent concerned
is prepared to go to considerable trouble to obtain the object of his
desire. Suppose that I frequently find myself with some distinctive
intense thirst for some specific fluid, and even that I in fact pass
much of my life pursuing and seeking that fluid. Still it would be
strange to say of me that I value the fluid concerned, that I attach
value to it or that I think it of value to me; it would be stranger
yet to invoke directly in any case purely of this kind more 'impersonal' talk of value. Any simple identification of valuing with wanting
will need amendment to take account of this.

Two complications should be mentioned so as to isolate the difficulty
here. (a) Value-talk might enter indirectly in any case of this kind
in which the constant pursuit of the object of desire leads the agent
concerned to neglect other valuings, be those valuings on his part
or on the part of the person who proffers the account of the agent's
case. (b) Value-talk of one kind or another can enter in similar-
looking cases in which the thought is legitimately invoked in the
accounting of the cases that, say, the agent concerned believes or
knows that the fluid concerned is necessary for his survival. But if
such a thought is legitimately invoked and serves to give some direct
place to the value-talk concerned, this merely shows that the case
concerned is not one of a desire purely of the 'reason-producing'
kind but is rather one of a more 'hybrid' character.

The other subclass of 'unmotivated desires', (2), was characterized in negative terms. The desires concerned lack the essential phenomenological character of 'reason-producing' desires, nor need a complete desirability* characterization of the object of any such desire make logical reference to the existence of that desire, it thus being possible for the putative desirability* of that object to 'transcend' the existence of the desire itself. (For the explanation of the asterisks, see p. 67). But nor is it the case that for a desire of this kind a complete desirability* characterization of its object must make logical reference to the existence of some other desire of the agent's. Nor, finally, is there any possibility in the case of a desire of this kind of the agent's producing some reason in support of the claim that the complete desirability* characterization is indeed one that serves to capture the desirability of the object. Such desires are those which most invite the thought: *he just wants it*.

It has been recognized here that there are desires of this kind, and it was further allowed that their objects need be neither trivial nor whimsical; it should now further be admitted that an agent could structure much of his life around the pursuit of the object of such a desire, could go to considerable trouble in the effort to satisfy such a desire. Yet even when the object of some desire of this kind is not trivial and when the trouble the agent concerned goes to is great, no more is naturally invited in accounting for such cases than strictly 'personal' value-talk: talk of the agent's *valuing* or *prizing* the object of his desire, perhaps talk of his *attaching value* to that object, perhaps even talk of that object's *mattering to him*. No value-talk of an 'impersonal' character finds a natural, direct place within the accounting for such cases. And the reason for that is not hard to find: the reason which refers to the very distinguishing feature of desires of this kind, the feature that nothing can be said in support of the claim that the presumed desirability* characterization of the object of the desire serves to capture that object's desirability. The matter begins and ends with (i) the agent's wanting in this way, and being disposed to go to considerable trouble to get, the non-trivial object concerned, and (ii) his valuing that object. Or, perhaps better, the matter begins and ends with the agent's wanting in this way that non-trivial object, and that way of wanting such an object *is* a way of valuing such an object. The tentative conclusion is, then, that once qualifications about the non-trivial character of the object of desire and about the agent's disposition to expend considerable effort in its pursuit are inserted the identification contemplated within Mrs Foot's careful scepticism is, in cases of desires of this second kind, substantially correct.

Within the class of Thomas Nagel's 'motivated desires' we distinguished a subclass (3) which was characterized in the following terms: for any desire within this subclass a complete desirability characterization of its object will logically make reference, not to the existence of the selfsame desire, but rather to the existence of some other desire had by the agent, whatever be the kind of this other desire. So while the putative desirability of the object of such a desire can 'transcend' the existence of that very desire it will not 'transcend' the existence of the other desire had by the agent, logical reference to which is made within the complete desirability characterization concerned. (This last claim needs qualification to take account of certain cases in which the other desire had by the agent falls within the remaining subclass of desires (4).) Moreover, in any particular case of this kind, the agent can support the claim that the desirability characterization concerned serves to capture the object's desirability by reference both to the existence of the other desire of his and to the relevant facts about the role of the object so characterized in the project of satisfying that other desire. Two seemingly obvious examples of desires of this third kind are, first, those in which the object of desire is a means to the object otherwise desired, and, second, those in which the object of desire is a constitutive part of the object otherwise desired.

In any case of a desire of this third kind it is perfectly natural to say that the agent values or attaches value to the object of his desire; and in certain cases it would be more or less natural to say of the object of desire that it is of, or has, instrumental or constitutive value for the agent concerned. It would even, I think, be more or less natural to talk in such cases in a yet more 'impersonal' way: to say, that is, that the object of desire has instrumental or constitutive value attached to it – attached to it, not strictly by the agent, but rather by the other desire had by the agent. That move into the 'impersonal' is of some significance: roughly speaking, given the existence of the agent's other desire together with the pertinent, instrumental or constitutive, factual considerations, the instrumental or constitutive object has instrumental or constitutive value for the agent whether or not the agent has the corresponding desire of this third kind. In such a case, still roughly speaking, the instrumental or constitutive object is at least worthy of desire upon the agent's part, would be at least a reasonable object of desire upon the agent's part, whether or not the agent in fact has the corresponding desire. Moreover, if in such a case reflection upon the agent's part about the circumstances gives rise to the previously lacking desire, then that desire can be understood as at least a reasonable response to the fact of its object's instrumental or constitutive value for the agent. The agent comes to value the object concerned because he recognizes that in the circumstances that object is of value for him. And finally, note that that description of that kind of reflective case can also be applied to cases otherwise similar in which there is no ratiocination on the agent's part: the possibility of the agent's reasonably invoking reasons for his desiring some object does not imply that the formation of that desire was the outcome of reflection.

If what has just been said is correct, it is obvious that considerable qualification is required to any proposal which attempts to identify the thought that something has value for an agent with the thought that the agent wants it or is prepared to go to trouble to get it.

(4) The final kind of desire distinguished was that exemplified by the members of the remaining subclass of Nagel's 'motivated desires', the subclass focused upon in the discussions both of Nagel and of John McDowell. A desire of this kind neither has some essential phenomenological character nor need a complete desirability characterization of its object logically make reference to the existence of the desire itself: thus the contrast with 'reason-producing desires' of kind (1). But nor need a complete desirability characterization of the object of a desire of this final kind logically make reference to the existence of some other desire had by the agent: thus the contrast with desires of kind (3). More positively, however, for any desire of this final kind there is the possibility that the agent within some specific context produces some reason in support of the claim that the complete desirability characterization of its object is indeed one that serves to capture the desirability of that object: he is not fated to rest with the thought that he just wants it. Thus the contrast with desires of kind (2).

It is in cases of action grounded upon desires of this kind that more completely 'impersonal' value-talk naturally comes to occupy a place within our accounting for them. The agent does what he does because he thinks that something – say, honesty or scientific truth – is a value, or is of value, or matters, or is desirable, or is worthy of desire. Of course more 'personal' value-talk can enter too in our accounts of such cases: the agent acts as he does because he values or prizes honesty or scientific truth. But from the agent's own perspective in such a case his valuing the thing concerned is a reasonable response at least to its value, to its desirability. And if he who proffers the accounting shares the agent's view of the matter, the level of 'impersonality' in his accounting may rise yet further: through the thought that the agent does what he does because he recognizes the value of, say, honesty, because he realizes that it matters, to the thought that the agent does what he does because of the value of honesty, because honesty matters.

An agent who so acts only then to find himself faced with doubt or even denial in relation to the supposed value upon the part of another might attempt, in diverse and contextually dependent ways, to ease that doubt or to rebut that denial. Perhaps he will fail to come up with anything which satisfies the other – or which satisfies even himself; but he may still continue, in a modest, non-dogmatic manner, with the conviction that there is *something* to be said in support of the presumed desirability of the object towards which his action was directed. He need be no more optimistic about his own capacity to support the pertinent claim of desirability, of 'impersonal' value, than he is about the openness of the other to appreciation of such support if once it be produced. Yet no such due caution within some particular conversational context nor even any such due general caution about the particular kind of desirability characterization at issue can serve to threaten the distinctiveness of desires of kind (4) and the correlate distinctiveness of the forms in which value-talk can be invoked within the accounts of those cases in which such desires are operative. Moreover, it is possible that both participants within such a dialogue be found within one and the same person; and if that is so, and if the dialogue ends with the persistence of the desire concerned, the agent may think of that desire as at least a reasonable response to the 'impersonal' desirability or value of its object. Any such case therefore represents a formidable challenge to even cautious formulations of general reductive identifications of the form: *being a value is nothing but being valued, which in turn is nothing but being desired.*

VALUE-INTERNALISM

Most of what has so far been said about Mrs Foot's careful scepticism has run along the directional line, so to say, from wanting to valuing; matters might be further clarified if that predominant direction is now reversed. That reversal brings us into contact with one of the most ancient of issues in philosophy; but it will help if we first try to isolate that issue from others with which it was frequently muddled.

Questions as to what has been called 'the psychological possibility of moral conduct' (Falk 1947–8: 493) seem to have been entangled within philosophers' discussions of ethics since at least the time of Socrates' efforts to still the doubts of Glaucon and of Adeimantus. Whatever assessment be made of the ancient history of philosophers' discussions of those questions, I think it clear that when what was presumed to be much the same debate surfaced in the present century its terms had by no means been much sharpened. Perhaps some progress was marked by a narrowing of focus to the relation to motivation of the very use of such words as 'ought', 'duty', 'obligation'. But that progress could only be slight as long as philosophers contented themselves with a misuse of the concept of motivation, imprecision in their use of 'use', reliance upon a supposedly pellucid notion of 'the moral "ought" ' and employment of supposedly equally pellucid notions of 'duty' and 'obligation'. And while some earlier, indefensible doctrines of 'motivation' were indeed largely abandoned, their place as the supposedly unproblematic case of 'motivation' was generally taken by the example of prudential motivation, with this being glossed in terms of ill-understood notions such as 'interest' and 'advantage'. Still, it is possible to identify one reasonably well-defined question involved both in that ancient history and in the contemporary debate; that question will be my concern here.

Donald Davidson has stated what he calls 'a mild form of internalism': 'if an agent judges that it would be better to do x than to do y, then he wants to do x more than he wants to do y'. About that doctrine he makes the following, admittedly inconclusive, remarks:

> It seems obvious enough, after all, that we may think x better, yet want y more. [The doctrine] is even easier to question if it is stated in the form: if an agent thinks he ought (or is obligated) to do x, then he wants to do x; for of course we often don't want to do what we think we ought. . . .
>
> It is easy to interpret [the doctrine] in a way that makes it false, but it is harder to believe there is not a natural reading that makes it true. For against our tendency to agree that we often believe we ought to do something and yet don't want to, there is also the opposite tendency to say that if someone really (sincerely) believes he ought, then his belief must show itself in his behaviour

(and hence, of course, in his inclination to act, or his desire). When we make a point of contrasting thinking we ought with wanting, this line continues, either we are using the phrase 'thinking we ought' to mean something like 'thinking it is what is required by the usual standards of the community' or we are restricting wanting to what is attractive on a purely selfish or personal basis.

(Davidson 1969: 27)

And Davidson concludes his remarks by contemplating the possibility that there is some other 'word or phrase we can convincingly substitute for "wants" ' within the initial statement of his 'mild internalism'.

His remarks are in fact largely directed towards the evaluation of a thesis quite distinct from the doctrine initially stated: a thesis about the connection between 'thinking we ought' and wanting. (Note that such a thesis is distinct too from any about the connection between 'thinking we morally ought' and wanting.) The doctrine initially stated, the 'mild internalism', is explicitly about the connection between *judging better to do* and *wanting more to do* – that is, the connection between comparative judgements of 'worth' of actions and comparative strengths of desires in relation to those actions. Now, the former, the comparative judgement, might arise in a given case from the agent's subscribing to some value, from his valuing something. In such a case, following our earlier terminological stipulation (p. 72), the comparative judgement concerned expresses a comparative evaluation on the part of the agent. So, in the kind of case I wish to consider here there are at least four possible factors in play:

1 the agent's *valuing* something – honesty, say, or clarity;
2 the agent's having some *general desire* directed towards instances of that thing, like honest actions or clear opinions;
3 the agent's *comparative evaluations* of things consequent upon his valuing, especially those evaluations expressed in terms of 'better to do', 'best to do'; and
4 the agent's *specific desires* in relation to particular contemplated actions.

The problem of what I shall call 'value-internalism' is that of accounting for the connections, if any, between these four possible factors; the problem, telescoping somewhat, of accounting for the connections if any between (1), the agent's valuing something, and (4), the agent's possible specific desires in relation to particular contemplated actions. An extreme 'value-internalist' holds that, except for cases in which an agent doltishly fails to fit together his desires and his beliefs, the connection is in some way necessary; but apart from that extreme there is a wide spectrum of possible opinions.

At an intuitive level the plausibility of any position on that spectrum which could reasonably be labelled 'internalist' will require some (non-question-begging) restriction of scope upon the kind of thing valued: a restriction, so to speak, to practical values, a restriction within (1) to practical valuings. But if once that restriction be formulated and inserted, it remains worthy of note that any 'internalist' position as here construed will still be a general one about all practical valuings. I think it fairly clear that so construed the issue of 'value-internalism' was indeed one of the issues enmeshed in the seemingly more specific debate about 'the psychological possibility of moral conduct'. But it should also be noted, as a final step towards sorting out the initial issues here, that the issue of 'value-internalism' has here been cast in (telescoped) terms of the connections of practical valuing with specific, action-directed desires and so precisely not in terms of such valuing's connections with action itself. That casting is dictated by a number of considerations: (a) my desire to avoid immersion in all the complexities that can intervene between desire and potential action upon desire (pp. 16–21); (b) my desire to side-step the distinct matter of any 'overriding' property supposedly found within certain kinds of practical valuings; and (c) my adherence to that part of current orthodoxy about reasons for acting which holds desire to be an essential component of any such reason for acting (pp. 54–5).

FROM VALUING TO WANTING: POTENTIAL UNMOTIVATED DESIRES

What I now wish to do is to consider this issue of 'value-internalism' in the light of the categorization of kinds of desire introduced in the last chapter and deployed within the first part of this discussion of valuing and wanting. More specifically, I want now to consider, in relation to each of those kinds of desire, whether there is any substantial possibility that, in a case where a desire of the kind concerned might have arisen, it could yet be the case both that the desire concerned does not arise and that the agent none the less continues to use the appropriate kind of value-talk without thereby making manifest some degree of insincerity on his part. In the course of this consideration it will at points prove necessary to replace the initial telescoping of the problem of 'value-internalism' by a microscoping, the focus then being *either* upon the question of whether there is any such possibility of an agent's so continuing to value something, as in (1), in the absence of the corresponding general desire, as in (2), *or* upon the question of whether there is any such possibility of an agent's so continuing with the pertinent comparative evaluation, as in (3), in the absence of the corresponding specific desire, as in (4). For in certain cases those questions seem to receive different answers.

No time need be lost upon 'the area shaped by potential "reason-producing desires" ', upon 'the area shaped by potential desires of kind (1)'. For we have seen that no kind of value-talk has any direct place in relation to any actual desire purely of this kind; moreover, talk of 'the area shaped by *potential* desires of this kind' is obscure when not irrelevant. But the remaining subclass of unmotivated desires, (2), requires a more patient examination.

In relation to certain members of this subclass and under certain conditions – roughly, where the contents of the desires concerned are neither trivial nor whimsical, and where the agent concerned expends great effort in the pursuit of the objects of those desires – we have seen that certain kinds of 'personal' value-talk can naturally find a place: talk of the agent's valuing or prizing the object of his desire, perhaps talk of his attaching value to that object, perhaps even talk of that object's mattering to him. None the less it is difficult to say the least to see how talk introduced in that way can then lend itself to the creation of (so to speak) a *potential space* between such valuing and such wanting, a potential space whereby it would be possible for such valuing to occur in the absence of such wanting. It is true that an agent with such a desire – say, a troublesome desire for social justice – has a desirability* characterization (p. 67) of the object of the desire, a characterization which logically makes no reference to the existence of that selfsame desire; still, there is nothing to make that characterization a *desirability** characterization except the existence of that desire. The matter, as we earlier tentatively suggested (pp. 74–5), seems to begin and end with the agent's wanting in this way that non-trivial object, that way of wanting such an object being his way of valuing that object. And this last identification precludes there being even a potential space between such valuing and such wanting.

It will prove instructive, however, to consider how one attempt to introduce such a space might be made. According to Judith Baker, H. P. Grice once contemplated the following kind of solution to the distinct problem of the connection between 'obligation' and 'motivation': 'if John thinks he ought to do some action *a*, then that requires that either John wants to *a* or he thinks that he ought to want to *a*' (Baker 1986: 472). The analogous proposal for valuing would be this: if John values something, then that requires that either John desires that thing or he values the having of such a desire.

Both the proposal contemplated by Grice and its analogue for the case of valuing pass over complications arising from conflicts, whether of 'obligations' or of valuings. More importantly, as with Grice's proposal, the analogue is successively to be applied: if in a given case John does not in fact desire the thing valued, then the same 'analysis' of valuing is to be applied to the then operative second disjunct. Judith Baker writes of the proposal about 'obligation' and 'motivation':

> In principle there is no end to such a regressive analysis. But the idea is that at some point real people will come to a stop and the original judgement of obligation will be cashed out in a desire. But there is no guarantee at what level.

> (ibid.)

The comparable idea in application to the analogue is that valuing will be 'cashed out' in a desire *at some level*: John's valuing requires either that he wants the thing concerned or that he wants to want it or that he wants to want to want it or. . . .

Once the possibility of desires of this second kind, (2), is recognized, there then is no good reason to deny the possibility of desires of this kind of levels higher than the first: the possibility of desires of this kind whose propositional contents relate to the existence of other potential desires of the agent concerned. So there is no good reason to doubt the coherence of the proposed account of valuing in the cases under consideration whereby John's valuing something is not equated with his desiring it (in this way) but is rather equated with his *either* desiring it (in this way) *or* desiring (in this way) to desire it *or* desiring (in this way) to desire to desire it *or* desiring (in this way). . . . None the less a difficulty faces this proposal.

Consider the suggestion that in some given case the agent's valuing something is 'cashed out' in, amounts to, his wanting (in this way) to want it: his having a second-level desire of kind (2). Now, how could it be that the agent's having that desire amounts to his valuing the object of the embedded first-order desire rather than to his valuing *the having of* the first-order desire? How can the desirability *of this kind* of the having of the first-order desire transmit itself (so to speak) to the object of that potential first-order desire? Given that the second-level desire is of kind (2), there is *ex hypothesi* no reason which can be adduced in support of the desirability of its object, of the desirability of this having of the potential first-order desire. The agent just has the second-level desire, just wants to have the potential first-order desire. So *ex hypothesi* there is no such reason which could serve in some way to transmit the desirability* concerned to the object of the potential first-order desire. If what the agent simply wants is to have the first-level desire concerned, that simple desire is satisfied by his coming to have that first-level desire; and if once that comes about, then there is nothing to be said, from the viewpoint shaped by the initial second-level simple desire, for his then seeking and pursuing the object of that first-level desire. He now has all that he, simply and originally, wanted to have. Of course he now has the first-level desire concerned and so might come to expend considerable time and trouble in the pursuit of *its* object: but why should he not see that as an unfortunate albeit foreseeable side-effect of the satisfaction of his simple and original second-level desire? Higher level desirings of kind (2) cannot consti-tute the valuing of the object of some potential first-level desire of that kind.

Suppose an agent to have a second-level desire of kind (2): he just wants to want some thing. Suppose further that thereby he comes somehow to have the corresponding first-level desire. That second supposition is not so straightforward. Given that the second-level desire is of kind (2), is just wanting, various factors which might otherwise have played some role in the generation of the first-level desire are ruled out of court: complete desirability* characterizations of the objects of desires of kind (2) do not logically make reference to the existence of desires had by the agent, nor is there any possibility of the agent's producing some reason in support of the claim that the complete desirability* characterization of the object of a desire of this kind is one that serves to capture the desirability of that object. Still, one possibility is that the agent take some drug which he knows will produce the first-level desire concerned.

Despite the obvious analogies between the desire brought about in this way and those desires within the first subclass, (3), of motivated desires, there is a crucial disanalogy too: in general terms, no complete desirability characterization of the object of the first-level desire thereby produced so as to satisfy the simple second-level desire of kind (2) need make logical reference to the existence of that second-level desire. There therefore seems no alternative, at least in general, in these cases of production of first-level desires to that of including the products within the same subclass of unmotivated desires, (2), in which the original second-level desires occur. One whim, we might say, has brought about another.

What of the question of the connection within this context between (3), an agent's comparative evaluations, and (4), his specific desires in relation to particular contemplated actions such as his wanting more to do *a* than to do *b*? At first glance the matter seems straightforward enough. Omitting certain necessary qualifications of detail, (a) it has here been stipulated that any such comparative evaluation on the agent's part is consequent upon some valuing of his, and (b) the conclusion has just been reached that within the area under consideration any such valuing is tantamount to the agent's having of the corresponding general desire of kind (2). It therefore seems that any case in which an agent sincerely subscribes to some particular comparative evaluation while yet lacking the corresponding specific desire will be a case of irrationality upon that agent's part: for given his general desire and his beliefs about the particular matter at hand, it seems that a principle of practical reason requires that he should have the corresponding specific desire. So while there is doubtless a potential space between the agent's evaluation and his having the corresponding specific desire, that space is of relatively little interest: for its realization, while not sufficient for doltishness, yet is sufficient for irrationality. While if in a given case the potential space is not realized -- if the agent comes in fact thereby to have the pertinent specific desire – the desire concerned will be a motivated desire of kind (3): any complete desirability characterization of its object, any characterization that serves to answer the question of why he more wants to do *a* than to do *b*, will logically make reference to the general desire on the agent's part (or to his valuing, but that valuing is tantamount in these cases to his desiring).

FROM VALUING TO WANTING: POTENTIAL MOTIVATED DESIRES

We might start consideration of the area shaped by potential desires of kind (3) by reflecting upon the suggestion that within this area any space between valuing or evaluating, on the one hand, and general or specific desires on the other, is no more than a manifestation of irrationality upon the part of the agent concerned, is no more than a manifestation of some transgression on his part of principles of practical reason. But whatever the initial appeal of such a suggestion its further elaboration would require that a great deal more work be done: first, in consideration of all the distinctive varieties of cases which fall under the very general characterization which has here been given of motivated desires of kind (3); next, in formulation of general principles of practical reason for each of the varieties so considered; and finally, in assessment of the suspicion that for some of the principles concerned to be defensible their application will need explicitly to be restricted to certain kinds of desires. So as to avoid immersion at this point within the details of any such further elaboration of the suggestion mentioned, I shall rest with the following thought: in the intuitively defensible cases of motivated desires of kind (3), the desires so 'motivated' are reasonable responses on the part of the agent to the facts of the cases, including the facts about the agent's other desires. Within these terms a rational response, one required by general principles of reason, is but *one kind* of reasonable response.

A general characterization, then, of cases instantiating the potential space within this area shaped by potential desires of kind (3) is the following: given his other desires and his beliefs about the pertinent matters of fact, the agent recognizes the value thereby attached to some object, and yet, while having nothing against that object, he simply has no desire for it: he recognizes that the object is at least worthy of desire, could reasonably be desired, but he does not in fact desire it. And then, as a characterization of a subclass of the possible cases picked out by that more general characterization, there remains the following: given his other desires, his beliefs about the pertinent matters of fact, and the general principles of practical reason, the agent recognizes the value thereby attached to some object, and yet, while having nothing against that object, he has no desire for it; he recognizes that the object merits desire, rationally would be desired, ought to be desired, but he does not in fact desire it. Moreover, in any given case in which some agent finds that the general potential space between valuing and desiring of kind (3) is realized, he might then go on to consider how in this case the space concerned could be eliminated, how in this case the lacking desire could be provoked. He could consider whether there is some changeable feature of his mental or personal life which is operative in the obstruction of the potential desire concerned; or he could consider the attempt to focus all his attention upon the other, 'motivating' desire which he in fact has, the attempt to focus upon its force or upon the attractiveness or desirability of its object; or he could consider the attempt to focus all his attention upon the exigencies of any principles of practical reason which might be in play; or, again, he could consider resort to some appropriate drug. And if such consideration issues in action, and if that action then results in the desire concerned, the agent will see that result, in varying degrees and in varying ways, as either a reasonable or a rational response on his part to the circumstances of the case. But, as before, that way of seeing desires of the general kind (3) does not require that any such process of reflection have preceded their existence.

In considering cases in which this general potential space between valuing and desiring of kind (3) is realized, it might perhaps be tempting to try to invoke anew the analogue for valuing of the proposal contemplated by Grice: to try to invoke the thought, that is, that while the agent concerned need have no desire for the object whose value is recognized yet in any such case the agent must either want to have that desire or want to want to have it or. . . . But whatever be the final worth of such an invocation, it should be noted that at least one possible motivation for it would be a manifestation of nothing better than confusion. The motivation is that of doing continuing justice to Philippa Foot's careful scepticism about there being any account of 'what we mean by saying that *anything* has value, or even that we value it, as opposed to wanting it or being prepared to go to trouble to get it'. The point here is not just that the invocation suggested does not exactly capture the sceptical thought there contemplated; it is also that inasmuch as that invocation approximates to that thought, so too does the account thus far given here. For on that account any pertinent judgement of desirability or value made by an agent in the absence of the corresponding specific desire on his part is anyway grounded upon some other desire actually had by him: the complete desirability characterization of the object of that judgement, of the object of the merely potential desire, will logically make reference to the existence of the other desire in fact had by the agent.

It was in the area determined by desires of the remaining kind of motivated desire, (4), that we found the most 'impersonal' forms of value-talk most naturally to have a place. In any case of a desire of this kind the complete desirability characterization of the object of that desire need make no logical reference to the existence of any desire had by the agent concerned; but, more positively, for any desire of this kind there is the possibility that the agent within some specific context produces some reason in support of the claim that the complete desirability characterization of its object is one that serves to capture the desirability of its object. And it seems difficult to deny that that positive defining characteristic of desires of kind (4) connects in some way with the distinctive ways in which value-talk naturally enters into the accounting for actual cases of action upon desires of this kind.

When any desire of this kind (4) occurs, there are at least the following three factors potentially in play (pp. 54–8):

(a) the agent's general desire – say, for honesty, or for scientific truth;
(b) the general desirability characterization had or accepted by the agent of the object of that desire – the general, and generally 'impersonal', value-invoking characterization of that object; and
(c) the various reasons which the agent might adduce in varying contexts in support of the claim that the complete desirability characterization of the object of desire is one that serves to capture the desirability of that object, in support of that invocation of 'impersonal' value-talk.

Now, we were earlier led to accept the substantive character of the completely general exclusive distinction between *desiring* some object and *having a desirability characterization* of it (pp. 48–9); so we must accept the substantive character of that general distinction in application to cases of kind (4), the substantive character of the distinction in such cases between (a) and (b). And that acceptance requires another: that of the substantive character of the question, in relation to the area shaped by potential desires of kind (4), as to whether there are possible cases in which (b) and (c) occur in the absence of (a) – the question, in relation to that area, of the possibility of cases of sincere reason-based claims as to values and of recognition of values without desirings. Moreover, the highest

level of generality of description of cases where desires of this kind
(4) do occur seems to suggest that there are real possibilities here.
That level of description runs as follows. Some reason as in (c)
reasonably elicits, produces as a reasonable response, the acceptance
of some general desirability characterization as in (b); and that
acceptance in turn reasonably elicits, reasonably gives rise to, the
corresponding desire as in (a) (pp. 57–8). Through recognition of
that process we can, distinctively and naturally, understand why the
agent has the desire which he in fact has. But if that is so, then it
seems that there is nothing impossible about a broadly similar
process of 'generation' which in fact comes to a halt with the
agent's acceptance of some general desirability characterization, that
acceptance not in fact giving rise to the corresponding desire.

About that *seeming* we should first note two points. First, there will
in this area be at most a very limited scope for replacement of the
general notion of a reasonable response by that more specific one
of a rational response, by that of a response required by general
principles of reason. As regards the potential relation or relations
between cases of (c) and of (b) the point is an obvious one: the
contextually-dependent character of any reason of kind (c) represents a formidable obstacle to the attempt to see any such relation
in terms of general principles of reason. The matter of the potential
relation or relations between cases of (b) and of (a) is less straightforward: so let us just note for the moment the striking history of
failure, of pure bluff, in attempts to show that there is some kind
of irrationality in every apparent case in which (b) occurs in the
absence of (a). And the second point to note relates to the matter
of the explanation of the difference between otherwise broadly
similar cases, the difference being whether or not the acceptance of
the general desirability characterization in fact gives rise to the
corresponding desire. Doubtless in many such cases the explanation
to be given will make reference to other mental and personal features
of the agents concerned; and doubtless in many of those many cases
the precise ways in which such reference is made will reveal that
what are in play are further variable valuings on the parts of the
agents concerned. But I know of no good argument which serves to
rule out the possibility of cases in which there are no explanations
cast in terms of the mental and personal lives of the agents of the
differences in their conative states, of the differences of their desires.

A more pressing worry about that *seeming* arises in the following
way. In accordance with what has so far been said here, cases in

which the general desire as in (a) does not occur can be separated
into two broad groups: those in which the agent's appreciation of
some reason as in (c) gives rise to his acceptance of some general
desirability characterization, to some putative recognition of some,
generally 'impersonal', value, and those in which it does not. But
just what is the content of the distinction so drawn? What is the
content of such talk of acceptance of some general desirability
characterization, of such value-talk, in the absence of the corresponding general desire? Isn't the criterion of the agent's sincere
acceptance of some general desirability characterization, of the sincerity of his talk of value, his having the corresponding desire?

But the general scepticism prompting that worry is in the nature
of the case vulnerable to the threat of the overlooked possibility.
Moreover, there is no good reason to presume that there must be
one criterion which serves to mark the distinction at issue in all such
cases. So, for example, much will depend upon the level of 'structural
complexity' of the general desirability characterization at issue in
the case concerned. In a case in which there is an appreciable level
of such complexity, the sincerity of the agent's acceptance of that
characterization could be made manifest through his acceptance of
other related desirability characterizations, that latter acceptance
indeed reasonably giving rise to the corresponding desires on his
part.

Another possibility will have occurred to the reader, that of invoking
once more some value-analogue of the distinct proposal contemplated by Grice. The suggestion might be made, for example, that
an agent's sincere acceptance of some general desirability characterization must be 'cashed out' in terms of some actual desire of the
agent's *at some level*: he must either have the corresponding general
desire, or want to have it, or want to want to have it, or. . . .

Under consideration are potential and actual desires of kind (4)
and the distinctive ways in which talk of desirability and of value
can naturally enter into the accountings of cases within the area
shaped by potential desires of that kind. Consider, then, a given
case within this area in which some agent judges something to be
of value: he thinks, say, that honesty is of value, is 'impersonally'
desirable, and potentially has various reasons which could be
adduced within varying contexts in support of that thought. If that
is so, then he will also think, say, *acting honestly* to be of value.
But it surely will also be the case that the agent concerned will think
desiring honesty to be of value (and so desiring honest action too).

And it surely will also be the case that the agent will think *desiring to desire honesty* to be of value. And so on. Quite how that process of 'transmission' is to be understood might well depend either upon any general views about value held by the agent concerned or upon the character of the particular value involved or upon both those things. So, for example, one possibility in any given particular case is that (each link in) the chain of desirings is thought to be of value only because the occurrence of (each link in) that chain is deemed a necessary means to the instantiation in the actual world of the value concerned; a distinct possibility is that the potential reasons which could be adduced within varying contexts in support of the claimed 'value-status' of the values concerned serve also to support the thought that (each link in) the chain of desirings is of some 'independent' value; while yet another possibility is that those reasons serve to reveal that the 'value-status' of the value concerned and of its instantiations in (say) acting is in some way derivative from the value of (each link in) the chain of desirings. But, to repeat, there seems nothing incoherent about the thought that which possibility is reasonably favoured, or that which combination of possibilities is reasonably favoured, might depend upon the character of the particular value at issue. Still, the conclusion remains that, within this area shaped by potential desires of kind (4), the thought that something is of value goes along with the thought that (each link in) the chain of corresponding desires is of value. And then, reflecting upon that potentially endless chain of thoughts of value, the suggestion might arise that for 'real people' some member of that chain of thoughts of value will be 'cashed out' in terms of the corresponding desire one level up in the chain. Moreover, such a suggestion, now made within the context of the immediately preceding reflections, might seem to have brought us closer to appreciation of some *argument* in favour of the truth of the value-analogue of the proposal contemplated by Grice.

Unfortunately difficulties remain over and above the obscure status of the claim about 'real people'. One relates to the starting-thought that one who thinks *honesty* to be of value will also think *desiring honesty* to be of value. Why would it not be enough, at least in certain cases, that the agent thinks *valuing honesty* to be of value (and so on for (each link in) the chain of valuings)? The threat of the question being begged is clear. In cases in which the desiring-*or*-valuing is deemed of value because it is a necessary means to the instantiation in the actual world of the value concerned this difficulty can be avoided: for given (a) acceptance of part of current orthodoxy about reasons for action in terms of the ineliminable role of desires within such reasons, together with (b) some plausible principle of practical reason in terms of means and ends, it follows that in such cases an agent who rests with the chain of (mere) valuings is thereby revealed to be irrational. But we have no reason as yet to generalize from such cases, to presume that all thoughts of the value of desiring or valuing are to be understood in the terms of those cases. And that connects with a second difficulty relating to the suggestion that for 'real people' some member of the pertinent chain of thoughts of value will be 'cashed out' in terms of the corresponding desire one level up in that chain. Doubtless for 'real people' that chain cannot go on forever; but why could it not just come to a halt with no such 'cashing out'? As before, in cases in which the desiring-*or*-valuing is deemed of value because it is a necessary means to the instantiation in the actual world of the values concerned the absence of any 'cashing out' in desire will make manifest some degree of irrationality on the part of the agent concerned; but as before, we have as yet no reason to generalize from such cases.

The provisional conclusion is thus that while some value-analogue of the proposal contemplated by Grice can serve as one criterion of an agent's sincere acceptance of some talk of value within this area, there is no reason to believe that it or anything else can serve as *the* criterion of such acceptance within this area. Whatever be the connections within the area shaped by potential desires of kind (4) between valuing and wanting, they resist encapsulation within any tidy identificatory formula of the kind which lurks behind Mrs Foot's careful scepticism.

THE SENSE OF SUBJECTIVITY, OF WORTH, OF MERIT

People on occasion say that issues about values are 'subjective'; and perhaps they say that more often of issues about moral values than of others. Philosophers too frequently say such things. I have no need to pay much attention to such voicings, be they from the mouths of normal people or of philosophers; none the less, I think it might help in the pursuit of the declared aims of this essay to consider some of the things which might be meant by such voicings. In so doing I shall consciously neglect the question as to 'the correct usage' of the word 'subjective'.

In cases of valuings within the area shaped by potential desires of kind (2), there is one meaning which might immediately be attached to the claim that such valuings are subjective: the meaning

encapsulated in the thought that in the case of such a valuing there
is nothing to be said in support of that valuing, together with the
thought that in the event of a difference of opinion about such a
valuing there is nothing that can be said for purposes of seeking a
reasonable resolution of the difference. And both the thoughts
there involved are correct. Moreover, there are further truths about
valuings of this kind which might be meant by a defender of the
claim of subjectivity. One is that, in any particular case of this kind,
the agent's valuing something just is his desiring it (in this way);
another is that in cases of this kind there is no natural place for
'impersonal' value-talk. A little more ambitiously, through the claim
of subjectivity the true thought might be being expressed that in
these cases there is nothing to be said for the thought that the
experience of valuing can count as a case of being presented with
some value-property or feature of the world which is independently
there – which is there to be experienced independently of any
particular experience of valuing. And the related truth might also
be being expressed that in cases within this area there is nothing to
be said for the thought that the agents' desires can be reasonable
responses to independent value-properties or value-features of the
world.

Hume wrote that 'when you pronounce any action or character
to be vicious, you mean nothing, but that from the constitution of
your nature you have a feeling or sentiment of blame from the
contemplation of it' (1888: 469). He continued: 'Vice and virtue,
therefore, may be compar'd to sounds, colours, heat and cold, which
according to modern philosophy, are not qualities in objects, but
perceptions in the mind.' Our concern is not yet with the matter of
moral valuings and moral judgements; but if we construe Hume's
remarks as being about cases of valuing within the area shaped by
potential desires of kind (2) while at the same time disregarding his
reference to 'meaning', the views so expressed are close indeed to
the subjectivist truths just now recognised. Such valuings are not
cases of being presented with 'qualities in objects', nor are the
desires in play reasonable responses to any such qualities. Indeed,
with such valuings and desirings we may need to be on the Humean
alert against the risk of spreading them upon the world which is
independently there, the danger of objectifying our valuings and
desirings precisely through taking them to be experiences of and
reasonable responses to value-qualities without the mind. But it
would be a further, mistaken move to conclude that that which is
thereby valued is itself 'in the mind', is the very experience or

'perception' of valuing (cf. McGinn 1983: 130). No valuing of this kind counts as a case of experience of some value-quality or value-feature to be found in objects without the mind; none the less, that which is valued, the subject of our value-predications, can yet be without the mind, can yet be, say, some 'action or character' of another.

The possible interpretations of the claim that valuings are subjective which render that claim true in relation to valuings within the area shaped by potential desires of kind (2) fail to render that same claim true in relation to the distinctive valuings within the area shaped by potential 'motivated' desires of kind (3). In cases of this kind there are things which can be said in support of any such valuing and with the aim of producing some reasonable resolution of any difference in such valuing: namely, through reference to the existence of the other, 'motivating' desire in play, together with reference to the relevant putative facts of the matter such as the pertinent instrumental or constitutive considerations. In this way a desirability characterization of the thing valued can be produced in cases of this kind which makes references neither to the agent's actually valuing it nor to his actually desiring it. That characterization purports to reveal why that thing is at least worthy of being valued; indeed that characterization might even purport to reveal why that thing ought to be valued, why it merits being valued. In cases of this kind there is also both a space for a distinction between the agent's valuing the thing concerned and his actually desiring it and a natural place for value-talk of a certain level of 'impersonality'. And, finally, in such cases the following thoughts can reasonably arise upon occasion: the experience of valuing counts as a case of being presented with some value – property or value-feature of the world which is independently there – which is there to be experienced independently of any particular experience of valuing it; and the agent's desire for the thing concerned is a reasonable response to independent value-properties or value-features of the world – independent, that is, of the particular agent's particular experience of wanting the thing concerned and of his valuing it.

That this flight from subjectivity, however, has carried us only a limited distance is brought out by consideration of cases in which the other desire in play, the 'motivating' desire, is one of kind (2). For in any such case, roughly speaking, both the force of the putative support for the agent's valuing and the plausibility of the hope for reasonable resolution of any difference in such valuing turn upon the matter of mere, non-reasonable fact as to whether others share this other, 'motivating' desire of kind (2). That matter has been conceded here to be, in more senses than one, subjective: in particular, it has tacitly been conceded that if that sharing does not in fact occur, there is nothing which can be said or done with an eye to producing a reasonable modification in that matter. So if that sharing does not in fact occur, again roughly speaking, both the force of the putative support for the agent's valuing and the plausibility of the hope for reasonable resolution of any difference in such valuing seem to evaporate. (That is so only *roughly speaking*: for in certain cases there is a clear possibility of reasonable criticism *of the motivated desire* of kind (3) even on the part of one who does not share the 'motivating' desire in play.)

None of that requires retraction of the other claims just now entered in relation to valuings within the area shaped by potential desires of kind (3), not even when the other, 'motivating' desire in play is of kind (2). But in cases where this other desire is of that kind or of kind (1), the other claims entered seem relatively anodyne. While, for example, some talk of 'independent' values can be allowed in such cases, the talk so allowed must be most cautiously and modestly construed: must be construed merely in terms of independence of the particular agent's particular experience of wanting the thing concerned and of valuing it. So construed that talk is quite compatible with the subjectivist's characteristic insistence upon actual human valuings and desirings being the source of all value: it is merely that in these cases that source, so to say, spreads itself further upon the world than in other, simpler cases.

It therefore becomes all the more urgent to consider the putative cases in which the other, 'motivating' desire is itself a 'motivated' one of kind (4); that in its turn makes it all the more urgent to consider the claim of subjectivity in relation to valuings within the area shaped by potential desires of that kind. In cases within this area there are once more things which can be said in support of any such valuing and with the aim of producing some reasonable resolution of any difference in such valuing: reasons can be adduced, that is, in support of the thought that the desirability characterization proffered is indeed one that captures the desirability of the thing concerned, is indeed one that serves to reveal that the thing concerned is at least worthy of being valued. But in contrast to the immediately preceding cases within the area shaped by potential desires of kind (3), in the present cases the things to be said will not now make reference to the existence of some other desire had by the agent: rather, they will be attempts to draw focused attention to some (value-) 'qualities in objects' without the mind, to some value-features of reality independent of the agent's actual desirings and valuings. The distinction in these cases between valuing and desiring; the natural place in these cases for completely 'impersonal' value-talk; the thought that in these cases valuing can count as a case of being presented with some value-property or 'quality in objects' which is there anyway and which is at least worthy of being valued independently of actual human desirings and valuings; the thought that in these cases an agent's desiring the thing concerned can be at least a reasonable response to the value independently had by that thing: all these now serve to mark out some considerable distance within the flight from subjectivity. In the briefest possible terms: our understanding of such cases is straightforwardly incompatible with the suggestion, descriptively understood, that actual human valuings and desirings are the source of all value. And a structurally similar incompatibility with any such subjectivist suggestion would emerge were those cases of valuing within the area shaped by potential desires of kind (3) in which the other, 'motivating' desire in play is of kind (4) to be considered.

It is none the less crucial to recognize that there remain various possible meanings which might be attached to the claim of subjectivity in accordance with which that claim is still compatible with the account given here of cases of valuing within the area shaped by potential desires of this final kind, (4). First, the subjectivist's claim might be that both the matter of the capacity for valuings of this kind together with that of quite which such valuings of this kind are in fact made will depend upon the nature of the 'subject', upon the nature of the person concerned: upon his physiological and psychological make-up, upon his needs, concerns and interests. And as long as that claim is not cast in terms designed to eliminate the area shaped by potential desires of kind (4) in favour of that shaped by potential desires of kind (3), there is no need to deny it here. That connects with a second possible truth behind the claim of subjectivity. We have held here that in cases of valuings within the area shaped by potential desires of kind (4) there are things which can be said with the aim of producing some reasonable resolution of any difference in such valuing: but that was not meant to imply great optimism either about the frequency of the realization of that aim or about its realization always being really possible. Features of the reasons-adducer and features of the reasons-receiver can easily combine to thwart the realization of that aim, and features of one or the other might suffice in a given case to render that aim unrealizable. Further, nothing said here about cases of such valuings is meant to license smugness, complacency or generalized certainty on a subject's part about his actual valuings of this kind at any given moment. Exactly the reverse is the case: once taking seriously the idea that such valuings purport to be cognitive responses to 'qualities in objects', which qualities are independently there, then caution will clearly be the order of the day. Our sensitivity to how the world is can always be bettered, in this as in any other case. The flight from subjectivity here being undertaken does not lead to the landing embrace of dogma (cf. Platts 1979: 247; 1980b: 70–1).

Those points should, now, scarcely be worth labouring; but there remains to be considered a further matter connecting with certain possible preoccupations of those who maintain the claim of subjectivity. This concerns the content in cases of valuings within the area shaped by potential desires of kind (4) of the thought that the object of any such valuing is deemed worthy of being desired. And perhaps the main point to be noted is the relative weakness (in a sense) of that thought. To hold that something is worthy of being valued and worthy of being desired is not yet to hold that it ought to be valued and ought to be desired: is not yet to hold, that is, that it merits being valued and being desired. (I think the element of linguistic stipulation in that way of putting the point is slight and anyway harmless.) The claim is rather that the thing concerned is a worthwhile object of such valuing and desiring: but ever so many things are worthwhile objects of such valuing and desiring. Think, say, of pursuit of the historical truth about the twelfth-century Renaissance: it can quite reasonably be held at the same time both that one who dedicates himself to the pursuit of that truth dedicates himself to some worthwhile end and yet also that, say, one who lives in blissful ignorance even of the existence of such a subject-matter can in no reasonable way be criticized. Moreover, even if someone indeed recognizes the value of the pursuit of the truth as to that subject-matter while yet having no desire himself to engage in it, it is very far from clear that there is as yet any ground for reasonable criticism of him.

It might prove useful to elaborate a little upon various ways in which that last, generally characterized, kind of case might be further developed. One possibility is that the person concerned either values the engagement in the pursuit at issue by others or desires that engagement. Another possibility is that the person concerned either values the 'non-hindrance' in the activity of others who are in fact engaged in that pursuit or desires such 'non-hindrance'. And another possibility is that the person concerned either values the giving of assistance to those others who are in fact engaged in that pursuit or desires the giving of such assistance. But all those cases as described are quite distinct from any in which the thought is defensibly invoked that the thing originally valued merits being valued and merits being desired, has being valued and being desired *owing* to it: any case in which the thing originally valued ought to be valued and ought to be desired.

At least some thought of that kind can be unproblematically invoked in description of certain actual cases. Think, for example, of the area shaped by potential desirings of kind (3) and of cases therein where the 'motivating' desire is either of kind (1) or of kind (2): a claim can naturally be invoked at least on occasion about what some agent ought to value and ought to desire. But such a claim is of course conditional upon, or relative to, the obtaining of the other, 'motivating' desire. Far more tendentious would be completely unrelativized claims to the effect that everybody ought to recognize some value of this kind, that everybody ought to value (in this way) the thing concerned, and to the effect that everybody ought to desire the thing in question: so that both ignorance and 'conative lack' would always be potentially reasonable objects of criticism. Nothing yet said here has been meant to count for, or against, the thesis that such claims can on occasion truly be made. So if the concern behind the claim of subjectivity is that of denying that thesis, this discussion has so far failed to address that concern. The point of what has just been said here has rather been that of trying to elucidate the comparative weakness of the various claims which have here been made by reliance upon the notion of worth, not that of merit.

TRANSCENDING THE SENSIBLY SUBJECTIVE?

A final matter of possible subjectivist concern relates to the appearance of what might be called 'transcendentalism' within the account so far given here of valuings within the area shaped by potential desires of kind (4). In view of what has been said in defence of the idea that a case of such valuing can count as a cognitive response to some value-property or value-feature which is independently there in objects without the mind, the thought might be invited that this account holds the existence of such value-properties or value-features – or, in apparently harmless abbreviation, the existence of values – to be completely independent of human valuings and desirings. And that might be judged rather hard to swallow.

Like so much else in this area the matter is perhaps best approached by a return to Hume. He held, as we have seen, that vice and virtue are at least usefully comparable to what have become known as secondary qualities, such as colours, which 'according to modern philosophy, are not qualities in objects, but perceptions in the mind'. That comparison, along with the presumed view of secondary qualities, has been instructively examined in various recent philosophical writings by some *most modern* philosophers, so I can keep my discussion here short with their help. But I should emphasize at the outset that my concern is still not yet with the theme of moral values and moral judgements: it remains that quite general one of valuings within the area shaped by potential desires of kind (4). What, then, is to be made of Hume's remarks if we consciously misconstrue them as if they were directed to that concern?

The first point to be noted is that in his discussion of secondary qualities such as colours, Hume, like many writers before and after him, runs together in an illegitimate way two quite different thoughts which might be expressed by saying that those qualities are 'subjective'. One is the thought, in the words of John McDowell, that a secondary quality 'is a property the ascription of which to an object is not adequately understood except as true, if it is true, in virtue of the object's disposition to present a certain sort of perceptual appearance' (McDowell 1982: 111); the other thought is that such qualities 'are not qualities in objects', so that experience of such qualities cannot be perceptual awareness of properties genuinely possessed by objects. Once those thoughts are distinguished there seems no good reason for thinking that acceptance of the first requires acceptance of the second: no good reason, that is, for thinking there to be some incoherence in the idea of a property which is genuinely possessed by objects and yet whose ascription to objects is to be understood in terms of those objects having a disposition to produce certain 'perceptions in the mind'. The ambiguity of the question 'Are there secondary qualities without the mind?' brings the point home neatly. That question can be answered affirmatively with the sense of holding that such qualities exist *outside of* the mind, are indeed properties genuinely possessed by *objects*, and can yet at the same time be answered negatively with the sense of holding that any veridical elucidation of our understanding of ascriptions of such qualities must *make reference to* potential effects produced in minds, produced in *subjects.*ʹ

None of that is designed to deny the possibility of there being qualities which are subjective in both of the senses distinguished; but let us none the less assume, what there is good reason to assume, that secondary qualities such as colours are subjective in only the first of those senses, allowing thereby that they are properties genuinely possessed by objects. And now let us note, within the context of that assumption, that the Humean suggestion is merely that there is a useful comparison between secondary qualities and the pertinent perceptual experiences, on the one hand, and values and valuings within the area shaped by potential desires of kind (4) on the other. That is: it would be at most a cheap victory over the Humean suggestion to rest merely with pointing out that there are differences between, say, colour-perceptions and valuings. There are many differences: but the specific Humean suggestion, the specific point of comparison at which we are now arriving, is untouched by at least many of those many differences. This is the suggestion tha·just as the ascription of some secondary quality to objects is to be understood in terms of those objects having a disposition in common to produce certain 'perceptions in the mind', so within the area shaped by potential desires of kind (4) the ascription of some specific value to objects is likewise to be understood in terms of those objects having a disposition in common to produce certain 'perceptions in the mind' – a disposition in common, say, to produce valuings (of this kind). And the point of the suggested comparison in the present context is not that of maintaining that such values are secondary qualities (any more than the point of rejection of the suggested comparison must be that of maintaining such values to be primary qualities): it is rather that of trying to free the account here given of the area shaped by potential desires of kind (4) from its appearance of (a certain kind of) 'transcendentalism'. It need not therefore count against the usefulness in the present context of the suggested comparison that there are, for example, important differences between the cases so compared as to how the dispositions involved are to be understood – the kinds of differences which in part lead David Wiggins to talk of 'a subjectivism of subjects and properties *mutually* adjusted' (Wiggins 1987: 199) and of '*appropriate*' reactions in subjects (ibid.: 187), or again those which in part lead John McDowell to talk of 'the contentiousness that is typical of values' and of 'objects that *merit*' the response concerned (McDowell 1982: 119). (In this discussion I shall allow the proponent of the Humean suggestion a more casual play with the notion of disposition than I think he is entitled to (cf. pp. 15–24); for my main point here emerges more clearly within the scope of this concession.)

While I doubt that the sense of 'subjectivity' positively involved in the suggestion so arrived at is one that has frequently been attached to the claim of subjectivity, at least in the mouths of normal people, still I think it fairly clear that that suggestion is compatible with the account so far given here of cases of valuing within the area shaped by potential desires of kind (4). That compatibility is secured through the combination within that suggestion of abandonment of the claim of subjectivity in Hume's second sense and the introduction of some pertinent notion of a disposition. None the less, I also think it fairly clear that the suggestion we have arrived at needs further elaboration: in part because its highly abstract character means that it covers too many distinct possibilities.

Let us, then, return once more to Hume himself. On his account (moral) values, just like colours, 'are not qualities in objects', but are rather the dangerously projectible products of 'the constitution of [our] nature'. So for Hume philosophical understanding of our talk of (moral) value should come to focus exclusively upon that 'constitution' – should come to focus exclusively, that is to say, upon the relevant dispositions in us, upon the relevant dispositions *in subjects*. For the suggestion just now arrived at here – Humean but not Hume's – the focus for understanding the pertinent sector of our talk of value in general seems initially quite distinct, seems initially to be upon dispositions *in objects*. But of course this focus is not *exclusively* upon dispositions in objects: for the pertinent dispositions are specified in terms of their potential effects 'in the mind', in terms of their potential mental effects *within subjects with certain dispositions*. So on the suggestion arrived at there are, loosely speaking, two kinds of dispositions in play: there are dispositions in objects, where those dispositions are specified in terms of their potential effects in certain disposition-bearing subjects, and there are dispositions in subjects, where those dispositions are specified in terms of their potential effects in relation to certain disposition-bearing objects. And thus the possibility is opened to view that because of features of the objects and features of the subjects particular examples of the two kinds of dispositions potentially in play do not *mesh* together (cf. Wiggins 1987).

According to this Humean suggestion, then, philosophical under-standing of talk of value within the area shaped by potential desires of kind (4) will require that attention be paid to two kinds of dispositions: dispositions in objects, where these dispositions are admittedly specified as dispositions to produce, say, valuings of those objects within certain disposition-bearing subjects, and dispositions in subjects, where these dispositions are specified as dispositions on the part of subjects to value certain disposition-bearing objects. And now the highly abstract character of the Humean suggestion can be appreciated just by confronting a seemingly simple question: Within the requisite specifications of dispositions in objects, exactly how is reference to the dispositions of subjects to be made?

In considering that question it is of importance to remember that the Humean suggestion has been construed here as having been put forward as a veridical descriptive account of (our understanding of) our talk of value within the area shaped by potential desires of kind (4). But consider now the following claims within that area:

(a) Pursuit of the historical truth about the twelfth-century Renaiss-ance would be worthwhile, would be worthy of value, even were it the case that human and similar beings not only did not in fact value it but in fact did not even have any disposition to value it.

(b) The preservation of innocent human or similar life ought to be valued, merits being valued, whether or not human and similar beings have even just the disposition to value it.

(c) Torture ought not to be valued, ought indeed to be disvalued, regardless of human dispositions in this respect.

Of course, one who makes such claims himself values the things concerned (or, in the torture case, makes manifest his disvaluing of the thing concerned); but the reach of his ascriptions of value across 'possible worlds' seems clearly to go beyond worlds in which that valuing occurs on his part or on anyone else's. Indeed, that reach seems to 'transcend' even the existence of dispositions to value the things concerned. There seems to be, if you like, an element of *necessity* within the contents of such thoughts of value.

If that prompts the objection that there would be no *point* to the expression of such thoughts of value within the context of an audi-ence lacking the dispositions concerned, the reply to be made has two parts. First, the lack of point to the expression of such a thought would not be the same as the falsity or the meaninglessness of the thought itself. And second, a possible reasonable point to the expression of a thought of value of this kind, within such a context, would be that of producing the relevant dispositions within the audience concerned *through the backing up of that thought by the adducing of reasons in support of the claim that the characterization therein deployed is indeed a desirability characterization.* (Remember that we are concerned with the area shaped by potential desires of kind (4).) Moreover, that brings to light other kinds of value-talk within this area which need, for descriptive purposes, to be taken account of: the kind of talk occurring in the claim that people ought to be disposed to value the particular things concerned regardless of their actual dispositions to value and the kind of talk occurring in the claim that certain dispositions to value are of value, are at least worthwhile, regardless of the actual dispositions to value of human and similar beings.

Within the area shaped by potential desires of kind (4) there are then certain distinctive ways of talking of value which need to be accommodated by the proponent of the Humean suggestion if that suggestion is to be acceptable as a veridical descriptive account of (our understanding of) all talk of value within that area. Perhaps there is some claim which both falls under the highly abstract initial Humean suggestion, is indeed a possible elaboration *of it*, and also serves to accommodate the distinctive ways of talking of value here at issue. Perhaps, for example, there is available to one seeking the requisite accommodation some suitable account of the *kind* of reference made within the specifications of the pertinent dispositions in objects, be the reference made to actual valuings, actual dispositions to value, the totality of actual dispositions to value or actually possible dispositions to value. What is clear is that even if the requisite accommodation proves to be technically possible, it is hardly likely to be so in terms which serve to save the subjectivist's characteristic insistence upon actual human valuings and desirings, or even just actual human dispositions to value and to desire, as the *source* of all value. Once the two kinds of dispositions involved in the Humean suggestion are distinguished – dispositions in objects and dispositions in subjects – and once consequently the distinctive character of the pertinent dispositions in objects is appreciated – the need to understand those dispositions in terms of worth or merit – then the possibility of some element of 'transcendence' has already been made clear. One concerned to save the subjectivist's characteristic insistence should have protested far earlier.

In this chapter I have tried to develop a theory of value and of valuing using the account of desire and its varieties presented in the preceding chapters. The starting-point was Philippa Foot's careful scepticism about 'what we mean by saying that *anything* has value, or even that we value it, as opposed to wanting it or being prepared to go to trouble to get it'. There is no short answer to that scepticism: it all depends upon the kind of wanting involved. Still, the results of this investigation are in the briefest possible terms the following:

1 'Reason-producing' desires supply no basis for talk of valuing, so the identification of wanting with valuing is incorrect when the wanting is of this kind.
2 For the other subclass of unmotivated desires, those whose objects are desired at random, the identification of wanting with one way of valuing is substantially correct once certain further conditions are imposed upon that wanting; but the truth of that identification supplies no basis for impersonal talk of values.
3 Within the first subclass of motivated desires, such as the desires for the means to (desired) ends, any simple identification of wanting with valuing is false: for there is a possibility of valuing without wanting. Perhaps more importantly, a cognitive account is given of valuings within the area shaped by potential desires of this kind; connectedly, a restricted kind of impersonal talk of value can be introduced in such cases. These claims are none the less compatible with the subjectivist's characteristic claim that actual desires are the source of all value.
4 Within the remaining subclass of motivated desires, that focused upon in the discussions of Nagel and McDowell, it is also true that any simple identification of wanting with valuing is false and that a cognitive account is given of valuings within the area shaped by potential desires of this kind. Moreover, a yet more impersonal level of talk of value can be introduced in such cases. But these claims in relation to this remaining subclass of motivated desires are incompatible with the truth of the subjectivist's insistence upon actual desires as the source of all value. Veridical appreciation of the character of these desires rules out in descriptive terms, not just identification of valuing with wanting, but also the vaguer subjectivist project of 'reducing' all valuing to wanting.

The cognitive account of valuings within the area shaped by potential desires of kind (4) was articulated in terms of a group of key elements (desires, desirability characterizations, desirability characteristics or features, reasons) and of certain relations between them (especially that of 'reasonably eliciting' or 'reasonably giving rise to'). But for full understanding of that account, more in the way of detailed articulation still needs to be said both about those components and, especially, about their pertinent relations. Some of what is needed will be found in the following part of this essay when attention is focused more narrowly upon the matter of morality.

Once thinking on the appropriate classification of moral desires, moral valuings and moral values within the terms of this theory of value and valuing, two thoughts are likely to seem initially obvious. One is that at least some moral valuings are understood in the terms of the area shaped by potential desires of kind (4), while certain other such valuings are understood within the terms of the area shaped by potential desires of the other motivated kind, (3). The other thought is that some of the moral valuings understood in the terms of the area shaped by potential desires of kind (4) are further understood in the more specific terms of cognitive responses to things which merit desire, which have desire owing to them, while other moral valuings of the same general kind are further understood in the weaker terms of cognitive responses to things which are merely worthy of desire, which are merely reasonable objects of desire. But obvious as those thoughts might initially seem, difficulties arise.

As regards the first thought, that of the understood cognitive character of certain moral valuings, an important difficulty stems from an argument of Hume's designed to show that *in reality* such an understanding of moral valuings would incorporate an illusion. That argument is indeed directed towards showing what in reality is the case; it is therefore compatible with the *descriptive* thought mentioned about our *understanding* of certain moral valuings. But if Hume's argument is a good one, we surely ought to try to change at least our understanding of those valuings. Moreover, and more importantly, to the extent to which that argument has filtered down into ordinary consciousness two possibilities arise: one is that acceptance of that argument sits uncomfortably alongside continuing adherence to the descriptive thought mentioned, the other is that that acceptance has displaced that thought. In the one case the *full* descriptive adequacy of the thought mentioned is threatened (and morality is indeed in a mess), in the other even the *partial* descriptive adequacy of the thought is threatened. I do not wish to enter into the historico-cultural question of whether Hume's argument has indeed filtered down into ordinary consciousness, although some of what is later said (in chapter 6) will serve to mark important distinctions between possible results of such filtration. Rather, in the following chapter I shall merely examine, and shall in fact be led to reject, that argument of Hume's; in the process some of the needed detailed articulation of the cognitive account of the pertinent moral valuings will be given.

The other initially obvious thought mentioned included the claim that certain moral valuings understood in cognitive and non-subjective terms are further understood in the more specific terms of cognitive responses to things which merit desire, which have desire owing to them. That seems to imply that any difference in such valuing is always a potentially reasonable object of discussion and criticism. But many proponents of 'moral relativism' have adduced theoretical arguments – some descriptive, some revisionary – purporting to show, in effect, that that seeming consequence is false. In the fifth chapter, therefore, I examine some representative arguments of 'moral relativists' so as to show that they show no such thing. In the course of that examination the importance of attention to specific reason-backed desirability characterizations for the purposes of philosophical understanding of moral thought and practice will emerge.

Some other questions about the connections with moral thought and practice of the theories of desire and value so far developed are considered in the second part of this essay: the question, for example, of the place of unmotivated desires of kinds (1) and (2) in that thought and practice. And some disconcerting features of our actual use of morality are also touched upon. But the governing aim of the second part of this essay is the quite general one of working towards an identification of the institution of morality through identification of central features of the theory internal to moral thought and practice.

Part Two

The philosopher supposes that the value of his philosophy lies in the whole, in the structure; but posterity finds its value in the stone which he used for building, and which is used many more times after that for building — better. Thus it finds the value in the fact that the structure can be destroyed and *nevertheless* retains value as building material.

(Nietzsche)

Moral concepts do not move about *within* a hard world set up by science and logic. They set up, for different purposes, a different world.

(Iris Murdoch)

4 Fact and action in Hume's moral theory

One of the marks, though not a necessary mark, of a really great philosopher is to make a really great mistake: that is to say, to give a persuasive and lastingly influential form to one of those fundamental misconceptions to which the human intellect is prone when it concerns itself with the ultimate categories of thought.

(Strawson)

I think a wickeder mind, and more obstinately bent on public mischief, I never knew.

(William Warburton on Hume)

THE MASTER ARGUMENT

Hume's examination of moral thought and practice ranges over a number of distinct claims relating to it; I wish to consider one central concern present in that examination, a concern which leads Hume to present a fascinating argument of great philosophical mastery. The concern is with the claim that the 'rules of morality . . . are . . . conclusions of reason' (Hume 1888: book III, part I, section I).

Hume's examination of that claim takes place within a picture of the mind as composed of at least two distinct faculties, that of reason and that of passion. Reason is the cognitive or intellectual faculty, the faculty of understanding, whose paradigm deliverance is perhaps that of beliefs. Passion is the active or conative faculty whose paradigm deliverance can be taken here to be that of desires and volitions. Cognitive states and conative states are distinct kinds of states: there is a sharp distinction, for example, between beliefs on the one hand and desires on the other. But also, and crucially, cognitive states and conative states are in at least one direction *in some way isolated*: no cognitive state alone of an agent can 'give rise to' a conative state of his. In Hume's words, 'reason alone can never produce any action, or give rise to volition' (1888: 414).

Whatever that doctrine of isolation amounts to, there are two claims, both true, which Hume is not thereby apparently committed to denying. The first is that a conative state can 'arise from' a cognitive state in combination with some other conative state. For example, my general desire to drink some water in combination with my belief that the glass in front of me contains water can 'give rise to' a desire to drink the contents of this glass. Hence there need be no inconsistency on Hume's part when he says, for example, that 'when we have the *prospect* of pain or pleasure from any object, we feel a *consequent emotion* of aversion or propensity, and are carry'd to avoid or embrace what will give us this uneasiness or satisfaction' (1888: 414, emphasis added). One with a general aversion or propensity as regards pain or pleasure can be led to an aversion or propensity *vis-à-vis* a particular object by the belief that that object will cause pain or pleasure. (But later (pp. 120–2, 127–8) a qualification will be made to this.)

The second claim that Hume apparently need not deny is that some ideas, such as those of emotions like pride, may require for their true application to a person the obtaining in that person both of some determinate cognitive state and of some determinate conative state. What Hume is apparently committed to is the possibility of disentangling the components of any such idea, of decompositionally analysing the conditions for its true application into the distinct sets of conditions for the true application of each of its component ideas, the one being that of some cognitive state, the other that of some conative state. Indeed, Hume need not even deny that the true application of some such ideas requires the obtaining of some relation between a cognitive state alone and some conative state; what he must deny is that the cognitive state alone 'gives rise to' the conative state.

Hume also draws a distinction within the workings of the faculty of reason. In one kind of employment the faculty of reason is deployed in the search for necessary truths, truths which say what has to be the case. According to Hume, truths of this kind are exclusively about the relations between ideas: the 'proper province' of the corresponding use of the faculty of reason is 'the world of ideas'. Moreover, the knowledge with which reason can provide us in relation to this 'province' is a priori knowledge: given that we have or possess the relevant ideas, we are thereby placed to achieve a priori knowledge of the relations between those ideas, a priori knowledge of necessary truths. But matters are different for the other kind of employment of the faculty of reason. Deploying reason in this second way what we search for are truths about the 'province' of 'realities': truths about the objects in the world, their properties, and especially their causal relations. For Hume any knowledge we can come by of such truths will be a posteriori: only through 'experience', through empirical investigation, can we come to obtain this kind of information. Moreover, Hume seems tacitly to have presumed that a posteriori knowledge of the 'province' of 'realities' will have as its object only contingent truths, truths about what is in fact the case although things might have been otherwise.

Notwithstanding the presence of many contentious points within Hume's way of marking the distinction between the two uses of the faculty of reason, his distinction is fundamental. Quite simply, upon reading the works of many philosophers prior to Hume – and even many later writers – it is unclear to which use of the faculty of reason they are referring by means of the mere word 'reason'. But there is a vast difference between a self-contradictory state and one of ignorance in relation to some matter of fact, just as there is a vast difference, for example, between the claim that an amoralist in some way contradicts himself and the claim that he is ignorant of some empirical truths.

None the less, Hume's arguments to show that the 'rules of morality . . . are not conclusions of reason' are directed equally against any attempt to found moral thought and practice upon either of the two uses of the faculty of reason. For those arguments are designed to show that no conclusion of reason, no state of the faculty of reason, could play the role in our lives which our moral ideas in fact play. I shall focus here upon one of those arguments, an argument corresponding to a more specific concern found as part of Hume's general concern with the refutation of any kind of 'rational-ism' within moral philosophy. The argument is designed to show that 'morality . . . consists not in any *matter of fact* which can be discover'd by the understanding' (Hume 1888: 468), and is focused upon the second, empirical use of the faculty of reason; none the less, it should be obvious how this form of argument can be generalized so as to count against any moral 'rationalism'.

Most of the materials deployed in this Humean argument against what I shall call 'moral factualism' are furnished by Hume himself in the course of his attempts to establish the following claims: first, 'that reason alone can never be a motive to any action of the will' (1888: book II, part III, section III); and second, that the 'rules of morality . . . are not conclusions of our reason' (ibid.: book III, part I, section I). And although I cast the argument in partly non-Humean terms, even this terminological distance is perhaps less than it superficially seems. That said we can now consider the argument, numbering its premises as they are introduced.

First (1), a matter of fact or truth is a possible object of knowledge: its status as such a matter is both secured by and exhausted by its being a possible object of knowledge. As Hume has it:

> Reason is the discovery of truth or falsehood. Truth or falsehood consists in an agreement or disagreement either to the *real* relations of ideas, or to *real* existence and matter of fact. What-ever, therefore, is not susceptible of this agreement or disagree-ment, is incapable of being true or false, and can never be an object of our reason.
>
> (Hume 1888: 458)

> If the thought and understanding were alone capable of fixing the boundaries of right and wrong, the character of virtuous and vicious either must lie in some relations of objects, or must be a matter of fact, which is discovered by our reasoning.
>
> (ibid.: 463)

> Morality . . . consists not in any *matter of fact*, which can be discover'd by the understanding. . . . But can there be any diffi-culty in proving, that vice and virtue are not matters of fact, whose existence we can infer by reason?
>
> (ibid.: 468)

Second (2), knowledge of any particular matter of fact or truth requires as regards the person with that knowledge only that he be in some determinate cognitive state, some specific state of the faculty of reason or understanding. As Hume puts it in his later work (*Enquiries Concerning Human Understanding and Concerning The Principles of Morals* 1902: 172): 'What is intelligible, what is evident, what is probable, what is true, procures only the cool assent of the understanding; and gratifying a speculative curiosity, puts an end to our researches.' But (3) no cognitive state of a person alone 'gives rise to' any conative state; the deliverances of the faculty of reason or understanding 'have no hold of the affections or set in motion the active powers of man' (Hume 1902: 172). Hence knowledge of any particular matter of fact or truth neither requires the obtaining within the person concerned of any conative state nor alone 'gives rise to' the existence of such a state.

Now (4), for a person to act or even just to have a reason for acting requires *at least* the obtaining within him of some conative state, requires *at least* that his 'active powers' be set in motion.

> The end of all moral speculations is to teach us our duty; and, by proper representations of the deformity of vice and beauty of virtue, beget correspondent habits, and engage us to avoid the one, and embrace the other. But is this ever to be expected from inferences and conclusions of the understanding, which of themselves have no hold of the affections or set in motion the active powers of man? They discover truths: but where the truths which they discover are indifferent, and beget no desire or aversion, they can have no influence on conduct and behaviour. . . .
>
> Extinguish all the warm feelings and prepossessions in favour of virtue, and all disgust or aversion to vice: render men totally indifferent towards these distinctions; and morality is no longer a practical study, nor has any tendency to regulate our lives and actions.
>
> (Hume 1902: 172)

Hence no knowledge of any particular matter of fact or truth alone gives a person any reason for acting; some additional, conative state needs to obtain for the person to have such a reason. And, to repeat, that additional conative state cannot 'arise from' the state of knowledge alone.

Yet (5), acceptance of some moral judgement can give, and at least on occasion does give, the person so accepting some reason for acting; indeed, acceptance of a moral judgement on occasion gives rise to action itself.

> If morality had naturally no influence on human passions and action, 'twere in vain to take such pains to inculcate it; and nothing wou'd be more fruitless than that multitude of rules and precepts, with which all moralists abound. Philosophy is commonly divided into *speculative* and *practical*; and as morality is always comprehended under the latter division, 'tis supposed to influence our passions and actions, and to go beyond the calm and indolent judgements of the understanding. And this is confirm'd by common experience, which informs us, that men are often govern'd by their duties, and are deter'd from some actions

by the opinion of injustice, and impell'd to others by that of
obligation.
   . . . Morals, therefore, have an influence on the actions and
affections. . . . Morals excite passions, and produce or prevent
actions.

(Hume 1888: 457)

It follows that acceptance of a moral judgement by a person is not
as regards that person just the obtaining within him of some cognitive
state and that such acceptance is not just a matter of the person's
having come by knowledge of some matter of fact or truth: 'The
rules of morality, therefore, are not conclusions of our reason' (ibid.:
457).

But now, a matter of moral fact or moral truth would have to be
no more and no less than both (i) a matter of fact or truth, and
(ii) that alone, recognition or knowledge of which determines the
acceptance by a person of the corresponding moral judgement that
the fact or truth obtains. So a matter of moral fact or moral truth
would have to be such both that (i) knowledge of it alone gives a
person no reason for acting, and also that (ii) knowledge of it alone
does give a person some reason for acting. Conclusion: there are no
moral facts, the matter of morality is not a matter of fact or truth.
The last word is Hume's: 'morality . . . consists not in any *matter
of fact*, which can be discover'd by the understanding' (1888: 468).

The argument purports not merely to refute moral factualism, the
idea that there are moral facts or truths at least some of which can
be known by us to obtain, but also to elucidate the content of that
which it denies. The key suggestion is the connection posited in (1)
between the notions of fact and knowledge: there is no more and
no less to a matter's being a matter of fact than its being a possible
object of knowledge. That suggestion is itself further developed by
the claim put forward in (2) about, so to say, the knower's constitutive contribution to his state of knowledge. Then given the additional
claims made in (3) and (4) about both the isolation of a cognitive
state alone *vis-à-vis* the conative states of a knower and what it is
for a person to have a reason for acting, we are led to the general
elucidatory conclusion that no matter of fact or truth is such that
knowledge of it by itself gives a person any reason for acting.

The connection between the notions of fact and knowledge from
which that general elucidation of the factual begins is not unproblematic; but note that neither the posited connection nor the final

general elucidation need carry any commitment to crude representative theories of concept-acquisition or of knowledge. Consider Hume once again: 'What is intelligible, what is evident, what is probable, what is true, procures only the cool assent of the understanding; *and gratifying a speculative curiosity, puts an end to our researches*' (1902: 172, emphasis added). Some matter of fact may come under investigation only because of the investigators' 'speculative curiosity'. More generally, some matter of fact may come under investigation only because of certain concerns, interests and needs the investigators happen to have: without those concerns, interests and needs the investigators would not have been led to shape the relevant conceptual resources nor to acquire the relevant evidence (cf. Platts 1983a). Some non-cognitive states of these (or other) types may be not just instrumental in but essential for the acquisition of the knowledge concerned. But that need not count against factualist doctrines as elucidated by the Humean argument. If any factualism were committed to the view that the relevant concepts and information are forced upon us regardless of 'all other considerations whatsoever', it could now scarcely be worth refuting.

Hume can now be seen to have adopted a strategy shared by a number of contemporary philosophers, that of approaching metaphysical questions of fact and value through considerations of philosophical psychology. Given the fruitlessness of most traditional 'direct' approaches to those metaphysical questions, the attraction of this change of tack is clear enough. But in any specific case of a philosopher's implementation of this strategy it is necessary to consider the question of the adequacy of the relevant parts of his philosophical psychology. We shall shortly return to that in the case of Hume; but first I wish to finish this brief sketch of that part of his investigations into the nature of morality which is here occupying us.

Given the argument which Hume has presented, how can persistence of attachment to the claim that morality is indeed a matter of fact or truth be explained? Historically speaking, the most interesting of the explanations which Hume gives is an explanation of how it is that people fail to recognize the truth of a premise of his argument: the premise, (4), that for a person to act or even just to have a reason for acting requires *at least* the obtaining within him of some conative state, requires *at least* that his 'active powers' be set in motion. Hume's explanation of the failure to recognize that truth is the following: there are certain 'calm passions' which simply are not felt, neither their existence nor their causal efficacy being discoverable by introspection (Hume 1888: 417); lacking the otherwise characteristic feel of passions, they therefore seem exactly like cognitive states, like states of the faculty of reason; but then, when those 'calm passions' operate to produce effects in the form of intentional actions, it consequently seems that states of the faculty of reason alone can indeed produce intentional actions. My reason for saying that that is Hume's most interesting explanation, historically speaking, of persisting attachment to the pertinent claim is simple: we see here the price which Hume is disposed to pay in order to maintain his theory of morality. And the price is high: recognition of the existence of 'calm passions' compels the abandonment of one of the fundamental principles of Hume's theory of ideas, the principle which holds that we cannot be mistaken about the contents of our own minds at any given moment. The conscious, systematic abandonment of that principle would have had far-reaching consequences within other parts of Hume's philosophy. And that Hume himself never followed through those consequences does not show that he was unaware of them, unaware of the price he was tacitly paying in order to maintain his account of the nature of moral thought and practice.

Finally, Hume presents us, in a surprisingly brief way, with his own positive ideas about the nature of morality. For the purposes of accounting for the practical nature of moral thought, Hume believes himself to have shown that nothing will be gained by the postulation of further properties in the objects towards which our moral thought is directed: any such 'objective' properties will be nothing more than further matters of fact, further possible objects of states of the faculty of reason, and so will leave quite unaccounted for the presumed connection between moral thought and action. Rather, what is needed for the purposes of accounting for that is something further *in us*: something adequately related to our faculty of passion (cf. Foot 1963: 74). What Hume postulates is a distinctive feeling of *moral approbation*. That feeling is agreeable or pleasing; indeed, Hume even tells us that there 'is no spectacle so fair and beautiful as a noble and generous action; nor any which gives us more abhorrence than one that is cruel and treacherous' (1888: 470). By this means Hume believes he can explain our tendency to perform actions whose contemplation produces so delightful a feeling; and so he thus believes he can explain the practical nature of our moral thought.

THE DOCTRINE OF ISOLATION

Hume said that 'reason alone can never produce any action, or give rise to volition' (1888: 414). It is perhaps tempting for the contemporary reader to construe this as no more than Hume's expression of that part of current orthodoxy which holds that any full articulation of an agent's reason for acting must make reference not just to the cognitive states of the agent such as his beliefs but also to his conative states, his desires or 'pro-attitudes'. But if that be all that the current orthodoxy really amounts to, I think the temptation should be resisted. (In this discussion I shall make Hume a gift of the notion of a reason for acting without wishing to suggest that he himself made free use of any such notion. Indeed, as will soon emerge, I think that on Hume's official account of reason there is no room for any such thing as a reason for acting. But the present gift makes it easier to draw out that point.)

Hume can be taken to have subscribed to at least part of this orthodoxy – that part, maintained in premise (4) of the Humean argument, which claims that for a person to have a reason for acting requires *at least* the obtaining within him of some conative state. The subscription is perhaps most vividly shown by Hume's invocation of the idea of 'calm passions'. And I know of no evidence to suggest that Hume would have denied the other element in the current orthodoxy, that the having of some reason for acting requires the obtaining of a cognitive state like belief. If the notion of having a reason for acting is tied to that of the possibility of acting upon the reason that is just as well since any such action needs at least some belief on the agent's part as to how, say, to seek and pursue the object of desire (cf. Williams 1981a). My point is rather that that part of current orthodoxy does not exhaust the content of Hume's claim.

If that were all that Hume meant then he might just as easily have put his point by saying that *passion* alone can never produce any action, or give rise to volition. He never did so. And while doubtless there were specific historical reasons for Hume's focusing upon the motivational powerlessness of reason, I think that the reconstructed Humean argument shows the point here to be not just historical. What Hume needs for the purposes of that argument is not just the mentioned part of current orthodoxy but also the claim that no cognitive state alone of a person 'gives rise to' any conative state. That addition, I am suggesting, is part of what Hume meant by his claim as to the motivational powerlessness of reason.

What does Hume's addition, the doctrine of isolation, amount to? And why should it be believed? Hume often writes as if the thesis of isolation is a merely causal one, the claim being that no cognitive state alone of a person causes any conative state. If that is the thesis, then of all philosophers Hume is the least well-placed to maintain it as an a priori truth since a major consequence of his discussion of causation is that what kinds of things can stand in causal relations to each other is never an a priori matter. Yet we never find in Hume's writings the results of any careful examination of 'objects with a strict philosophic eye' designed to support his crucial addition. Instead we find the following argument:

> A passion is an original existence, or, if you will, modification of existence, and contains not any representative quality, which renders it a copy of any other existence or modification. When I am angry, I am actually possest with the passion, and in that emotion have no more a reference to any other object, than when I am thirsty, or sick, or more than five foot high. 'Tis impossible, therefore, that this passion can be oppos'd by, or be contradictory to truth and reason; since this contradiction consists in the disagreement of ideas, consider'd as copies, with those objects, which they represent.
>
> (Hume 1888: 415)

> Reason is the discovery of truth or falsehood. Truth or falsehood consists in an agreement or disagreement either to the *real* relations of ideas, or to *real* existence and matter of fact. Whatever, therefore, is not susceptible of this agreement or disagreement, is incapable of being true or false, and can never be an object of our reason. Now 'tis evident our passions, volitions, and actions, are not susceptible of any such agreement or disagreement; being original facts and realities, compleat in themselves, and implying no reference to other passions, volitions, and actions. 'Tis impossible, therefore, they can be pronounced either true or false, and be either contrary or conformable to reason.
>
> (ibid.: 458)

One of the few philosophers both to have seen the importance of this argument and explicitly to have construed it as an attempted defence of the merely causal thesis of isolation is Barry Stroud. On this interpretation, Hume is emphasizing the abstract nature of the entities, propositions, which are the only 'objects of reason'. Being abstract entities, these objects of reason can have no causal influence. Such influence is restricted to 'original existences' or 'modifications of existence'. But then Hume makes the further 'questionable' assumption that reason itself can be identified with the totality of the objects of reason. And Stroud objects that this 'seems to leave out altogether the notion of reason as a faculty of the mind, or reasoning as a mental process' (Stroud 1977: 158–61).

The interpretation is ingenious; but it makes of this argument of Hume's a remarkable irrelevance. The point is not just the questionableness of Hume's supposed assumption as to what reason is. Even conceding that to Hume, his argument so construed does nothing to show that a cognitive *state* of a person cannot alone cause some conative *state* of that person. But on the merely causal interpretation of the thesis of isolation, the seeming possibility that is 'left out altogether' is exactly the possibility that Hume needs to deny for the purposes of his argument against moral factualism.

Note also that on this interpretation, since 'reason' cannot cause anything it cannot even cause cognitive states such as belief. Yet Hume's argument lays emphasis upon some supposed distinctive feature of the passions: their lack of 'any representative quality', their being 'original facts and realities, compleat in themselves'. But on Stroud's interpretation this emphasis is quite unnecessary: for that interpretation, the causal powerlessness of 'reason' is a universal truth and the only one needed. Remarks about its (non-) effects would be beside the point.

(Some might think there to be a quicker, more direct way of eliminating the merely causal interpretation of the thesis that no cognitive state alone 'gives rise to' any conative state: namely, by reference to Hume's discussion of pride in book II of the *Treatise*. And it is true that Hume there repeatedly holds the cause of pride to be a belief. But aside from familiar doubts about the consistency of different books of the *Treatise*, I think Donald Davidson has given the correct reading of those causal claims: 'Both belief and attitude, reason and passion, are necessary to cause pride. But the relevant attitudes . . . are, Hume thinks, universal. . . . Where men differ is in their gifts, and hence in what they believe to be their gifts; this is therefore what needs to be mentioned in explaining pride, even if it is the "inactive" principle' (Davidson 1976: 286).)

If better is to be done by Hume it will prove necessary, I think, to abandon the merely causal interpretation of the thesis of isolation. That is, the question of whether a cognitive state can alone cause the existence of some conative state must be sharply distinguished from the question of whether a cognitive state can alone 'reasonably cause' the existence of such a conative state – the question, in Humean terms, of whether a cognitive state can alone give rise to a conative state *in virtue of* some 'reasonable connection' between the propositional contents of those states.

One possibility opened to view by the drawing of this distinction is that Hume thought there to be no such real relation as reasonable causation: the idea of such a relation is incoherent. The argument for that thought might, schematically, be as follows. Although both cognitive and conative states indeed have propositional contents, those contents and their relations of reason are irrelevant for the matter of any causal relations involving those states. If, for example, some particular cognitive state which is a state of belief causes some 'modification of existence' which is a state of desire then as regards the causal relation obtaining between those states the matter of their propositional contents is irrelevant – it is not *material* for causal powers. Causal efficacy is blind to any relations reason may detect between the propositional contents of such states: within the terms of the causal nexus, of the famed cement of the universe, 'modifications of existence' no more have propositional contents than does a man's being more than 5 foot high. As Hume writes:

> The understanding exerts itself after two different ways, as it judges from demonstration or probability; as it regards the abstract relations of our ideas, or those relations of objects, of which experience only gives us information. I believe it scarce will be asserted, that the first species of reasoning alone is ever the cause of any action. As it's proper province is the world of ideas, and as the will always places us in that of realities, demonstration and volition seem, upon that account, to be totally remov'd, from each other.
>
> (Hume 1888: 413)

So the province of reasoning is the world of ideas whereas causality, like the will, places us in that of realities. On the present interpretation, Hume holds the notion of reasonable causation to be the incoherent consequence of an attempt to unite those two provinces within a federal structure.

Thus understood, Hume is effectively adopting one of the perennially popular responses to the great problem of how the causal role of mental states can be reconciled with the rationalizing role of the propositional contents of such states: he denies that such a reconciliation is possible and then reacts by dismissing the ideal structure of rationalization in favour of the concrete, naturalistic foundation of causality.

Perhaps that is what Hume should have meant (given other elements of his philosophical system); but I doubt it is what he did mean. On this interpretation Hume ought also to have denied that even a process through which a person's deductive reasoning leads to some change in his beliefs can be a reasonable causal process, can embody a change which comes about in virtue of some 'reasonable connection' between the propositional contents of the beliefs concerned. I suspect Hume might have enjoyed this consequence. But the matter does not end there. On this same interpretation Hume also ought to make the same denial as regards the generation of the desire for health from the combination of a hatred of pain and the belief that sickness is painful. Such a generation must be understood as merely causal. Indeed, the same denial has to be made about the generation of intention and action by some combination of belief and desire. If my desire to drink water and my belief that this is water combine to generate my intentional action of drinking this, this process too must be understood as a merely causal one which does not in the least occur because of the propositional contents of my mental states.

But that is at best very puzzling. Why, of all my beliefs, is it that which is that *this is water* which is held to combine with the desire so as to generate my action? Is it just that we implausibly think ourselves to have observed some 'constant conjunction' between such belief-desire pairs, on the one hand, and drinkings of water on the other? Surely not: for the action to be intentional under that description it has to be generated by such a pair since only thus is it rationalized under that description. That is an a priori remark about the concept of intentional action, about the conditions under which it is possible for that concept to have application. Properly understood, therefore, it does not conflict with Hume's claim about the looseness and independence of all beings in the universe (Hume 1888: 466). The view this present interpretation attributes to Hume can therefore be maintained only by abandoning employment of the concept of intentional action itself – a concept one might expect to figure large in any treatise of *human* nature. (Note too that one convinced of Davidson's reading of Hume's discussion of pride will see the present interpretation as in immediate conflict with the whole of that discussion. And note also that on this interpretation Hume would be committed to denying the first of the claims mentioned above (p. 110); his remarks about the role of the 'prospect of pain or pleasure' (Hume 1888: 414) would have to be interpreted in merely causal terms.)

A further worry for a proponent of this interpretation is an allied textual point touched upon earlier. On both occasions Hume presents his argument as turning upon the status of the *passions* as 'original existences', 'modifications of existence', 'original facts and realities, compleat in themselves'. Yet upon the current interpretation Hume could just as well have made his point by assigning the same status to cognitive states, to states of the faculty of reason (hence my remarks above about deductive reasoning). It is true that Stroud claims that a person's discovering or believing something is 'just as much' a 'modification of existence' as is his being angry or his being more than 5 feet tall. But it is surely clear that, aside from any merely terminological issue, Hume wishes to draw attention to some feature supposedly distinctive of the passions as the foundation for his thesis of isolation. The ground of that wish is what we have yet to understand.

Note finally that it is not at all clear how, upon this interpretation, the remainder of the Humean argument against moral factualism is to be modified so that it is then both valid and with plausible premises. The difficulty is obvious: for the claim that no cognitive state alone reasonably causes any conative state to do the work required of it in yielding the conclusion that knowledge of a matter of moral fact or truth would have contradictory properties, it seems that it will prove necessary to invoke the notion of reasonable causation within some *positive* claim about either the general notion of having a reason for acting or the reason-giving character of moral judgements. But any such positive claim is *ex hypothesi* incoherent.

Consider once more Hume's actual words when presenting the argument at issue:

A passion is an original existence, or, if you will, modification of existence, *and contains not any representative quality, which renders it a copy of any other existence or modification.* . . . 'Tis impossible, therefore, that this passion can be oppos'd by, or be contradictory to truth and reason; since this contradiction consists in the disagreement of ideas, *consider'd as copies*, with those objects, which they *represent*.

(Hume 1888: 415, emphases added)

Let us say, initially and tentatively, that both somebody's *believing that p* and his *desiring that q* are propositional states of that person, each being 'composed of' some propositional attitude (believing and desiring respectively in those examples) together with some propositional content (*p* and *q* respectively). Thus one who believes that *p* is not thereby in the same propositional state as one who believes that *q*, nor is one who believes that *p* thereby in the same propositional state as one who desires that *p* (as is most clearly marked in those languages requiring a sharp subjunctive formulation of the contents of desires).

Now, for a believing-state that *p* reasonably to cause a desiring-state that *q* the believing-state has to cause the desiring-state in virtue of some relation of reason holding between the propositional contents *p* and *q*. Hume is clearly, I think, trying to characterize some fundamental difference between, say, believing-states and desiring-states, which difference shows such a case of reasonable causation to be an impossibility. But just what is that supposed difference?

Believing-states 'contain some representative quality which renders them copies of other existences or modifications', desiring-states do not. The former at least purport to represent how things are, and are thereby at least thought of as 'originating' in that *presence* which they *re-present*. By contrast desiring-states do not purport to represent how things are, and are thereby at least thought to 'originate' within the desirer: they are '*original* facts and realities, compleat in themselves' (Hume 1888: 458, emphasis added). Now Hume was notoriously at least negligent about the distinction between concepts and propositions and in consequence at least negligent of the ways in which the significance of a proposition can be determined by the significance of its constitutive concepts. He also seems to have thought – *very* roughly speaking – that the matter of the significance of propositions is determined 'genetically', by those 'existences' causally responsible for the propositions' coming to mind. Those two features of Hume's thought may have combined with his view that the passions are 'original existences', that they 'originate' within us, not without from other 'existences', to produce an inclination to think of the passions as having no significant content: to think that is, that they are not really *propositional* states at all (cf. Kenny 1963: 25 n. 1). Thus Hume himself: 'When I am angry, I am actually possest with the passion, and in that emotion have no more a reference to any other object, than when I am thirsty, or sick, or more than five foot high' (1888: 415). But then if Hume thought that the passions such as desires had no propositional contents, he would rightly have thought it obvious that no other 'beings in the universe' could reasonably cause them; so he would have thought it obvious that cognitive states could not do so.

This interpretation has much textual support; I think it clearly answers to one inclination within Hume's mind. But, first, it attributes to Hume a (now stunning) error: the denial of the propositional-state status of the passions precludes any possibility of accounting for the rationalizing role of reasons for acting; it will hence ultimately preclude employment of the concept of intentional action. Second, the interpretation focuses upon a needless error found at one point within Hume's system of thought without considering how that overall system could have enabled Hume to avoid the error. Thus Davidson's comment upon the interpretation:

> The criticism is confused. What Hume *called* the passion had no 'representative quality'; but the pattern of elements he called on to make a passion what it is certainly did. The valid criticism is that what Hume called the passion has no place in the pattern.
> (Davidson 1976: 288)

Third, it is again unclear how on this interpretation the validity of Hume's argument is to be preserved. And finally, there is a philosophically more interesting interpretation of Hume, together with a diagnosis of his error, which has at least as much textual support.

Perhaps Hume did not mean to deny that the passions have propositional contents; rather, perhaps what he meant to deny is that such contents are *representative* contents or supposed *copies*. So understood, and passing aside later complications in Hume's account of belief, his initial point is similar to that made by G. E. M. Anscombe in terms of the different 'directions of fit' which may obtain between mental states and the world (Anscombe 1958: section 2; and cf. above, pp. 48–9). A believing-state purports to represent how the world is, purports to fit with how the world is. If such 'fit' is lacking, then it is the believing-state which should be changed in order to obtain the requisite 'fit'. Believing-states aim, *inter alia*, at the truth, and it is a crucial failing in such a state if it misses that target. But desiring-states, like other conative states, do not purport to represent how things are, do not purport to 'fit' with how the world is. If no such 'fit' obtains, then, roughly speaking, there is no onus upon the desirer to modify his desiring-state in order to achieve such a 'fit'; rather, the desiring one has reason to try to change how the world is so that it will then 'fit' with (the content of) his desiring-state. While a desiring-state might apparently hit the target of truth, that is never its aim. ('Apparently' because of complexities introduced by the subjunctive character of the contents of such states.)

But all that gives us is an elucidation of the general distinction between cognitive and conative states; as yet it says nothing about the possible, or impossible, relations between such states. It clearly does not follow from that distinction that no believing-state can alone cause a desiring-state, nor does it follow that desiring-states are not propositional states at all. For the purposes of salvaging a modified version of the Humean argument what I think is needed is this: the thought that from this distinction between believing-states and desiring-states it follows that no believing-state can alone reasonably cause any desiring-state. But, crucially, that will not be so because of any incoherence in the relational notion of reasonable causation. That notion is deemed coherent, thereby opening the possibility of a modified version of Hume's argument against moral factualism in which positive use is made of that notion. Rather, presuming that notion coherent, the thought is that it is shown to have no application between believing-states (alone) and desiring-states by the distinction of kind between those states to which Hume has drawn attention. But why might that thought seem reasonable?

In one of his most famous passages Hume wrote:

I cannot forbear adding to these reasonings an observation, which may, perhaps, be found of some importance. In every system of morality, which I have hitherto met with, I have always remark'd, that the author proceeds for some time in the ordinary way of reasoning, and establishes the being of a God, or makes observations concerning human affairs; when of a sudden I am surpriz'd to find, that instead of the usual copulation of propositions, *is*, and *is not*, I meet with no proposition that is not connected with an *ought*, or an *ought not*. This change is imperceptible; but is, however, of the last consequence. For as this *ought*, or *ought not*, expresses some new relation or affirmation, 'tis necessary that it shou'd be observ'd and explain'd; and at the same time that a reason should be given, *for what seems altogether inconceivable*, how this new relation can be a deduction from others, which are entirely different from it. . . . [T]his small attention wou'd subvert all the vulgar systems of morality, *and let us see, that the distinction of vice and virtue is not founded merely on the relations of objects, nor is perceiv'd by reason.*

(Hume 1888: 469–70, final two italicizations added)

Nobody could say that this passage has been neglected by subsequent philosophers; but we have not worried sufficiently, I think, about its location, textually and philosophically, at the end of Hume's arguments designed to show that moral distinctions are not derived from reason.

The suggested interpretation of Hume begins from the supposition that for him the relation of reasonable causation (of 'giving rise to') is a hybrid composed of at least two utterly distinct *kinds* of elements: relations of reason obtaining in 'the world of ideas', such relations being candidates for a priori knowledge, on the one hand, and causal relations obtaining in the world of realities on the other, such relations being candidates only for a posteriori knowledge. Thus reasonable causation occurs if a causal relation obtains between propositional states in the world of realities in virtue of some relation of reason obtaining between the propositional contents of those states in the world of ideas. That being so some a priori consideration of reason could indeed suffice to establish in some cases that the relation of reasonable causation does *not* apply. (Any positive truth involving the relation would be a possible object of only empirical knowledge.) That is, upon such a view of the relation it would indeed seem possible to determine a priori that some kinds of things could not reasonably cause certain other kinds of things.

Hume claims to know a priori that it is 'altogether inconceivable' that there be any reasonable relation between an indicative *is*-proposition and an *ought*-proposition such that the latter follows from the former. That is just a matter of some 'small attention'. But suppose Hume also thought, as others have, of desires as pieces of (self-directed) advice; or suppose he thought that a natural expression of a desire could take the form of an *ought*-proposition; or suppose he merely thought the subjunctive propositional content of a desire to be far more like an *ought*-proposition than an indicative *is*-proposition. Then he would also think that his 'small attention' would show the impossibility of any cognitive state alone, with its indicative propositional content, reasonably causing a conative state.

Given the structure of his argument, he would thereby indeed think that his 'small attention' shows 'that the distinction of vice and virtue is not . . . perceived by reason' (Hume 1888: 470).

SOME DIFFICULTIES

On this interpretation Hume simply assumes without argument, through his reliance upon the notion of reasonable causation, that 'ideal relations' of reason can be in some way reconciled with the naturalistic realities of causal relations. It would be unfair to berate Hume for that mere assumption. But there are two further points on which he must be criticized.

First, the matter of his 'small attention' is treated in far too simplistic a way. There is no more than a blank assertion as to the 'altogether inconceivable'. That is an instance of a general failing in his philosophy, well described and diagnosed by Stroud:

> Hume's treatment of the whole subject of 'reasoning from ideas alone' is rudimentary and perfunctory. He accepts almost uncritically talk of 'the same' and 'distinct' ideas, and of 'the relations of ideas', as if they inhabited a determinate objective domain immediately open to our minds for inspection. The theory of ideas encourages this picture of a set of autonomous, interconnected 'things' among which certain relations can be discovered to hold merely in virtue of our 'possessing' the ideas in question. Hume's confident assertions about which ideas are 'the same', and which 'distinct', with their consequences about what is, and what is not, 'absolutely' impossible are an expression of this picture.
>
> (Stroud 1977: 240)

But in the present context a second stricture is more important: Hume's conception of 'the world of ideas' renders the project of reconciling reason and causality an impossible one. On Hume's picture, the one is deemed to have as its proper province the world of ideas, the other that of realities; and it is a mere sleight of hand to suggest that propositional states can somehow bridge the gap between the two provinces. Those provinces could not even be within mental shooting-distance of each other. For reasonable causation as Hume understands it to occur between two propositional states, the one causes the other in virtue of some relation of reason in the world of ideas between the propositions that are the contents of those states. But what does the *in virtue of* signify here? *It cannot be causal since the relations of reason between propositions in the world of ideas, like the propositions themselves, are abstract 'beings'.* But what for Hume could it be other than causal? I conclude that Hume should in consistency have held the relation of reasonable causation to be incoherent (cf. pp. 120–2); he came close to the reason why he should have held that when stressing that the provinces of reason and will are 'totally remov'd, from each other' (Hume 1888: 413). (That is why my initial gift to Hume of the notion of a reason for acting must now be taken back (cf. p. 117.)

Hume makes rational connections and causal connections so remote from one another that it becomes impossible to make sense of reasonable causation as something that happens in the natural world. More specifically, it becomes impossible to make sense of *reasoning* as something that happens in the natural world. It would require at least another book to consider possible reactions to this problem and to defend some general theory of reasoning and reason which escapes it without thereby falling into the difficulties of psychologism. For the moment I merely wish to emphasize that my discussion has focused upon the role played in the generation of that problem by Hume's picture of reason as the source of a priori knowledge of 'recondite facts about some mysterious super-sensible entities with a life of their own' (Stroud 1977: 245) only because I think the deficiencies of that picture are most readily appreciated. But I also suspect that any adequate account of this matter will need also to modify the Humean picture of the realm of causal connections as, so to speak, brute and senseless: for only in this way could the relation of reasonable causation be rescued from the hybrid status assigned to it within Hume's theory, and I suspect that rescuing to be a prerequisite for success in the pertinent theoretical endeavour.

REASONABLE CAUSATION OF DESIRES

I wish to elaborate and exemplify just a little more so as to avert various misunderstandings which might arise as to the exact points at which I wish to take issue with Hume's discussion of morality. But first two disclaimers. (a) Hume seems primarily to have been concerned with (a certain powerlessness of) the principles governing deductive and inductive reasoning, the principles of theoretical reason, thinking them to exhaust the claims of theoretical reason; but I shall be more concerned with a distinct possible role for 'reason'. (b) Yet I shall not be primarily concerned with the familiar, anti-Humean suggestion that there are principles of practical reason overlooked by Hume, principles required by rationality and which should govern practical deliberation. That is (combining the disclaimers): if the notions of rationality and irrationality are tied to those of obedience to or transgression of principles of theoretical or practical reason, it will shortly emerge that my main concern here is not with matters of rationality and of irrationality. Doubtless there are cases of potential reasonable causation where the fact that the potential 'reasonable effect' does not occur marks out some element of irrationality on the part of the subject concerned; but in the cases of reasonable causation that will concern me here that need not be so. In these cases the absence of the potential reasonable effect does not suffice to establish the presence of irrationality.

Those disclaimers having been entered, let us move to more positive matters. In any case in which one set of propositional states reasonably causes, 'gives rise to', some other set of propositional states, recognition of that reasonable causation enables us distinctively to understand why the reasonable effect came about. The questioning of *why*, as distinctively and naturally construed, is brought to an agreed end (cf. pp. 27–9, 57–8, 96–7). Yet, to repeat, if in a structurally similar case the potential reasonable effect does not in fact come about, it need not follow that in this case there is some element of irrationality. Some relatively unproblematic cases of such reasonable causation are the following:

1 Some belief-desire pair gives rise to a corresponding intention to act.
2 The intention to perform some particular kind of action in fact gives rise to an action of that kind.
3 The further intention with which some kind of action might be performed in fact gives rise to an action of that kind.
4 A subject's belief that another's action directed at the subject manifests ill-will gives rise to resentment in the subject.
5 A subject's belief that some situation in which he finds himself is dangerous gives rise to fear on his part.

In these cases we can understand why the effect reasonably came about; but if in other, structurally similar, cases no such effect is forthcoming, it need not follow that in these other cases the agent transgresses some principle of theoretical or practical reason. We accept the reasonableness of the relation between the propositional states involved; we tacitly accept the reasonableness of the distinct relation between the propositional contents of those propositional states. But that latter reasonableness need not reduce itself to any matter of *principles* of theoretical or practical reason. It thus remains an open question whether in any particular case in which the potential reasonable effect does not occur there is some element of irrationality upon the subject's part; that will turn upon the matter of how the absence of the potential but unrealized reasonable effect is to be accounted for. It is enough for my purposes that the accountings in various such cases may leave untouched the issue of the subject's subscription to principles of rationality, may leave untouched the issue of his rationality.

Let us now turn to another kind of case. Person A has recently suffered the death of his beloved wife; B and C are both close friends of A, yet while B has a strong, manifest desire to help A in every way possible and for all the time needed, C has not.

Considering the case of B in a little more detail, we might articulate it in the following terms (cf. pp. 54–8):

1 First there is B's *desire*: his desire, say, to help A in every way possible and for all the time needed.
2 Then there is some *desirability characterization* had by B of the object of his desire: say, that of helping a bereaved friend as far as is possible.
3 Finally there are the *reasons* which B might offer, were that his style, in support of that desirability characterization.

Even taking into account the matter of B's style, quite which reasons he will adduce in support of his desirability characterization will depend upon the specific conversational context in which he finds himself. But now suppose that B is talking with C, and that B reasonably comes to think C's lack of a desire like his is owing, not to clumsiness or embarrassment on C's part, nor to C's being merely a fair-weather friend, nor to any general coldness on C's part, nor to C's having some weaker, distinctive conception of what friendship is and of what it requires, but rather to C's having a distinctive, and far from uncommon, view of what the bereaved A's situation is like. Perhaps C thinks of A's situation as being closely comparable in terms of its salient features to that of one whose loved one has gone to live in some distant land; or perhaps C thinks of A's situation as being closely comparable in terms of its salient features to that of one who has recently undergone a painful divorce.

Features of C's own life story might naturally be operative in C's conceiving of A's situation in such terms: our own minds do have a great propensity to spread themselves upon the minds of others. But whether that is so or not B anyway need not think ill of C. Yet were it his style B might try to change C's view of A's situation: that is, B might try to change C's conception both of what death is and of the salient features of the situation of one who has experienced the death of a loved one. B might, for example, when faced with the analogies used by C as here described, attempt to communicate to C some more vivid appreciation of what it is like to live with some most intense emotion directed towards a complete absence *in* the world. Any such attempt is scarcely likely to take the form of either some argument derived from principles of reason or some argument grounded upon the results of scientific investi-gation, nor is the matter of the likelihood of B's succeeding in his attempts separable from general questions about what C is like; yet none of that shows that all that is available in such a case is mere psychological manipulation. (Something *resembling* scientific investigation might none the less help C in certain specific situations. In their investigation of the links between stress and illness (*Getting Well Again*), Simonton, Simonton and Creighton report the efforts of Holmes and Rahe to design a scale that assigns numerical values to stressful events. Death of spouse comes top at 100, divorce second at 73: but the 'distance' between those two is close to that between the latter and marital reconciliation (which is assigned 45)!)

B's concern is not of course that of merely correcting some cognitive inadequacy on C's part, is not that of merely correcting C's misconception of what A's situation is like. His concern is rather to do that so as *thereby* to produce a change in C's conative states, a change in C's desires. If this further change in fact occurs we can understand why it occurs in terms of the change in C's view of the facts of the matter of A's situation. We can understand C's newly found desire as a reasonable effect of the change in his cognitive states. Indeed that is, I think, how we would naturally understand it. Yet this need not imply that were the cognitive change to occur without bringing about the conative change C would thereby make manifest some element of irrationality, would thereby make manifest some transgression on his part of principles of reason. Compare cases of emotions like fear and resentment: does the fact that we can understand the genesis of such an emotion in one person at a given time in terms of his conception of the facts of the matter show that in structurally and cognitively similar cases where no such emotion is generated there must be some element of irrationality present?

It is important to distinguish two points made here. First, I have claimed that we often understand why various aspects of our mental lives come about in terms which assume there to be relations of reasonable causation instantiated between certain groups of cognitive states alone and certain conative states. And when considering the reasonable relations between the propositional contents of such propositional states, I claim that we hold there to be reasonable relations between certain sets of indicative, *is*-propositions and certain subjunctive propositions which might perhaps naturally be expressed through *ought*-claims. That first point, then, relates to consequences of an alternative to Hume's view of reason and reasoning; but those consequences bring us to the second point aimed at a related mistake to be found within Hume's theory of motivation. Hume admits one way in which the correction of some belief about a matter of fact can bring about a change in an agent's desires, one way in which states of the faculty of reason can affect an agent's motivational states. Very roughly speaking, the possibility he admits can arise when some more general desire has combined with some false factual belief to give rise to some more specific desire. We have seen reason to doubt whether Hume should in consistency have admitted this possibility (pp. 127–8); but the present point is a different one. Once appreciating the first, anti-Humean point made here, a further possibility, equally anti-Humean, will be recognized in the terrain of motivation: this is that an agent's desires can reasonably be modified through the correction of some mistake within his cognitive states, where that reasonable change between propositional states is the 'causal counterpart' of some reasonable relation between the contents of the cognitive states alone and the contents of his desires – is the 'causal counterpart' of some reasonable relation between some set composed exclusively of *is*-propositions and certain subjunctive or *ought*-propositions. I tried to exemplify this possibility by the case in which correction of C's misconception of what death is gives rise to the specified change in his desires; but the existence of this *kind* of possibility is of course independent (in one direction) of the intuitiveness of the example given.

On the account of the matter given here there are at least three ways in which B might fail to achieve his aim of modifying C's desires in relation to the bereaved A: (i) B might fail to achieve the requisite modification in C's views about what death is; (ii) although B achieves that modification, none the less C fails to see the force of B's reason as a reason for subscribing to the pertinent desirability characterization; and (iii) while C comes to share B's desirability characterization yet C does not come to share B's desire. The first case, (i), will be thought of by B as one in which C remains in a state of ignorance about some matter of fact; and it is likely that the second case, (ii), will be thought of by B in the same terms. (That will surely be the case if the potential desire in play is, and is recognized by B as being, of kind (4) within the taxonomy of desire presented in Chapter 2.) While in both the second and third cases, (ii) and (iii), B might think of C as exemplifying the phenomenon of a potential reasonable effect not in fact occurring. What makes the notion of a desirability characterization so important is the dual role which some of its exemplars play within the structure of certain cases: in these cases failure to subscribe to the desirability characterization would be a manifestation of ignorance about some matter of fact, while subscription to that characterization could have as a reasonable effect the obtaining of some conative state of desire.

MORALITY AND ACTION

According to the late J. L. Mackie

there is no indeterminacy or lack of clarity about the main point [Hume] is making. This is that the essential fact of the matter, when virtue is distinguished from vice, or right actions from wrong, is simply that people have different feelings or sentiments with regard to them.

(Mackie 1980: 64)

But just as it is rarely obvious what is obvious – the obvious is rarely *apparent* – so it is rarely clear what is clear; I think there is more behind Hume's 'main point' than meets the eye. (Of course, what is in play here may merely be a difference of interests between Mackie and myself. Mackie's claim – that Hume supposes that a moral attitude is a matter of feeling and that moral judgements are expressions of such feelings – might be clear enough in the context of opposing those philosophers who have not begun to appreciate the point.) Much of the shady background will not be considered here. The difficulties which arise, for example, from Hume's distinction between natural and artificial virtues will not be considered, nor will the views, if any, of Hume as to the semantic character of moral judgements. And I shall not consider the ramifications of the following remarks made by Hume in his later writings (although I confess I should have loved to linger over his example of 'a very small variation of the object'):

> Extinguish all the warm feelings and prepossessions in favour of virtue, and all disgust or aversion to vice: render men totally indifferent towards these distinctions; and morality is no longer a practical study, nor has any tendency to regulate our lives and actions.
>
> (Hume 1902: 172)

> A very small variation of the object, even where the same qualities are preserved, will destroy a sentiment. Thus, the same beauty, transferred to a different sex, excites no amorous passion, where nature is not extremely perverted.
>
> (ibid.: 213 n. 1)

> Celibacy, fasting, penance, mortification, self-denial, humility, silence, solitude, and the whole train of monkish virtues; for what reason are they everywhere rejected by men of sense, but because they serve to no manner of purpose; neither advance a man's fortune in the world, nor render him a more valuable member of society; neither qualify him for the entertainment of company, nor increase his power of self-enjoyment?
>
> (ibid.: 270)

Rather, I wish to focus upon 'the main point' of Hume's proposed solution to *his* problem about the connections between morality and action. In general terms that solution, to repeat, is the following: whether it be due to nature or to artifice, the fact is that seeing certain kinds of actions gives us a special kind of pleasure whereas seeing certain other kinds of actions gives us a special kind of pain; we therefore have a natural disposition to carry out actions of the former kinds and to shun those of the latter kinds.

Perhaps the first thing to note is that Hume held another belief which *required* that his explanation of the presumed connections between morality and action take that general form. He subscribed to what Barry Stroud has called 'a monolithic doctrine of motivation' according to which any chain of desires comes to end with the desire for pleasure or the avoidance of pain (Stroud 1977: 170). And if all motivation is grounded upon that natural desire, moral motivation is too.

Nobody need deny that many human desires should be understood in terms of pleasure or the avoidance of pain (cf. pp. 60–1). Many appetitive desires, for example, are disagreeable or even painful when not satisfied and their satisfaction, by contrast, is agreeable or even pleasurable, in part owing to the elimination of the disagreeableness or painfulness which goes with their unsatisfied state. But as a universal thesis about human motivations Hume's doctrine is indefensible – think of desires whose contents refer to times after one's death, or even of desires whose contents include the condition that one not know of their realization. That doctrine therefore gives us no reason to hold that Hume's account of the motivational basis of morality *must* be correct. Still, one who agrees with this rejection of Hume's monolithic doctrine of motivation could yet hold that the result of applying that doctrine to the particular case of moral motivation does indeed provide the correct account of that case – as a matter of mere fact. But even this claim runs into difficulties, a principal, untheoretical one of which is that it clashes with a remarkably firm intuition. Let us suppose that we do indeed always experience some intense pleasure upon seeing instances of some morally good kind of action; none the less, the intuition is, the prospect of experiencing such a pleasure could not constitute the *moral* motivation for performing some action of that kind. The prospect of that pleasure could well be considered a welcome *side-effect* of performing the action; but if that prospect constitutes the motivation for performing the action the motivation is not a moral one. In *Les Liaisons Dangereuses* Valmont decides at one point to try to live 'morally' and later describes the results of his experiment in the following terms: 'I was astonished at the pleasure to be derived from doing good, and I am now tempted to think that what we call virtuous people have less claim to merit than we are led to believe' (quoted in Dent 1984: 44 n. 4). Valmont's observation cuts both ways: it registers the fact that an account along Hume's lines might serve to explain many *seemingly* moral actions while at the same time expressing the intuition that, precisely because of that, the actions thus explained would lack moral merit. (That intuition is untouched by doubts that might well be felt about the veridicality of Valmont, playfully deciding now to adopt morality, as a model of even the hypocritical 'moral' agent.) Or consider Aubrey's story of how, outside St Paul's Cathedral, an Anglican clergyman who had seen Hobbes giving alms to a poor man asked Hobbes if he would have given the alms had not Christ commanded it. Hobbes replied that he gave the alms not only because it pleased the poor man but also because it pleased him, Hobbes, to see the poor man pleased. Hobbes's theoretical consistency is evident; but the suspicion that he was a moral man brings with it the suspicion that he was lying. (The story is cited in MacIntyre 1966: 135.)

That is no more than the expression of an intuition that goes against Hume's account of moral motivation; it would gain in interest were Hume to have shared that intuition. An interesting question arises as to why Hume insisted upon the distinctive character of the pleasures and pains which for him constituted the groundings of moral motivations. One possibility is that through this insistence Hume hoped to mark off moral from other motivational considerations; another is that he was trying to prepare the ground for incorporation within his theory of the ancient doctrine that moral considerations for acting outweigh other such considerations. But a third possibility is that within the context of his monolithic doctrine of motivation Hume hoped thereby to mark a distance between moral and other motivations. The Humean account of moral motivation does not, that is, see that motivation in terms of the pursuit of mere pleasure, but rather in terms of the pursuit of a distinctive kind of pleasure; and so, the suggestion might be, the moral agent is distinguished from the mere pleasure-seeker. In this way the Humean account might perhaps try to retain some conception of the *dignity* or the *sublimity* of morality – to put the point in most un-Humean terms. But even passing over the issue of textual support for attribution of any such strategy to Hume, it remains unclear that that strategy accommodates the apparently clashing intuition. In order to show the 'naturalness' of moral motivation, it is essential within the terms of Hume's account that production of the distinctive pleasure not depend upon the experiencer's thinking that, say, the morally correct has been done. Yet in the absence of that forbidden addition, it is still the case that moral motivation is grounded upon the pursuit of one's maximum natural pleasure; and notwithstanding the possible sophistications just mentioned, that claim still conflicts with the intuition that has here occupied us.

It remains the case that one of Hume's great contributions to moral philosophy is his emphasis upon the practical nature of morality together with his insistence upon the need to examine that nature within the terms of an acceptable philosophical psychology. I have tried to indicate some of the reasons for thinking that the philosophical psychology he himself relies upon is not acceptable; I must now berate him upon another point.

Generally speaking, Hume is disposed neither to repetitiveness nor to vagueness in the explanation of his own ideas. But his descriptions and discussions of the practical nature of morality go against that general rule. The following passages are fair samples:

> If morality had naturally no influence on human passions and actions, 'twere in vain to take such pains to inculcate it; and nothing wou'd be more fruitless than that multitude of rules and precepts, with which all moralists abound. . . . [C]ommon experience . . . informs us, that men are often govern'd by their duties, and are deter'd from some actions by the opinion of injustice, and impell'd to others by that of obligation.
>
> (Hume 1888: 457)

> The end of all moral speculations is to teach us our duty; and, by proper representations of the deformity of vice and beauty of virtue, beget correspondent habits, and engage us to avoid the one, and embrace the other. . . . What is honourable, what is fair, what is becoming, what is noble, what is generous, takes possession of the heart, and animates us to embrace and maintain it.
>
> (Hume 1902: 172)

> [H]eroic virtue, being as unusual, is as little natural as the most brutal barbarity.
>
> (Hume 1888: 475)

So the aim or purpose of moral thought is to modify our behaviour through the modification of our 'habits'; sometimes that thought achieves its purpose but sometimes it does not, while the extreme demands of morality are rarely acted upon. All of that seems more or less correct; at the same time none of it seems much use for purposes of theoretical clarification of the practical nature of morality.

Still, fairness to Hume requires that we recognize the general difficulty within philosophy of producing any interestingly exact description of a given phenomenon in terms which do not presuppose some contentious theory of the phenomenon concerned. And that renders it unsurprising that Hume's otherwise anodyne descriptions of the practical nature of morality are supplemented by the following, tangential but far more interesting and far more theoretical, remarks:

Take any action allow'd to be vicious: Wilful murder, for instance. Examine it in all lights, and see if you can find that matter of fact, or real existence, which you call *vice*. In which-ever way you take it, you find only certain passions, motives, volitions and thoughts. There is no other matter of fact in the case. The vice entirely escapes you, as long as you consider the object. You never can find it, till you turn your reflexion into your own breast, and find a sentiment of disapprobation, which arises in you, towards this action. Here is a matter of fact; but 'tis the object of feeling, not of reason. It lies in yourself, not in the object. So that when you pronounce any action or character to be vicious, you mean nothing, but that from the constitution of your nature you have a feeling or sentiment of blame from the contemplation of it.

(Hume 1888: 468–9)

This is one of the passages which prompted Mackie to remark that 'there is no indeterminacy or lack of clarity about the main point [Hume] is making' (1980: 64); but I still think that there is still more behind this 'main point' than meets the eye.

A rough gloss upon Hume's views as to the practical nature of morality might now run as follows. Each time that a person sincerely accepts a moral judgement about an action already performed he has some feeling, pleasing or disagreeable depending upon the case, directed towards the object of that judgement. It is therefore the case that each time that a person sincerely accepts a moral judgement about some as yet unperformed action, he has the prospect of experiencing some feeling, pleasing or disagreeable depending upon the case, which prospect would be realized were it to be the case both that the action be in fact performed and that he be aware of that performance. Faced with such a prospect the person will therefore have a corresponding desire: the desire that the action be performed in the case in which the prospective feeling is pleasing (together with the desire that he be aware of that performance), the desire that the action not be performed in the case in which the prospective feeling is disagreeable (or the desire that he not be aware of that performance). It is therefore the case, roughly speaking, that each time a person sincerely accepts a moral judgement about some particular action, he has a desire directed towards the matter of the realization of the object of that judgement.

Some brief comments should be made upon this gloss. First, the content of these claims of Hume's about the practical nature of morality depends upon his conception of desire. We have seen that, through acceptance of the existence of 'calm passions' (pp. 115–16), Hume abandons the otherwise standard empiricist thought that what distinguishes desires is their feel. We have also seen reason to doubt an orthodoxy of Hume interpretation which holds him to deny the propositional attitude status of desires (pp. 123–4). What, then, remains to distinguish desires from other propositional attitudes? It seems as if all that remains – and there is ample textual evidence for its presence – is the thought that desires are dispositions or propensities to act, tendencies to try to obtain the objects of the desires. But we have seen, in the first chapter, reason to doubt the substance of any such thought; that same doubt therefore infects Hume's more theoretical account of the practical nature of morality. Second, the gloss given goes beyond anything said by Hume in at least two ways: first, the element of feeling is distinguished in general terms from that of desire in the interest of reducing the vagueness of talk of 'sentiments'; and second, the case of an already performed action is distinguished from the case of an as yet merely potential action in the interest of revealing more clearly the theoretical apparatus deployed by Hume. (Of course, despite his acceptance of 'calm passions', Hume's thought on desire is focused, like that of other active power theorists (p. 68), upon 'reason-producing' desires; in relation to those desires the application of the general distinction between the elements of feeling and desire is problematic.) And the third comment is that the gloss differs from anything said by Hume in its articulation of the problematic role played by the agent's awareness of the performance of the action concerned. Why not just avert one's eyes from the evil actions of others? It is worthy of note, however, that neglect of that role will come naturally to one whose sole concern is with an agent's moral judgements about his own actions.

FACT AND FEELING

Belief about a matter of fact can interact with some antecedent desire to give rise to a new desire. My belief that there is a bottle of vodka in the refrigerator can combine with my desire to drink vodka to produce the desire to open the refrigerator. But that does not show that the question of whether there is a bottle of vodka in the refrigerator is no matter of fact. Hume sometimes writes as if that model of the generation of new desires is the appropriate one for the generation of moral desires. We naturally have a general desire for pleasure and avoidance of pain; that desire can combine with the belief, say, that we shall feel a distinctive pleasure upon contemplating a certain kind of action to produce a desire to perform actions of that kind. But aside from the question of Hume's right to use that model (pp. 127–8), if that were his considered view of the matter it would seem to be a consequence that morality is indeed a matter of fact: a matter of which actions in fact issue upon contemplation in the special pleasures and pains concerned (cf. Hume 1888: 468–9, cited above, pp. 137–8). The requisite connection between beliefs about that matter of fact and active powers would be secured by the general desire for pleasure and the avoidance of pain.

For the purposes of his argument against moral factualism it might seem that Hume needs something like the following: the idea that there is a connection between any sincere moral judgement and a corresponding desire *independently of* other desires had by the agent. And perhaps the most Humean way of trying to ground that idea is through identification, at least in part, of the moral judgement and the corresponding desire. Sincerely to accept a moral judgement *is*, at least in part, to have the corresponding desire independently of one's other desires. But how can that claim be reconciled with the monolithic doctrine of motivation? The general desire for pleasure and avoidance of pain can play no role in the *generation* of moral desires if morality is not to be a matter of fact. But what, then, is the relation between that general desire and the mass of specific desires necessarily involved in sincere acceptance of moral judgements? How can we even be sure that those specific desires do not tell against the monolithic doctrine of motivation?

Somewhat ironically, it might seem that the solution to that puzzle has been given by contemporary anti-Humeans. When Thomas Nagel introduced the distinction between motivated and unmotivated desires, his third account of motivated desires drew an analogy between the ascription of them and the ascription of beliefs in general principles of logical inference (cf. p. 49). As Nagel then put it:

> [T]he temptation to postulate a desire at the root of every motivation is similar to the temptation to postulate a belief behind every inference. Now we can see that the reply in both cases is

the same: that this is true in the trivial sense that a desire or belief is always present when reasons motivate or convince – but not that the desire or belief explains the motivation or conclusion, or provides a reason for it. If someone draws conclusions in accordance with a principle of logic such as *modus ponens*, it is appropriate to ascribe to him the belief that the principle is true; but that belief is explained by the *same* thing which explains his inferences in accordance with the principle.

(Nagel 1970: 30–1)

There are elements in play here which Hume cannot in consistency accept; but what might seem open to him to accept is the distinction between the ascription of a general desire because of its role in the generation of further desires and the ascription of such a desire because of the 'accordance' or conformity between that desire and a mass of more particular desires made manifest in a person's conduct. And if Hume were to hold that the ascription of the general desire invoked within his monolithic doctrine of motivation is of that second kind, it might seem that that doctrine could then be reconciled with denial of the claim that morality is a matter of fact.

Such an attempt at reconciliation would, however, carry with it a considerable cost. The problem would not just be the dramatic anticipation of nature involved in Hume's continuing adherence to his monolithic doctrine of motivation, nor the fact that that adherence seems to fly in the face of facts about the sheer diversity of the objects of human desire, nor the obstacle for that doctrine which actual cases of moral motivation represent in accordance with our earlier discussion of Valmont's case (pp. 135–6). There would now be a further difficulty: if the attempt at reconciliation invokes in the way indicated some analogue of Nagel's notion of a motivated desire, it is necessary to show how the distinction can then be drawn between the object of desire and a foreseeable side-effect of its realization. More specifically: within the terms of the contemplated attempt at reconciliation, how could Hume justify the thought that pleasure and avoidance of pain is the object of such a motivated desire as opposed to being merely the foreseeable side-effect of the realization of the objects of distinct particular desires?

I suspect the historical truth about Hume's own view of the matter to be less *recherché*. He wrote:

The vice entirely escapes you, as long as you consider the object.

You never can find it, till you turn your reflexion into your own breast, and find a sentiment of disapprobation, which arises in you, towards this action. *Here is a matter of fact; but 'tis the object of feeling not of reason.*

(Hume 1888: 468–9, emphasis added)

Morality, therefore, is more properly felt than judged of. . . .

(ibid.: 470)

Such remarks prompted a famous retort on the part of Thomas Reid:

Let us apply this reasoning to the office of a judge. In a case that comes before him, he must be made acquainted with all the objects, and all their relations. After this, his understanding has no further room to operate. Nothing remains, on his part, but to feel the right or the wrong; and mankind have, very absurdly, called him a *judge*; he ought to be called a *feeler*.

(Reid 1969: 474)

My concern here is not with the philosophical force of that pleasing enough retort: the present point is a more historical one. Suppose that Hume's enquiries into the nature of morality, like so many of his philosophical enquiries, are to be understood, at least officially, as being undertaken from a first-person point of view: as being undertaken, that is, by a person who is trying to understand what is going on when, say, he himself makes moral judgements, *which understanding is to shun recourse to the views of others upon the matter.* Suppose further that within such terms his disapprobations and the like are objects of feeling, not of reason: perhaps, that is, his sentiments of disapprobation are possible objects of knowledge for others and thus, so to say, matters of fact *for them*, but from his own point of view such sentiments are objects of feeling, not of reason or knowledge, and so are precisely not matters of fact *for him.* Then, within the terms of the first-person point of view and of the consequent understanding of the Humean notion of 'a matter of fact', morality on Hume's account of it indeed turns out not to be 'a matter of fact' – and turns out not to be that in a way which is compatible with the monolithic doctrine of motivation. And so, rephrasing Mackie's claim a little, we might now say this: *from the Humean viewpoint,* the essential point about the way in which *I* distinguish virtue from vice, or right actions from wrong, is that *I* have different *feelings or sentiments* with regard to them. But the little is neither slight nor simple: neither the primacy nor even the coherence of the presumed point of view thus made explicit is beyond dispute; the exclusive distinction within this context between feeling and knowledge is tendentious; and the operative notion of 'a matter of fact' is now distant from the seemingly more or less commonplace one with which we were presented at the outset of this reconstruction.

In the first part of this essay a theory of value was developed which included a cognitive and non-subjective treatment of the members of a certain class of valuings, and it was then suggested that in intuitive terms at least some moral valuings are members of that class. In the present chapter I have examined an argument of Hume's which were it a good one would apparently show that such a cognitive and non-subjective treatment of any moral valuing could be descriptively correct only at the price of revealing that valuing to incorporate an illusion (cf. p. 104); but I have tried to show that the argument is not a good one. In particular I have criticized the premise of the argument which claims that no cognitive state can alone 'give rise to' a conative state; in the process I hope to have articulated further the all-important details of the pertinent cognitive and non-subjective treatment (pp. 128–33). But through consideration of Hume's account of the practical nature of morality presumed within his argument I have also tried to make clear the very special character of the target at which that argument is directed; the perhaps unexpected upshot is that even had Hume's argument been a good one it would not have counted *directly* against the pertinent cognitive and non-subjective treatment of moral valuings.

5 The reach of morality

Philosophers have measur'd mountains,
Fathom'd the depths of seas, of states and kings,
Walk'd with a staff to heav'n, and traced fountains:
But there are two vast, spacious things,
The which to measure it doth more behove:
Yet few there are that sound them; Sinne and Love.

(George Herbert)

Well did that great man, I think it was Sir Walter Scott, but if
it warn't, 'twas little Bartley, the bookmaker, say, that there was
no young man wot would not rather have a himputation on his
morality than on his 'orsemanship.

(R. S. Surtees)

THE INTERNAL QUESTIONS

Thomas Nagel once remarked that the issue over the 'extent' of
morality is 'one of the deepest in ethical theory'. He added:

Many have felt it an objection to utilitarianism that it makes
ethics swallow up everything, leaving only one optimal choice, or
a small set of equally optimal alternatives, permissible for any
person at any time. Those who offer this objection differ over
the size and shape of the range of choices that should be left
to individual inclination after the ethical boundaries have been
drawn.

(Nagel 1978: 116 n.7)

If we focus not upon utilitarianism but upon the issue, and so on
the threat of ethics swallowing up everything, worse can be done by

way of a first step than that of distinguishing three questions about the 'extent' of morality within an individual's life:

1 What is the *area* of morality? That is: to how much of our lives are moral concepts applicable? Which parts of our lives have, potentially, a moral dimension?
2 Whatever be the area, so understood, of morality, should we always seek out the pertinent moral aspects within that area? Within that area, should we always go in search of the potential moral dimension?
3 What is the *domain* of morality? Once having recorded the moral aspects of some specific situation, should we for example always act exclusively on the basis of those moral considerations? Within its area of application, as here understood, should morality be sovereign? When should moral considerations be overriding?

The question about the area of morality has often received an implicit answer through the examples upon which philosophers have chosen to focus. Thus some philosophers focus exclusively upon cases which are strikingly mundane and frequently trivial; more importantly, the cases are narrowly circumscribed in terms of the kinds of circumstances in which they can arise. The recurrent obsession, for example, with the paying of debts, the keeping of promises, the obeying of traffic signals. No one need deny that moral aspects can be found in examples of those kinds: but if the area of morality is restricted in that way – if those are the paradigm cases of the application of moral thought – then it is difficult to understand the worry Nagel mentions: how could such a morality swallow up very much?

Philosophers of a very different style apparently see the central applications of moral thought in moments of great and tortuous decision. Should we bomb Hiroshima? Should I try to assassinate Hitler? How should I behave within the Warsaw ghetto? No one need deny that moral aspects are found in examples of those kinds: indeed, it is clear that deep moral issues arise in such cases. But if the area of morality is restricted in that way – if those are indeed the paradigm cases of the application of moral thought – then, luckily, for the vast majority of normal human lives there is little danger of morality swallowing up anything.

The difference of style can mask the similarity between the ideas involved in each position. One aspect of that similarity is now clear: each position, albeit in a distinctive way, isolates morality from at least much of human life. But another aspect of the similarity should be noted: each position focuses upon contexts of decisions to act. No one could deny the thought that morality is practical; but it is far from obvious that the relations of moral thought to practice are as straightforward as those positions represent them as being.

In *The Sovereignty of Good* Iris Murdoch gave vivid expression to a markedly different stance:

> The area of morals, and ergo of moral philosophy, can now be seen, not as a hole-and-corner matter of debts and promises, but as covering the whole of our mode of living and the quality of our relations with the world.
>
> (Murdoch 1970: 97)

Doubtless there are many ways of reconstructing the arguments that led Miss Murdoch to that conception of the area of morality (as here understood); I shall merely reconstruct the simplest. Moral thought is indeed directed, at least in part, towards questions about action, towards questions of the form 'What shall I do?' But when certain common answers are given to those questions – 'Do that', 'That is what you should do', 'That is what you must do', 'That is the best thing to do' – the interest and substance of the answers depends upon their being potentially backed up by reasons: reasons which will be cast either in terms of some vocabulary like that of the traditional vices and virtues (loyalty, honesty, courage, etc.) or in terms of yet more mundane evaluative vocabulary (unimaginative, snobbish, abusive, etc.). Compare Wittgenstein's observation that we only call a picture 'beautiful' when we cannot be bothered to think of anything more specific to say about it. So in this sense, the vocabularies of specific vices and specific virtues and of the yet more mundane evaluations are the primary vocabularies of morality. But now we should note, first, that those vocabularies are not limited in their application to contexts of deciding to act, and second that there is very little in human life which is immune in principle to the application of such vocabulary. The life of a person is nearly totally a perpetual *possibility* of vice and virtue, of value and disvalue. But then, given the primacy of the corresponding vocabularies, the area of morality is indeed nearly 'the whole of our mode of living and the quality of our relations with the world'. One cannot put oneself outside the reach of morality just by not borrowing money, refusing to make promises and shunning the use of the car – not even in combination with the luck of never finding oneself within a great dilemma. (Here and throughout this chapter the term 'reasons' has a wider usage than that which it has received so far in this essay: it should now be understood as covering both what have so far been called 'desirability characterizations' and what have earlier been called 'reasons' (cf. p. 54). In the present context that distinction is unimportant; moreover, as will become clear, most of the examples of what will now be called 'reasons' are examples, in earlier terms, of 'desirability characterizations'. But the naturalness of my usage now of talk of 'reasons' outweighs, I think, any slight risk of confusion.)

It is peculiarly difficult to argue well in favour of a thesis that strikes one as obvious. I suspect that what in this case has hidden that obviousness most frequently is a confusion of that thesis about the area of morality with a similar thesis about the domain of morality. The same Miss Murdoch tells us, for example, that moral philosophy 'is the examination of the most important of all human activities' (1970: 78); she later remarks that the arts 'show us the absolute pointlessness of virtue while exhibiting its supreme importance' (ibid.: 86); again, she claims that a 'genuine sense of mortality enables us to see virtue as the only thing of worth' (ibid.: 99); and she closes by remarking upon 'the pointlessness of virtue and its unique value and the endless extent of its demand' (ibid.: 104). But perhaps most vividly for our present purposes she claims 'that nothing in life is of any value except the attempt to be virtuous' (ibid.: 87). Searching for a relatively classic, relatively rigorous, expression of a similarly strong view we might stumble upon Brentano: 'To further the good throughout this great whole so far as possible – this is clearly the correct end in life, and all our actions should be centred around it' (Brentano 1969: 32). And it is noteworthy that even as careful a contemporary writer as David Wiggins seems to presume that the question of life's having a meaning comes to turn, in doubtless subtle ways, upon the question of whether certain kinds of moral judgement 'can be plainly and straightforwardly *true*' (Wiggins 1976: 87).

   In what follows I may merely be exhibiting my lack of grasp of Murdoch's notion of *virtue*, of Brentano's notion of *the good*, and of Wiggins's notion of *the moral*. If that is so, what I shall say in a moment should at least start to make that clear. But prior to that I should express something close to incredulity at these claims: incredulity, for example, at the idea that morality and virtue play such exalted roles in the very idea of (a) life's having meaning, and incredulity at Brentano's claim about what is *clearly* the correct end in life about which *all* our actions should be centred.

An empire-building propensity of a seemingly specific conception of morality can be succoured, of course illegitimately, by a tendency to expand the reach of the concept of morality: a tendency to permit the *concept* of morality to swallow up far too much. Once indulging that tendency, sight will be lost of the *singularity* of morality itself (to adapt Bernard Williams's useful expression). But in fighting off that tendency it will not prove necessary to give some characterization or general 'definition' of 'morality'. It should be enough for present purposes that we appreciate examples of various modes of thought which are practical and yet not moral.

Some weeks after the earthquakes of Mexico of 1985 I found myself travelling by taxi in the provincial city of Guadalajara. After asking after the situation in Mexico City, the taxi-driver informed me that the earthquakes had been a punishment from God for the vice-ridden lifestyle of the inhabitants of the capital city. I did not enquire for further details of his explanation; but I was reminded of the Emperor Justinian's claim that the cause of earthquakes is homosexuality. None the less, beneath the surface similarities on which I had seized there were profound differences between the ideas of Justinian and those of my taxi-driver.

Even for one who has the concept of morality, the question 'What should I do?' does not have to be equivalent to the question 'What morally should I do?'; indeed, one who knows the answer to the latter question can coherently persist in worrying about the former. While if someone lacks the concept of morality, as Justinian did, any supposed equivalence between what might be called 'the general practical question', on the one hand, and the moral one on the other cannot be correct. Justinian's judgement was not and could not have been a moral one. The examples can be multiplied: the overriding Homeric respect for the cunning of a general in terms of his ability to deceive his opponents; the code of honour made manifest in the practice of duelling; the dictates of Mexican (or English) *machismo*. None of those is, nor tries to be, a phenomenon exemplifying moral thought. Pleasingly alien as those examples might seem, reference to them is not essential for purposes of indicating the singularity of morality. For we are all now familiar with other practical values which can be brought to bear upon the general practical question 'What should I do?'. No great weight need be placed upon the matter of prudence – and fortunately so, since the concept itself is a matter of almost as great an unclarity as is the matter of the place for prudential considerations within moral thought. Far clearer cases are provided by the distinctive practical values to be found within the practice of etiquette, within the law, in relation to the preservation and appreciation of works of art, in relation to practices partly constitutive of cultural identity and even, I think, within politics (remember Hume's observation that good political philosophy is not necessarily good moral philosophy). Alongside that list of relatively 'formal' values, we might append other, less 'formal' ones: aside from the matter of humour, there are those values, for example, reflected in distinctive 'individual ideals' about forms of life (cf. Strawson 1961), those that give expression to, and shape, the distinctive characters and personalities of individuals, and those which arise within distinctive personal relationships such as love and friendship.

Each of those things valued can bear upon the general practical question 'What should I do?'; and each can continue so to bear even when morality itself speaks upon the question. The thesis that morality alone should always determine our answer to the question is neither trivial nor obvious. Even if we pass over the obvious difficulties which arise for the *should* as it occurs in the thesis, we must note, and reject, another manœuvre designed to reveal the thesis as obvious, another manœuvre designed to make it evident that morality should swallow up everything: the manœuvre which takes the form of claiming that the values of all those other things are derivative from moral values. Think of the claim, for example, that the only reason we have to preserve great works of art is that we have a moral obligation to preserve them. Any such claim serves merely to record the determination to treat morality itself as a catchall. Rejection of that determination does not *require* the denial of the thought that morality should perhaps somehow respect the places of these other values; it might simply register that they have their own places.

One last example of an attempt to side-step the difficulties here. In *A Theory of Reasons For Action*, David Richards proposed the following principle:

> a principle of mutual love requiring that people should not show personal affection and love to others on the basis of arbitrary physical characteristics alone, but rather on the basis of traits of personality and character related to acting on moral principles. . . .

> (Richards 1971: 94)

How could an evidently intelligent man come to write such a thing? I think part of the answer is fairly clear: Richards saw that if we do not incorporate personal relationships such as love and friendship within morality from the outset, then those relationships can acquire a force or even authority in motivational terms which is capable of threatening the authority of morality. So to try to preserve the authority of morality – its dominion – Richards tried to re-interpret the nature of such personal relationships so that this threat could never arise. Personal relationships are to be seen as a kind of moral relationship; thus what morality says cannot conflict with what the personal relationships say. But before we rush to embrace this morally sanitized principle of love, we need first to ask whether we really want human life to be governed by any such principle. And if doubt is felt on that score, we need just remember an alternative 'solution': that of accepting the irreducible plurality of *kinds* of practical values within human life, and the consequent need in that life to face up to conflicts between those values. (There is also surely operative in Richards's thought here that view of rules as the primary concept of moral life which Alasdair MacIntyre deems the stance characteristic of modernity: 'Qualities of character . . . generally come to be prized only because they will lead us to follow the right set of rules' (MacIntyre 1981: 112). On this, in other contexts most important, point see also McDowell 1979 and Warnock 1971. Richards's principle of mutual love seems to me a *reductio ad absurdum* of the marriage of that stance with the exaggeration of morality's domain.)

The main points insisted upon here have been first, the distinctiveness of the question about the area of morality from that about its domain, and second, the difficulty of the latter question in the light of the plurality of practical values. Maybe a life free from morality would be solitary, poor, nasty, brutish and short; yet it is not clear that a life in which morality is an all-powerful sovereign within its vast area would be notably better. Thought and imagination should be directed, for instance, towards the character of a way of life in which moral considerations always ride sovereign over the individual ideals of agents, over the expression and development of their characters and personalities, over the motivations arising within their personal relationships like love and friendship, hatred and enmity. It is not just that we are not as the practitioners of such a way of life would be; rather, we know that if we were to become like that, we should have lost too much. Too much of our selves, of others' selves and of the relations between those selves. Once losing all that, we might as well have lost everything: for indeed, we should have lost *our* lives.

Another possibility should be touched upon before leaving these difficulties about the internal reach of morality. The suggestion might arise that we need to distinguish some favoured subclass of the cases in which morality speaks upon the general practical question 'What should I do?' – the cases, say, where morality *orders*. The contrast so relied upon between a moral *requirement or demand* and a mere moral *consideration* seems anyway to be required by our thoughts about supererogation and heroism (cf. Urmson 1958). And now, the suggestion continues, we should merely hold that in cases of that favoured subclass morality's voice is overriding. By this strategy, the thought is, we can answer the question about the domain of morality; and yet, the thought or hope continues, that domain will be in general but a small part of the area of morality. And thus, the thought ends, there will now be no danger of morality's coming to swallow up 'the whole of our mode of living' at the expense of all other evaluative considerations.

The implementation of that strategy is a difficult matter. There is no reason to believe it has to take the form of some general characterization of the favoured subclass of cases, some general characterization of what it is that makes for there being a moral requirement or demand, where the characterization does not itself employ the idea of a moral requirement or demand. (That form is instantiated in the independently unappealing attempt to implement the strategy through a mere listing of moral requirements and the circumstances which give rise to them, along the lines of an encyclopedia of codified duties: for any such attempt lends itself to the giving of a characterization, untidy as it might be, of that general kind.)

But just how, then, is the strategy to be implemented? One suggestive possibility trades upon our earlier discussion of the falsity of the atomistic view of desirability perception (pp. 41–3). There it was claimed that one can seem to see some feature of an action as desirable while attending only to that feature and yet come to see it as having no desirability at all within the context of the action as a whole. That could be construed as no more than the description of a psychological reality, of a psychological fact. But the following suggestion might now arise: in the presence of a requirement something that would otherwise have been a reason for acting differently, that would otherwise have been a desirability consideration, is no reason at all for acting differently, is not a desirability consideration; so a requirement is in play when one who sees things straight will come to see that apparently desirable features of other courses of action open to him are merely apparently so; and so the agent who sees things straight in such a context will exemplify the psychological reality just now described. That is a remark about an *effect*, falling under the general description just now given of the psychological reality, within the psychology of one who sees things straight. But this last notion requires that whether something is a reason or not – whether something is really a desirable feature – is, at least in the pertinent cases, an objective matter, not constituted by any psychological facts. (Compare the earlier discussion of the 'subjectivity' of values on pp. 98–9; but note the closing remarks on p. 97.) Thus this way of connecting the notion of a requirement with agents' psychology does not require the thought that any psychological effect falling under the general description given here of the pertinent psychological reality makes manifest the presence of some requirement: error is always possible. Indeed, this way of connecting the notion of a requirement with agents' psychology does not even require the thought that the occurrence of the pertinent psychological reality makes manifest the *presumed* presence of some requirement: the description given of the pertinent psychological reality is indeed general. And now, finally, to complete the suggestion under consideration, it might be added – just as a piece of phenomenology – that in cases where the requirement in play is a moral one the agent who sees things straight and so experiences the psychological effect described thereby experiences the 'sublimity' of moral requirements.

Many will have wished to protest from early on against the terms in which this possible implementation of the strategy has here been described – without thereby having to deny either the occurrence of the pertinent psychological reality as initially described or the philosophical interest of thoughts expressed by saying 'I had to do it' or 'I couldn't have done otherwise' (cf. Williams 1981b). But my point now is a simpler one: even conceding the contentious terms in which it has been described, this implementation fails to resolve the question of the domain of morality. The proposed elucidation of the notion of a requirement or demand is initially a perfectly general one since there seems no good reason for thinking that all requirements are moral requirements, for thinking that other practical values cannot issue in requirements. But that being so, imagine the situation of an agent who finds himself placed so as *either* to increase his sensitivity to moral requirements *or* to increase his sensitivity to requirements of some other kind. Nothing said here, concessions included, has given him any reason at all to go for the first option. (Things might have seemed different if the reference to the 'sublimity' of moral requirements had been meant as something more than just a piece of phenomenology, as in certain Kantian theories; but I have never caught even a glimpse of what that something is supposed to be.)

It is in a way sad that that strategy runs into difficulties: for otherwise it could have prompted an interesting suggestion about the remaining question of those initially distinguished about the internal reach of morality. Taking its cue from a familiar manœuvre in philosophical discussions of scepticism in general, the prompted suggestion would have been this: that we should seek out the moral aspects of a situation when there is some specific reason for suspecting there to be some requirement or demand of morality in the offing. Part of the interest of that suggestion would have arisen from the urgent need to say something about the remaining question – urgent because of a further possible threat of morality's swallowing up too much, *too much time*. Once appreciating the vast area of morality, together with accepting merely that moral considerations always bear upon questions of what one should do, the threat might emerge that we shall think of ourselves as bound always to hunt out the potential moral considerations within each situation. The prompted suggestion would have given us more time for our selves, and others' too. Instead of perhaps holding there to be a constant overriding moral requirement to hunt for any pertinent moral consideration, the suggestion would have been that there is a constant, overriding moral requirement not to pass over any specific reason for suspecting there to be some *other* moral requirement in the offing. It would thus have been no proof of immorality to respond to the further possible threat of morality's swallowing up too much by retorting that constant seeking out of the moral dimension would be (too much of) a waste of time.

The due prestige of science will most surely be undermined by treating it in a 'scientistic' manner, by seeing it as the source of answers to all theoretical questions, the scientific and the non-scientific alike (cf. Platts 1983b: 2–3). In a similar fashion, the due prestige of morality will most surely be undermined – most surely has been undermined I think – by treating it in a 'moralistic' manner: by seeing it as the source of answers to all practical questions, the moral and the non-moral alike. This discussion of questions about the internal reach of morality has been intentionally problematic and general: has intentionally emphasized general problems which seem to me to cast considerable doubt upon unthinking, or even thinking, 'moralism'.

MORAL DISCREPANCIES

It must now be impossible to doubt that the moral ideas and practices of different people and of different peoples have frequently differed greatly. Even the least 'relativist' of moral philosophers, Kant, insisted upon the need for his students to occupy themselves with the details of such differences; and since Kant's time, awareness of those differences, and perhaps of those details, has become commonplace. Yet before attempting to draw any conclusion about the nature of morality from the agreed fact of moral discrepancies, philosophical prudence suggests that we should first register the vagueness of the agreed fact by noting some of the discrepancies between discrepancies. That is, our initial concern should be with the *kind* of conceptual apparatus to be used in the description of moral discrepancies; and if here there be theory, it need not yet be moral theory.

Earlier in this chapter we saw various examples of systems of practical thought which were not systems of moral thought: that of the Emperor Justinian, the Homeric code of respect, the code of honour made manifest in duelling, even the nearer phenomenon of *machismo*. Nothing was said as to what distinguishes such systems of practical thought from moral systems; none the less, at the present intuitive level, the examples serve to emphasize the requirement that when considering putative cases of moral discrepancies, it is essential to be reasonably sure that the systems of thought being compared are all indeed systems of *moral* thought. Cases of confrontation between some system of moral thought, on the one hand, and some other non-moral system of practical thought on the other, look to be quite different. Whatever be the content of the thought that each of two systems is indeed a system of moral thought, for the moment let me just stipulate that all the examples I shall mention are to be understood *as if* that thought is true of them (unless of course the context makes it clear that the stipulation is not then operative).

One other preliminary point: a difference of practice, however striking, need not be a manifestation of a difference of (*ex hypothesi* moral) values. The concepts of given moral values, and the general moral principles which contain those concepts, are often highly abstract: their role in determining specific practices is mediated, among other things, by the beliefs of agents about many matters of empirical fact. So differences of practices need not have anything to do with a difference of values: they might simply arise from differences of beliefs about matters of fact. The movement from general moral principles to specific concrete actions is often of a complex kind: if once we lose sight of that complexity we shall be led to detect discrepancies of moral values and principles where there are none.

CONCEPTS AND CONCEPTIONS

Those preliminary points are worth mentioning only because of frequent neglect of them: vague talk of 'different moral ideas' can aid that neglect. But that same vagueness can aid other, more important, neglects. Perhaps the most important and most common is that of the distinction between differences of moral concepts and differences of moral conceptions.

Let me introduce the explanation of the general distinction between concepts and conceptions by means of three, non-moral examples. The first example comes from the natural sciences (cf. Platts 1980a; Wiggins 1980: 77–86). Suppose that two scientists introduce the expression 'electron' as referring to the subatomic particle responsible for such-and-such an effect in a cloud-chamber. Each scientist then goes on to construct a theory which purports to explain, in a scientific, law-based manner, the observed effect. None the less the theories thus constructed differ in terms of the fundamental laws governing electrons: they differ, that is, in the fundamental properties they attribute to electrons. I shall say that such a case is that of a *shared concept*, that of an electron, alongside that of *different conceptions* of what an electron is. That is, first, there is a shared concept, that of an electron, because the best interpretation on the part of one scientist of the other's use of the term 'electron' is obtained by pairing it with his own use of the same term: 'By "electron" he is referring to electrons.' The term has the same literal meaning in each of their mouths; they are talking about the same subject. And that is what makes it the case that their different theoretical beliefs about the properties of electrons are, logically speaking, in immediate conflict. And what makes that possible is the presupposition of a shared referent prior to, and independently of, the formation of theoretical beliefs about the properties of the shared referent: that is, the prior, partial 'fixing of the reference' of the term 'electron'. But note, second, that what makes it the case that none the less there are different conceptions of an electron is the difference within their respective theories about the fundamental laws governing electrons. They have different beliefs about *what* an electron *is*, about the *nature* of electrons, about the *essential properties* of electrons. The difference in those modal beliefs is what constitutes their difference of conception. They may also differ in other beliefs about mere contingencies involving electrons: one may believe that there are more electrons in the atmosphere of Pluto than in that of Venus, the other may deny it. But such a difference of beliefs will not constitute a difference of conception (although it might in a given case prove to have arisen from such a difference); the beliefs which go to make up a scientist's conception of what an electron is are of a quite different character.

In this example taken from the natural sciences it is clear how the difference of conception might be resolved: namely, by deployment of the usual scientific methods involving observation, experimentation and theory construction. For present purposes we need not linger over the question of whether there must always be one right answer to a question like 'What is an electron?'; it is enough that there are many wrong answers. What should be emphasized before leaving this example is that what pressures us *in these cases* into trying to answer the question is its univocity in relation to the different scientific theories – the fact that in these cases there is indeed a shared concept and a consequent immediate logical incompatibility of beliefs. Cases of difference of concepts would produce quite distinctive confrontations.

The second example to be considered is not mine: it is taken, with slight modification, from a most important paper by W. B. Gallie (1955–6). Consider a concept like that of *the champions* in relation, say, to a game such as football, where that concept is not to be understood in 'formalistic' terms such as that of 'the league champions' or 'the Cup winners', but rather in terms tantamount to those of *who best play football*. So understood, the question of who the champions are can provoke seemingly endless and notably passionate debate; and that, according to Gallie, is to be explained in terms of the *essential contestedness* of the concept involved. Gallie gives the following seven characteristics of any such essentially contested concept: (I) it is 'appraisive' of some given activity; (II) the activity concerned is of an 'internally complex character'; (III) there are rival orderings in terms of importance of the component parts or features of the activity; (IV) the activity admits of considerable modification in the light of changing, and perhaps unforeseen, circumstances; (V) within disputes each party recognizes that its own use of the concept involved is contested by those of other parties, and each party has at least some appreciation of the 'different criteria' in the light of which the other parties claim to be applying the concept in question; (VI) the concept derives from an 'original exemplar' whose authority is acknowledged by all the contestant users of the concept; and (VII) it is plausible that the disputes about 'the correct use' of the concept will enable the original exemplar's achievement 'to be sustained and/or developed in optimum fashion'.

Those characteristics are indeed found in the concept of the champions just now mentioned; and doubtless Gallie is right in thinking them also to be found in other more important concepts (art, democracy, social justice, a Christian life). But the present interest of the concepts and disputes characterized by Gallie is that they provide another kind of exemplification of cases of difference of conception within a framework of shared concepts.

The concepts now at issue are distinctively evaluative or 'appraisive'. How could such a concept be shared within a context of disputes about its application? The general theoretical answer as to when the concept is shared is now familiar: when the best theory of interpretation of the disputants reveals them to be talking of the same subject. But Gallie's discussion enables us to say a little more: perhaps most notably, that what makes such concept sharing possible is the prior, partial agreement upon one use of the concept – the prior agreement as to the 'original exemplar', the prior, partial agreement as to some 'paradigm exemplars' of the concept concerned. (Note that Gallie was writing well before certain current theories of reference became fashionable.) And that possibility-facilitating consideration is supplemented by others: appreciation of the 'different criteria' used by others, and even the common end of sustaining and developing the original exemplar's achievement.

The clearer the possibility of the concept's being shared is made, the more problematic might seem the next question: how is it possible for different conceptions of what it is, for example, to play football well to arise? Again Gallie enables us to say something on the question. Notwithstanding the prior, partial agreement as to the 'paradigm exemplars' of the activity concerned, differences can arise about how to go on from those exemplars (and about quite what is going on in any such going on). The internal complexity of the activity paradigmatically exemplified, the consequently possible 'rival orderings' of its component parts or features, and the 'open' character of the activity in relation to changing circumstances: these can give rise, in natural and intelligible ways, to different conceptions of what it is for the activity to be performed well (and so to different ideas as to what made the original exemplars *paradigms*). Recognition of that can serve to explain a notable fact: that in many of these debates, both of the adversaries can be found within one and the same person. And recognition and understanding of that might well serve to control the common propensity to identify any external adversary with the devil's handyman.

This second example has obvious similarities to, and just as obvious differences from, the first example taken from the natural sciences. The most obvious similarity is the key role played in securing the sharing of concepts by a prior, partial 'fixing of the reference' of the expression concerned, while one obvious difference is the evaluative nature of the concepts involved in the second kind of example. But further, important differences emerge if the matter of how differences of conception might be resolved is considered. In the first kind of example it is clear that deployment of the methods of natural science is the basis of resolution of differences of conception. Now, in the second kind of example the results of such deployment might sometimes serve to undermine certain misconceptions; and the potential for such undermining might be increased by additional recourse to the methods of the social sciences and other similar methods of investigation. Conceptions can rest in complex ways upon presumptions about the corresponding matters of fact. But even in the absence of error in such presumptions about those matters of fact, the disputes in this second kind of example can reasonably and intelligibly continue. Such disputes can usually be understood as turning, primarily, upon the question of the ordering in terms of importance – of salience – of the component parts or features of the activity concerned; and that question can often be understood as turning upon other questions both about the best form of adaptation of the activity to new circumstances and about quite what constitutes a positive development of that activity. Such

questions no more frequently lend themselves to deductively rea-
soned resolution than they lend themselves to straightforwardly
scientific decision; but that no more shows that such questions
represent a blank impasse than it shows that putative answers to
them cannot be more, or less, reasonable. Attempts to change
another's way of seeing the paradigm exemplars of the activity
concerned, like attempts to make him vividly imagine or appreciate
what the activity would be like were his favoured conception of it
to be realized, need not be studies in mere manipulation.

To accept that notions like the unreasonable, the blinkered and
the blind can be in play in these disputes between rival conceptions
of some activity is not yet to accept any thought of *the one true
conception*. Gallie seemed to think it at least possibly desirable that
such disputes continue without end; but that thought presupposed
the idea of an activity's being 'sustained and/or developed in optimum fashion'. Were that last idea to be understood in terms of the
limit of *the* 'optimum fashion', Gallie's position would be analogous
to that which holds a plurality of rival scientific theories of the
natural world to be desirable for the pursuit of *the* true scientific
theory of the world in the light of familiar facts about the infinite
complexity of the natural world and our own, limited, epistemic
capacities in relation to that world. But no such position is required
by Gallie's talk of 'optimum fashion', and I anyway doubt that it
could correctly be attributed to him. Consider a pertinent example,
that of a football team. We evidently have the concept of a good
football team and also that of one football team's being better than
another; so unsurprisingly we also have the concept of the best
actual team. But do we have a concept of the best possible team,
of the absolutely perfect team? Surely not: just what would the *score*
be? All that Gallie's talk of 'optimum fashion' requires is the concept
of the comparative ordering in application to actual cases and to
specific, imaginable possibilities: it does not require any idea of the
absolute end-point of that ordering. In at least the overwhelming
majority of examples of this kind we have no such idea: if thought
of *the one true conception* of the activity concerned is tied to thought
of such an end-point then there is no such conception to be had.
Recognition of that fact might also have a salutary effect: that of
serving to control the propensity towards senseless hyperbole within
disputes of this second kind between rival conceptions.

Despite those differences about the forms and possibilities of
resolution of differences of conception, the final account of conceptions in this second kind of example is not that different from that

in the first, scientific kind of example. The beliefs determining a given person's conception of what, say, a Christian life is are certain modal beliefs: his beliefs about what a Christian life is, about the nature of a Christian life and about what a Christian life requires. It is perhaps true that within examples of this second kind there will occur a greater element of relativization to specific circumstances within the contents of these modal beliefs; but that element of relativization implies no diminishing of objectivity. And it is doubtless true that other differences of belief about matters of fact – about whether for example more people lead Christian lives in Sussex than in Yorkshire – may be consequential upon differences of conception: but, as before, that does nothing to undermine the distinctive character of the beliefs which constitute a given person's conception of, say, a Christian life.

The final example to be considered is not mine either: it is taken, with considerable and tendentious modification, from Philippa Foot's discussion of moral relativism (Foot 1978: 153). Consider certain judgements of taste: judgements about who is good-looking, about which foods and drinks taste good, about which colours combine well in furnishings or clothes. It seems undeniable that such judgements can differ greatly as between different cultures, different generations, different social classes and groups, even different individuals. Pacal was doubtless held to be good-looking by the ancient Maya, Nureyev is by us; the French have quite different views upon what is palatable from the inhabitants of Nebraska; Indian culture seems far more prone to combinations of strong colours than is that of Surbiton. The natural, pre-philosophical description of any such case presupposes that the differing judgements are about the same thing. That is, the natural description presupposes that the same concept is in play despite the great differences of judgements using that concept. But how is such a sharing of concept possible against the background of radically divergent judgement?

One contrast with the first two kinds of example is immediately clear: no help is now to be had from the idea of a prior, partial 'fixing of the reference' of the expression concerned. Exactly the reverse is the case: a large part of what explains the differences of judgements about who is good-looking is the fact of the differences between the paradigms of the good-looking as between Mayan culture and ours. But how, then, can the same concept be in play?

Once again the general theoretical answer to that question will be grounded upon the theory of interpretation; but, also again, a little more can be said. Mrs Foot seems to suggest that the clue is to be found in the generality of the concepts at issue: '[The most suitable examples arise] where we need set no limit to the variations in the application of an expression, or rather no limits to its application within a given domain' (Foot 1978: 154). Still, that generality might seem to bring with it a threat of vacuity – as if the expression 'nice' were the most favoured case. It is therefore important to see that within Mrs Foot's discussion another consideration might be in play which could be invoked at this point. At an intuitive level the specimen concepts mentioned by Foot are perhaps understood in dispositional terms: so that a good-looking person, for example, is one who tends to produce some distinctive agreeable sensation in one who experiences him (he *looks good*). And now the thought might be that what makes possible the sharing of the concept despite the great variations in its application is the sharing of the 'sensational response' produced by its putative exemplars.

It is perhaps also natural to say that the ancient Maya held distinctive beliefs about what it is to be good-looking, about the nature of the good-looking. And then, for one who has followed this discussion thus far, it might seem natural to say that the Maya had some distinctive conception of what it is to be good-looking. But before saying that, we should reflect upon the fact that 'no one set of [the opinions about who is good-looking] appears to have any more claim to truth than any other' (Foot 1978: 154). While there can be a certain degree of 'local objectivity' in judgements about who is good-looking as made within a given community or group which agrees upon some paradigms of the good-looking and upon various 'criteria' for being good-looking, yet once considering another community or group with radically different opinions it seems that there is nothing to be said. Indeed, the idea that the ancient Maya were mistaken, or unreasonable, or blinkered, or blind in their judgements about who was good-looking seems no better than the expression of unthinking imperialism. Given that I wish to anchor the notion of a conception in terms of certain distinctive modal beliefs – beliefs, for example, about the nature, the essence, of the good-looking – I prefer to say that the consequence of liberation from unthinking imperialism is the abandonment of any conception of what it is to be good-looking. Any conception will be a misconception. We may still have to talk of our imperialist's 'conception' of the good-looking; but so to talk is already to mark his error.

That has been an attempt to introduce in general terms the distinctions between, and some of the complexities of the distinctions between, difference in concepts, difference in conceptions and difference of 'mere' beliefs as regards some matter of fact. Assuming those distinctions to apply *in one or another way* within the moral sphere, the unsurprising result emerges that a difference in moral practice can be the manifestation of different kinds of complementary difference: of concepts, of conceptions, of 'mere' beliefs and of the various combinations of those things. Again, there is nothing here that should startle us. Concepts like that of justice – or democracy, or corruption, or loyalty – are highly abstract, as are general moral principles which contain them. The role of such concepts and principles in determining specific practices is mediated by many additional elements: the beliefs of the agent concerned about many matters of fact, his other values (his other evaluative concepts, moral or non-moral), his conceptions of the relevant values, his beliefs within a given context about the relations between those values. Simple talk of 'different moral ideas' serves only to obliterate the complexity of that mediation and to make of the idea of the recognition of moral discrepancies a useless, complexity-masking truism.

It is important to recognize that each of the differences mentioned – of concepts, of conceptions, of 'mere' beliefs – is a difference of degree. Many philosophers of science have focused upon a supposed limit in the case of scientific concepts: they have focused, that is, upon the supposedly possible case of two scientific theories which purport to apply to the same, or almost the same, domain of experience, but whose basic terms purport to refer to entities of radically different natures – that is, whose basic concepts are radically different. That supposed possibility is roughly what has come to be known as that of *radical incommensurability* between rival scientific conceptual schemes: the practitioners of such rival theories live, we are told, within different worlds. Whether or not there really is such a possibility in the scientific case is not my concern here; all I want here to *indicate* is a reason for thinking that differences of moral concepts will fall short of that supposed limit. The point, in brief, is this: if once we determine to use the expression 'morality' in a way that respects the singularity of morality, that respects for example the distinctiveness of moral value as but one kind of practical value, then I think we shall be forced to recognize that any *moral* conceptual scheme will share certain concepts with our own: the concepts, for example, of justice, of harm, of well-being and perhaps of happiness.

Other moralities might include quite different conceptions of what those things are; but if not even those concepts are shared, I cannot see how other schemes of thought can be deemed to be rival *moralities*.

Two final observations to close this section. First, it is perhaps a little unclear as a matter of linguistic intuition whether talk of 'a different morality' applies to those cases in which some other group weighs differently moral values as compared with other, non-moral values; and it is comparably unclear whether such a difference of weighting is always to count as a difference of conception of the moral values concerned (cf. p. 56). But what matters is not the settling of those largely terminological doubts, but is rather the recognition of this (I think widespread) phenomenon. And second, although it has been assumed here that the distinctions between concepts, conceptions and 'mere' beliefs apply in one way or another within the moral sphere, nothing has yet been said about in quite which way(s) they apply. We introduced, and refined, the distinctions through a consideration of three different kinds of examples: but we have said nothing about to which kind of example any *specific* moral discrepancy most closely approximates.

THE EXTERNAL QUESTIONS

If once we consider some morality different from our own what should our attitude be? And how do answers to that question relate to the matter of the objectivity of moral thought? These questions place us firmly within the terrain of the issue of 'moral relativism'; but the terrain where we are thus placed is not perhaps so firm.

Moral philosophers have usually come none too well out of their excursions into this terrain. Starting from an emphasis upon the fact of moral discrepancies, and combining that with some claim about the subjective nature of morality, they have wished to draw some 'relativist' conclusion positing restrictions, usually considerable, upon the possibility of moral criticism of societies with moralities different from one's own. Nearly all such attempts to establish a 'relativist' conclusion have failed in clear and uninteresting ways. A brief listing of the most common failings may serve to clear the ground a little.

1 The requirement that the other system of thought being considered be itself a system of moral thought is forgotten.

2 The conclusion drawn by the supposed 'relativist' is in fact some 'absolute' moral principle – say, to the effect that morally speaking no society ought to criticize any morally distinct society (cf. Williams 1972: 22–3).

3 No notice is taken of the obvious explanations of moral discrepancies in terms of the different circumstances under which others live – explanations which are often compatible with a 'non-relativistic' conception of morality (cf. Platts, 1979: 248–9).

4 The fact is overlooked that the relativity of, for example, some predicate is compatible with the idea that that predicate have 'absolute' conditions of application once the parameters of its relativity are made explicit (think of the relativity, for example, of 'is grammatical' as a predicate of sentences to a given language).

5 The category of that whose recognition is determined by human needs, concerns and interests is assumed to coincide with that of the subjective (cf. Platts 1983a: 147–8); in a similar manner, the two uses of 'subjectivity' run together by Hume (cf. pp. 98–9) are not distinguished (cf. Wiggins 1987: 201–2).

6 It is assumed that one who denies the 'relativistic' restriction upon the possibilities of moral criticism of a morally distinct society must condemn the members of that other society; it is similarly assumed that acceptance of some 'relativistic' thesis is one and the only reasonable way of grounding the value of tolerance.

7 It is presumed that recognition of the supposedly subjective nature of morality precludes any reasonable possibility of acting upon our own morality in dealings or engagements with morally distinct societies (cf. Foot 1978: 161–2).

8 The variety of kinds of moral discrepancies that can occur is disregarded.

9 The fact that talk of 'different conceptions of the same thing' usually occurs within the context of the possibility of reasonable debate between rival conceptions is overlooked.

The listing is far from exhaustive, nor are all the failings specified independent of one another; still, that listing enables us to side-step a number of needless pitfalls. At the same time there surely are genuine questions about, so to say, the *external reach* of moralities. We may move closer to appreciation of some of those questions if we focus once again upon the distinction between differences of concept and differences of conception, and then consider one general difficulty arising for certain kinds of 'relativism', for certain proposed ways of restricting the possibilities for moral criticism between different moralities.

Consider two groups or societies which differ in their moral concepts. In general there need be nothing surprising about such a case. Given, for example, the notable differences in the circumstances of life of the bourgeoisie of Madrid and of the Hopi Indians of North America, it would rather be surprising were they to have exactly the same moral concepts. But to accept the naturalness and intelligibility of such differences of concepts is not to preclude the possibility that one of the groups or societies might reasonably criticize, in moral terms, the moral conceptual framework of the other. In many actual moral debates the point at issue is exactly that of whether certain moral concepts should be employed: those of the distinctive Christian virtues and vices, those of patriotism and nationalism, perhaps even sexist and racist concepts. It is true that there is an interesting theoretical question as to the kind and degree of understanding of any concept at issue in such a debate available to one who rejects the concept's use; but in many cases that rejection need not imply absolute incomprehension. It is also true that the stubborn and often vile nature of many human beings must rule out any great optimism about the real possibilities for reasonable change within their framework of moral concepts: 'The devil is an optimist if he thinks he can make people meaner.' But the existence of blind alleys does not establish the pointlessness of travelling (not even in Mexico City).

An instructive question arises for cases of difference of moral concepts: why could not the two systems of moral concepts be in some way combined? One possible answer is that, precisely due to the evaluative, practical nature of the concepts involved, the resultant 'combined scheme' might turn out to be practically inconsistent: it might turn out that the combined scheme both morally require that an agent perform a certain action and at the same time morally require that he not perform it. But many have held that such practical inconsistency will arise within any adequate moral framework given the existence of genuine moral dilemmas. And anyway there is another way of combining two systems of moral concepts which will not immediately produce that supposed difficulty: in the style of someone who works in the mornings as a nuclear physicist while dedicating his afternoons to the study of Jane Austen's novels. Where does someone go wrong who lives each day with the moral scheme of one of the groups until noon and then switches to that of the other group?

Doubtless many different considerations might serve to determine that a person does not in fact morally criticize such a combination of different systems of moral concepts; and those same consider- ations might serve to determine that a person does not in fact morally criticize some framework of moral concepts different from his own. Apart from mere inertia, some of those considerations are the following:

1 the person thinks that the point does not matter enough, say, because he thinks or suspects that the other's scheme does nobody any harm;
2 the person thinks that nothing turns on the difference in terms of realistic possibilities of adoption of the other moral scheme, as with historically distant schemes of moral thought;
3 the person thinks that the moral criticism contemplated will have no effect on the other, be this because of some specific belief about the other or because of some general belief to the effect that nobody heeds such criticism;
4 the person has a fear of being, or seeming to be, morally smug;
5 the person has a fear of behaving in a dictatorial, imperialist or colonialist manner;
6 the person is in general terms tolerant of, or even has some general love for, diversity;
7 the person is not sure that there is any error or incoherence within the other's moral scheme, be this because of some general scepticism about his own 'epistemic' capacities or because of some more specific scepticism in relation to the particular case;
8 the person suspects there to be no substantial moral difference between his and the other's moral schemes: perhaps he thinks of the differences as amounting merely to a difference of conven- tional means to agreed ends; or perhaps he thinks of the difference as amounting merely to morally acceptable differences in the light of different roles within different social structures;
9 the person thinks that, in view of other, non-moral features of the other's life, isolated moral judgement about the other would be beside the point, tasteless or even ridiculous (maybe, for example, he judges the other to be a quite outstanding artist, or even just a remarkably witty person).

That rag-bag of a list is inevitably incomplete. Yet while recognizing the potential efficacy of the considerations mentioned in the braking of moral criticism of distinct moral frameworks, and even while recognizing that such braking might often be justified, still we should not lose sight of the at least apparent possibility of legitimate moral criticism of other moral frameworks – or of our own; for that possibility seems to be presupposed by our thought upon *moral* matters. Consider again the attempts to combine different systems of moral concepts: it is surely a part of our ideas about what moral thought is that we reject in this area the kind of unrestricted 'tolerance' which would unconditionally permit all such combinations; and it is also surely a part of those ideas that we do not think of that rejection as merely psychological revulsion. Consider direct combination of two different schemes of moral concepts: we believe, it seems to me, that in at least many cases the new moral dilemmas which would arise within the combined scheme would be illusory, would be nothing more than the products of a mistaken scheme; and in at least many cases we believe that, I think, because we also believe that at least one of the schemes thus combined would be, in one way or another, mistaken. Likewise we reject the completely general possibility of a systematic switch at noon because we believe that in at least many cases one of the schemes thus combined would be, in one way or another, mistaken. But if that is right as a description of our thinking upon these matters, then it is clear that that thinking presupposes the possible application of the notion *mistaken* to systems of moral concepts; and that in its turn presupposes the possibility of criticism between different systems of moral concepts. What that shows is the at least revisionary character of any completely general denial of the possibility of meaningful moral criticism between different systems of moral concepts. The same at least revisionary character is detectable in the comparable general denial of the possibility of meaningful moral criticism between adherents to different moral conceptions within a framework of shared moral concepts: crudely, both the persistence of discussion and debate within some cases of this kind and our attitude in some cases towards the possibility of a midday switch seem indicative of a conviction that in many cases something is at issue other than mere psychological revulsion and that something can be attempted other than mere psychological manipulation.

Doubtless the extreme 'relativist' position still has manœuvres open to it, beginning perhaps with the explicit embracing of the at least revisionary character of the proposed restrictions. But a more promising strategy for one concerned to find some truth in 'relativism' is quite other: namely, that of searching for some more specific 'relativistic' restriction upon the possibilities for meaningful moral criticism between different moralities. If once we pay due attention to important distinctions *within* our moral thought, the hope of the 'relativist' might now be, we shall find more cautious restrictions upon the possibilities of meaningful moral criticism which at least do not conflict with the general structure of that thought and which might even be required by it.

ONE CONTEMPORARY RELATIVISM

That strategy has recently been explored in a number of different ways. Gilbert Harman, for example, has held that an important 'relativist' restriction upon the possibility of meaningful moral criticism between moralities comes to light if once we distinguish different kinds of moral judgements. The members of one group or society can say that some member of another group with different moral practices is '(literally) a savage or . . . (literally) inhuman, evil, a betrayer, a traitor, or an enemy' (Harman 1975: 190); they can also say that it ought morally not to be the case that the members of the other society do what they do, that it is a terrible thing that they act as they do. But as regards an action whose moral evaluation by the members of the first group or society is based upon some part of their moral system which is not shared by the other group or society, it makes no sense for members of the first group to say of some member of the other group that he morally ought, or ought not, to perform the action concerned, nor to say that he was morally right, or wrong, to have performed it. The reason for that restriction, according to Harman, is that these last judgements are 'inner judgements' and it is a feature of such judgements that they can only be made about a person if it is supposed that the person is capable of being motivated by the relevant considerations. In the kind of case specified the difference between the moralities of the groups or societies shows, *ex hypothesi*, that the supposition does not hold for the action at issue.

Two distinct claims are presumed by Harman's 'relativist' restriction:

1 There is a class of judgements, the 'inner', the making of which
   in relation to a given audience has sense or point only if it is

supposed that the audience is capable of being motivated by the relevant considerations.

2 Judgements about what a person morally ought, or morally ought not, to do, along with judgements about whether the person was morally right, or morally wrong, to have done something, are 'inner judgements'.

What might the arguments for those claims be? Perhaps the most interesting, whether it was Harman's or not, is the following: consider *certain* judgements saying that some particular person has a reason for doing, or for not doing, some particular thing. If a person has a reason for acting of any kind, it must surely be possible for him to act upon the reason: if there is no such possibility, what is the sense to saying that *he has* the reason? Now, the distinguishing feature of the *kind* of judgements of reasons now under consideration is that the possibility of the agent's acting upon the reason concerned requires that that reason be connected in some *specific* way with the agent's actual stock of desires, with the agent's actual 'motivational set': if there is not *that* connection – if the reason in favour of performing the action concerned touches neither his actual stock of desires nor any enlarged stock of desires to which he might reasonably be led from his actual stock by the elimination of needless ignorance on his part about 'mere' matters of fact and the elimination of needless deficiencies in his logical reasoning – then there is no sense to saying that he has a reason for acting *of this kind*. Such judgements of reasons are 'inner judgements'; and I can see no reason for denying there to be a class of such judgements. (At least: I see no reason for denying that as long as it is not presumed that that class of judgements – of *uses* of sentences, if you like – can be identified in general by reference to some class of sentences themselves.)

If it could now be shown that judgements about what a person ought morally to do, or about what it would be morally right for him to do, are always tantamount to judgements of reasons *of that kind*, Harman's 'relativistic' restriction would be established. How might that be shown? One relatively extreme argument is this: these moral judgements clearly purport to give reasons for acting, are clearly judgements of reasons; but the *only* coherent judgements of reasons are those of the specific kind described in the first part of this argument; so either those moral judgements are incoherent or they are tantamount to 'inner judgements'; the generally unproblematic nature of the use of such moral judgements making the first option of incoherence implausible, it can therefore reasonably be concluded that such judgements are indeed 'inner judgements'. Another, seemingly more moderate, argument is this: the moral judgements concerned clearly purport to give reasons for acting, are clearly judgements of reasons; moreover, at least on occasion agents subsequently act upon those reasons; but such cases of action upon those reasons are properly understood only in terms of that specific account of acting upon a reason which was presupposed within the first part of this argument; so again the moral judgements concerned are revealed to be 'inner judgements'. Quite how moderate this second argument is will depend upon the further reasons to be given for the claim that cases of action upon these moral reasons are properly understood only in terms of that specific account of acting upon a reason presupposed in the first part of the overall argument: if the claim is that that is the only coherent account of acting upon a reason which can be given the air of moderation disappears. But even if the claim is, more moderately, that that account of acting upon a reason is as a matter merely of fact the correct account of action upon moral reasons, doubts might well awaken.

The first point to be noted is now an old friend: the bald judgement that a person morally ought to do some particular thing or would be morally right to do it – or even that he has a reason to do it – is remarkably uninteresting if it is both the beginning and the end of the matter (cf. pp. 146–7). The interest and worth of any such judgement depends on its potential backing by some detailed specification of why he ought to do it, some detailed specification of the reason for doing it – some detailed specification, in Harman's terms, of *the relevant moral considerations*. But now suppose in some given case that such backing is indeed forthcoming: some detailed specification of the action concerned is produced as a way of backing up the claim that the person concerned morally ought to do it. Then the second point to be noted is that it is now far from obvious that the profferred account of how the backed-up judgement operates in motivational terms is always correct.

The proffered account is in a clear sense a (modified) Humean one. The person on the receiving end of the moral judgement has some initial stock of beliefs and desires (his 'motivational set'). In the simplest Humean case the backed-up judgement connects directly with that stock in such a way that the agent should reasonably come to have a desire to perform the action concerned. But the backed-up judgement might have another, indirect connection with that initial stock by having the same kind of direct connection with some hypothetical modified stock standing in a specific relation to the person's actual stock: the relation being that the hypothetical modified stock of beliefs and desires would reasonably arise from the person's actual stock were the person to be freed from needless error in his beliefs about 'mere' matters of fact and from needless deficiencies in his powers of reasoning (cf. Williams 1981a). The (modified) Humean suggestion at play is then that a backed-up judgement can have motivational efficacy only if it stands in some appropriate connection, direct or indirect, with the agent's actual stock of beliefs and desires – only if, that is, it stands in the appropriate direct connection either to the agent's actual stock of beliefs and desires or to some such hypothetical modified stock. But if the person's actual desires are appreciably different from those of the person proffering the moral judgement, that condition might well not be satisfied; and there will then be no sense, the thought of the 'relativist' is, to the proffering of the backed-up moral judgement about what the person ought to do or has a reason to do.

But just why is that Humean account deemed to be *the* correct one? A sleight of hand can often be detected at this point. Those wishing to defend the universal applicability of that account frequently proceed by arguing against what is perhaps the best known rival account: the rival account which purports to show that Reason requires that a person have certain desires, be susceptible to certain motivational considerations, regardless of what his actual desires might be. More specifically, this rival account purports to show that a person will indeed be susceptible to certain specific moral motivational considerations on pain of being *irrational*. But defenders of the (modified) Humean account need have no difficulty in showing that the claim of irrationality is in general nothing but bluff; and they then conclude that their own alternative account of the matter is obviously correct.

But that result is not so easily obtained: Hume and Kant, or Humeans and Kantians, do not exhaust the options here. This can be seen in more than one way. One worry about the (modified) Humean account is this: even in the cases which seem best to fit that account – for example, a case in which the person who is on the receiving end of the proffered moral judgement has the pertinent general desire (say, to be loyal to his family) – there is a disregard of the matter of how that desire is to be understood and so of the question of the kind of desire it is. The issue is not, at least in

general, whether it is a desire required by Reason; the issue is
rather, at least in general, whether the person's desire is reasonable,
is understood as a reasonable response to his view of the facts of
the matter (cf. pp. 128–33). And that points to a distinctive possible
motivational role for the backed-up judgements at issue, a role
neither Kantian nor Humean: he who proffers the judgement need
not presume the antecedent presence of the pertinent general desire
either in the person's actual stock of desires or in the hypothetical
modified stock; rather, his aim in proffering the *backed-up* judgement is that of trying to change the person's view of the facts of the
matter in the hope the changed view will reasonably elicit a desire
in the person to perform the action concerned.

The first part of this essay included an attempt to articulate and
defend the philosophical psychology required by this distinctive
option. But the idea of such an option is nothing new, being at least
as old as Socrates would have been were he still to be alive, so there
is little excuse in terms of present originality for the sleight of hand
involved in attempts to defend some Humean account of all these
matters by mere rebuttal of the Kantian account. Once the alternative option is recognized as just that, there emerges the possibility
that some backed-up judgements of reasons, while not being 'inner
judgements' as that notion is understood by (modified) Humean
theories, are not thereby isolated from the possibility that the persons
receiving the judgements act upon the reasons given.

That has an important bearing upon Harman's 'relativist' restriction
upon the possibility of meaningful moral criticism between different
moralities. The restriction can now be expressed like this: as regards
an action whose moral evaluation by the members of one group
depends upon some susceptibilities to motivation of theirs which are
not shared by the members of the other group, it makes no sense
for members of that first group to make 'internal judgements' about
some member or members of the other group in relation to the
action concerned. Now, in the light of what has been said here,
there are a number of unclarities within Harman's discussion. The
immediately pertinent one relates to the question as to how talk of
'susceptibility to motivation', of being 'capable of being motivated
by the relevant considerations', is to be understood. On balance it
seems that Harman's intended model is an unmodified Humean one:
such talk is to be understood in terms of direct connections with the
person's actual stock of desires (and 'goals' and 'intentions' and
'habits' and 'dispositions'). None the less let us suppose that the

arguments later given by Bernard Williams (in Williams 1981a) in favour of the modified Humean model are acceptable to Harman. Even with this amplification of the possibilities of meaningful moral criticism, one further possibility is disregarded: namely, that the proffering of a backed-up moral judgement of reasons be an attempt to change the person's view of the facts of the matter in the hope that the changed view will then reasonably elicit a moral desire in the person receiving the judgement to perform the action concerned. That distinctive point to the making of a moral judgement is, implicitly and incorrectly, ruled out by the 'relativist' restriction. And once freed of too easy a comprehensive attachment to some Humean, or even modified Humean, model of motivation, we shall feel no inclination, I think, to say that the judgement so made is not 'a full-fledged moral judgement' (Harman 1975: 195) nor to say that in cases of this kind there is the pretence that the person on the receiving end of the judgement 'is susceptible to certain moral considerations in an effort to make that person or others susceptible to those considerations' (ibid.: p. 193). (That last phrase of Harman's, incidentally, strongly supports the attribution to him of an *unmodified* Humean account of motivation. Note also that the points insisted upon here count against Harman's literally relativist logical form proposals as well as against his conventional account of the nature of morality. But also note that that last phrase of Harman's – in virtue of 'or others' – might prompt us to recognize the further case in which the point of making some backed-up judgement of reasons is the attempt to change some other person's view of the facts of the matter, some person other than he who is strictly on the receiving end of the judgement. Think, for example, of the making of such a backed-up judgement about *foreigners*, where the intended audience of the judgement is some part of the home population; but note also that within such a context there are many other possible points to the making of such a judgement – flattery of the home population for example.)

Explicit recognition should be given here to an important point. There is a good question about when it is really possible to change a person's view of the facts of the matter and also an interesting subsidiary question about when there is a reasonable hope that that change of view will elicit the corresponding desire to act. Here there is indeed a vast terrain of 'relativist' problems. Doubtless answers to these questions will make reference to the character and personality of the person concerned, and more specifically to his desires. But we need note only two points here. First, for the matter of 'moral relativism' *as here understood* it is essential that the person concerned have some morality (neither Harman's Martians nor Harman's Hitler clearly satisfy this condition (1975: 191–3)). And second, there is no reason to presume that the references made to the person's desires within the answers to those questions will serve to re-instate as comprehensively correct some Humean or modified Humean account of motivation.

Two closing comments upon Harman's provocative defence of 'moral relativism'. It is clear that a difference of moral concepts constitutes for Harman a difference of motivational susceptibilities: if a person does not have the concepts of the pertinent moral considerations he can hardly be 'susceptible' to motivation by them (on Harman's understanding of 'susceptibility'). But matters are not so straightforward in cases of differences of conceptions within a framework of shared moral concepts. If Harman continues with his original unmodified Humean account of motivation, such a case seems to constitute a difference of motivational susceptibilities. But if Harman were to accept the modified Humean model of motivation the matter is not so simple. The difference of conception is likely to make itself manifest in a difference of action and judgement and of actual desire; but what counts upon the modified Humean model is some hypothetical, modified stock of desires to which the person concerned could reasonably be led given his actual desires. The question then arises as to whether one employing this modified Humean model will recognize as a pertinent case of such reasonable modification of a stock of desires one in which that modification comes about through some reasonable modification of the person's actual conception; if that is recognized as a pertinent case, then the further question arises of whether the employer of the modified Humean model thinks of this process of reasonable modification of conception as potentially converging upon the one, true conception. If the employer of the modified Humean model were to think that, he would not think of a difference of actual conception as a difference of motivational susceptibilities as he understands that notion. But it seems, to say the very least, unlikely that any kind of Humean will think any such thing.

The other closing comment upon Harman's discussion relates to the following: he claims that by contrast with more traditional relativist arguments his relativism is neutral upon the question of the objectivity or subjectivity of moral thought. Much of what has been said here, in terms of supplementary arguments perhaps required for Harman's position and in terms of its needed clarification, seems to suggest the presence of subjectivist tendencies within any full development and articulation of his relativism. The final point to be noted is that the obvious ways of trying to cast doubt upon the coherence of the distinctive judgements of reasons, the distinctive *uses* of sentences about reasons, which have here been invoked against Harman's relativist restriction, as upon the coherence of related judgements to the effect that some particular person morally ought to be motivated by some moral consideration and ought morally to have the concept of the relevant moral consideration (cf. p. 102), all presuppose some (revisionary) subjectivist thesis. So against his declared aims, Harman's relativism seems likely to come to rest upon a subjectivism as undefended as it is revisionary.

ANOTHER CONTEMPORARY RELATIVISM

Another recent exploration of the possibilities of a cautious 'moral relativism' is found in the writings of Bernard Williams (1974–5; 1985: ch. 9). In the course of those writings Williams's views changed upon a number of points; what follows is therefore a brief *reconstruction* of one 'relativist' position suggested by parts of those writings rather than a position which can now clearly be attributed to Williams.

The core of the 'relativist' position emerges in cases exemplifying the following possibility in relation to two groups or societies S_1 and S_2 with 'incompatible' sets of moral beliefs: due to certain factors, such as industrialization, the growth of knowledge, or even the March of History, there is no group – neither S_1 nor S_2 nor any other group – for whom there is an authentic possibility of their taking on, and living according to, the moral beliefs of S_1 and a comparable possibility of their taking on, and living according to, the moral beliefs of S_2, where the possibilities denied are understood in terms such that they would have had to have been compatible with at least a minimum of sanity – with, that is, the retaining of a hold upon reality – and with at least a minimum of rationality (that last, compound condition determines much of the content of the idea of an authentic possibility, or impossibility, of taking on, and living according to, some set of beliefs). In terms of a sane and rational living of some set of moral beliefs, in such a 'confrontation' between the two societies there is no real practical decision at issue: for no group or society is the question 'Which of the sets of moral beliefs should we adopt and live by?' a genuine practical question. In

Williams's terms, the 'confrontation' is 'notional' not 'real' (Williams 1985: 160–1). For example: owing perhaps to some infantile nostalgia members of contemporary Mexican society might believe that they could, here and now, authentically take on the moral beliefs of the pre-Columbian Aztecs; but unless those members lose both their sanity and their rationality the most that they can do is to ape, in a grotesque manner, the *trimmings* of Aztec moral life; and the same is true as regards the real possibilities of adopting Aztec morality for any other group or society now in existence.

The ease of sane and rational adoption of some set of moral beliefs is, when possible, a matter of degree; but for the kind of 'moral relativism' now at issue the key is the cut-off point where there ceases to be any such possibility. Why that is supposed to be so emerges in the following way. First, we are invited to distinguish a class of very general moral judgements about the moral acceptability of a society's overall moral beliefs and so about the general moral structures found within that society. So, for example, judgements about the behaviour and character of individuals within the given society are not at issue. Then, at an intuitive level, we are asked by the 'relativist' to consider the question of what could be the 'point or substance' (Williams 1974–5; 142) of the making by members of one society of such a very general moral judgement about the moral acceptability of some other society's morality in a case where the relation between the two societies is like that between S_1 and S_2, in a case where the confrontation between their moralities is 'notional'. Intuitively, the 'relativist' suggests, there would in such a case be no sense, no 'point or substance', to the making of such a judgement.

Moreover, the 'relativist' claims to be able to explain and to *justify* that intuition. The making of such a very general moral judgement about another society's morality acquires 'point or substance' only within a context of a genuine practical question, only within a context where some group exists which is faced with an authentic option between the two moralities concerned. Why is that the only consideration which could give 'point or substance' to the making of those judgements? Compare the structurally similar case where the sets of beliefs concerned are scientific ones: say, contemporary combustion theory as compared with phlogiston theory. And suppose that, given the requirements of sanity and rationality together with the growth of scientific knowledge and education, there is no authentic possibility of any existing group or society taking on belief in phlogiston theory. That does not seem to preclude the possibility that subscribers to contemporary combustion theory make meaningful general judgements about the scientific unacceptability of phlogiston theory. The subscribers are not restricted to scientific evaluation of particular phlogiston theorists: they can also remark that phlogiston theory is false by indicating its specific scientific inadequacies. Why, then, is there no comparable possibility in the moral case which could give 'point or substance' to the making of comparably general moral judgements about the moral acceptability of some other system of moral beliefs even within the context of a 'notional' confrontation? Because, this 'moral relativist' claims, there is no possibility in the moral case of *objective* general criticism of other sets of moral beliefs: there is no question of applying notions of truth or falsity to such very general moral judgements because there is nothing which could be said, done or investigated to give substance to the application of those notions. We may continue to call the other system of moral beliefs 'false' if we wish; but that talk serves merely to register our rejection of that set of moral beliefs. That is the (notion of) truth in 'moral relativism'.

The 'moral relativism' that thus emerges is indeed cautious: it postulates a restriction upon the making of only a limited class of moral judgements, and that restriction is held to come into play only within a specific kind of confrontational context. The final claim of the 'relativist' is then this: given the lack of objectivity of general judgements about the moral acceptability of sets of moral beliefs, it follows that when the confrontational context is 'notional' as between two such sets there is no 'point or substance' to the making by subscribers to one of those sets of such general judgements about the other set.

It is true that far more needs to be said in explanation and exemplification of the terms within which this 'moral relativism' is cast. It is also true that there is the possibility of further reasonable weakening of the restriction proposed upon moral judgement: this might be achieved either by consideration of other practical sources of 'point or substance' which could arise within cases of 'notional' confrontation or by consideration of other cases in which, 'notionality' and subjectivity notwithstanding, there is sufficient relation of some determinate kind between the two sets of moral beliefs to give 'point or substance' to the making of the relevant moral judgements (cf. MacIntyre 1981: ch. 17; Williams 1985: 165–7). But a more direct puzzle arises about the restriction proposed by this kind of 'moral relativist'.

Let us concede his presumption of the lack of objectivity of his favoured judgements. If that is so, how could there be any 'point or substance' to the making of such a judgement even within a confrontational context which is real? The thought of the 'relativist', presumably, is that such judgements within such a context can have 'point or substance' through their influence upon the practical deliberations of the group or society responsible for the 'reality' of the confrontation. But here we stumble upon the first cousin of an old friend: the mere affirmation of the 'moral unacceptability' of some set of moral beliefs as much lacks interest as does the mere affirmation that a person morally ought to perform some specified action (cf. p. 170). Any claim of either kind has substantial interest only if it is potentially backed up by judgements about more specific considerations. Yet the denial by this 'moral relativist' of objectivity in his favoured class of judgements is tantamount to the denial, at least in general, of the possibility of any such potential backing for those judgements. It is thus mysterious how it can be that for this 'relativist' his general moral judgements have 'point or substance' even within a confrontational context of a 'real' character.

THE PROSPECTS FOR A REASONABLE RELATIVISM?

That brings us to the last of the contemporary examinations of the possibilities for a cautious 'moral relativism' that I wish to consider. In a most interesting paper (Foot 1978) Philippa Foot, aside from pressing an objection against Bernard Williams similar to that which I have just urged against my more hypothetical 'moral relativist', undertakes two main tasks: first, that of describing some general structure which can be discerned within classes of judgements which are clearly 'relativistic'; and second, that of exploring the difficulties which arise for attempts to hold that that general relativist structure is instantiated within moral thought and discourse.

For purposes of her first task Mrs Foot focuses upon judgements of taste: judgements about who is good-looking, about which foods and drinks taste good, about which colours combine well in furnishings or clothes. Following our discussion earlier in this chapter of such judgements (pp. 160–1), we can begin by noting two of their pertinent characteristics:

1 such judgements can differ greatly as between different cultures, different generations, different social classes and groups and different individuals; and

2 no one set of such judgements has any more claim to truth than any other: the degree of 'local objectivity' found in such judgements does not begin to count against the thought that there is nothing to be said as between communities or groups with radically different tastes.

We also noted a worry about how different sets of such judgements can be about the same thing, can invoke the same concept, given the claims (1) and (2). So trading upon that earlier discussion we can note two further elements within the relativistic structure of tastes:

3 the concepts involved in the judgements are 'rather general'(Foot 1978: 154); moreover,
4 the concepts involved in the judgements are perhaps informally understood in dispositional terms, the dispositions concerned being to produce distinctive sensations and reactions in those experiencing the objects of those judgements.

So much for the general relativist structure discernible in Mrs Foot's examples; what now of the question whether that structure is found within moral thought and discourse? Mrs Foot's discussion focuses principally upon the matter of whether claim (2) is true in application to moral judgements. As she notes, the idea behind this kind of 'moral relativism' is familiar: it is the idea that in any case of a difference of moral opinions, discussion between the parties to the difference will quickly break down, will quickly result in a stand off, so that there is then no reasonable point to persistence in the making of moral judgements about the other party. On this matter Foot makes two points. First, the 'moral relativist' merely asserts that that is how things turn out, not deigning to consider details of discussions within such contexts of moral difference in order to support his assertion. Once abstracting away from tiredness, boredom and impatience, it is clear a priori neither where nor how such discussions end. The moral Mrs Foot wishes to draw is that, like it or not, moral philosophers need to pay far more attention to cases of moral discussion found in history and in literature. And second, the problem with the idea of the 'relativist' is not just its a priori character: if once we descend to consider details of actual discussions within contexts of moral difference we shall come up against the difficulty posed by our limited understanding of many of the concepts involved in those discussions. Mrs Foot mentions as examples those of *value* and of *happiness*: in my terms here, without more adequate conceptions of those things we shall be unable to achieve the requisite understanding of discussions in which they figure.

Thus Mrs Foot's discussion of this 'moral relativism' ends upon a clearly agnostic note: before we can come to any reasonable conclusion about the truth or falsity of such a 'relativism' we shall need to have paid more attention to details of discussion within contexts of moral difference and to have given more thought to the nature of certain key concepts frequently figuring in such discussion. But while Mrs Foot's observations seem to me substantially correct, I also think it likely that the difficulties facing this kind of 'moral relativism' are yet more considerable.

First, it is worth noting, but only to reject, the manœuvre which tries to establish that there is nothing reasonably to be said within contexts of differences of moral opinions by showing there is no possibility in general of one of the party's showing the other to be *irrational*. Given the absence, at least in general, of any such procedure of Pure Universal Reason as a means of resolution of differences of moral beliefs, this 'relativist' wishes to draw the conclusion that in general there is no procedure for the resolution of those differences, that there is in general nothing that can reasonably be said with an eye to such resolution. But the difficulty facing that wish is by now clear: from the fact that there is no procedure of Pure Universal Reason for the resolution of moral differences it does not follow that there is nothing which can reasonably be said for such purposes. Kant and Hume no more exhaust the possibilities here than they do within the general theory of motivation. There are many different things which might reasonably be said within different contexts of moral difference. Matters are likely to be different in cases of partial difference of moral concepts from how they are in cases of difference of conceptions; and matters are likely to be distinctively different when what is at issue is the balancing of moral considerations against other evaluative ones. But unsurprisingly I should wish to emphasize one specific possibility as regards what can reasonably be said in some discussions: this is the possibility of producing a backed-up moral judgement with the intention of trying to produce a reasonable change in the other party's set of moral beliefs through production of a reasonable change in their view of the facts of the matter. Whether that possibility arises in a given case will doubtless depend upon the character of the other party and its moral beliefs; so here is another large and problematic terrain which needs to be charted before we can come to any reasonable conclusions about 'relativist' restrictions upon the possibilities of meaningful moral criticism between different moralities.

The second point to be noted relates to a distinctive difficulty facing the kind of 'moral relativism' at issue, a difficulty related to elements (3) and (4) of the general relativist structure. Which moral concepts are supposed capable of transcending radical differences of judgements involving them even though nothing can be said for purposes of a reasonable resolution of those differences? The condition of appreciable generality seems to rule out the candidature, for example, of the concepts of specific vices and virtues. Perhaps the most likely concepts to satisfy that condition are either those of *the morally best action, what morally ought to be done, moral duty* and perhaps *the morally good*, or those, like Williams's *moral acceptability*, which are used in very general moral judgements about moralities, about overall sets of moral beliefs and practices. In either case the resultant 'moral relativism' faces two new difficulties: that of making plausible the claim that such concepts are dispositional in nature in some way sufficiently similar to that presumed in (4), the final element of the general relativist structure; and that of defending the interest of the resultant 'relativist' restriction in the light of the uninterest of moral judgements expressed in terms of those concepts when those judgements lack any backing in judgements about more specific considerations. That point has already given us now boring enough reason to resist having much interest in the making of such boring judgements. And finally we should note a difficulty which faces any 'moral relativism' that opts in favour of concepts like *the morally best action, what morally ought to be done* and *moral duty*. What distinguishes that 'relativism' from the position of one who (rightly) rejects a conception of morality as a 'calculus of action'? Or from the position of one who (rightly) insists upon the general difficulty of determining exactly what morality requires in terms of action? Any *distinctive* 'relativist' braking of moral judgement is still far from evident.

Perhaps, as so often in philosophy, it is the journey, not the arrival, that matters. None the less, notwithstanding the subtlety of these recent explorations of the possibilities for some cautious 'relativist' restriction upon meaningful moral criticism between different moralities, it is none too clear that much progress has been made towards a defensible formulation of any such restriction. Of course good questions for further investigation have cropped up during this consideration of these recent explorations; but those same questions could have arisen, and perhaps more clearly, without the 'theoretical frameworks' of 'moral relativisms'.

Perhaps, again as so often in philosophy, the matter of theory is misleading. Perhaps in this case, that is, some vague and ill-defined 'moral relativist' attitude has come to gain whatever attraction it has through the negative force of its criticisms – sometimes moral, sometimes philosophical, sometimes justified, sometimes not – of supposed errors within other views of differing degrees of 'theoreticity'. So perhaps, for the purposes of saving 'the truth in moral relativism', there is little more that can usefully be done other than the investigation in piecemeal, scarcely theoretical, ways of the diverse considerations which can in fact make of the making of moral judgements between different moralities a somewhat senseless, or even distasteful, activity. There are genuine and important enough *practical* questions about the external reach of morality just as there are about its internal reach; and there are important connections between the two kinds of questions. So, for example, moral judgements about the moralities of other societies may need to be weighed alongside other kinds of judgements about other aspects of those societies. Presumably the problematic internal questions for us have their counterparts for members of another society; and if those members resolve their questions with different forms or balances – if they have, say, different views as to the domain of morality – it need not be clear that there is much interest in isolated moral judgements of their way of resolution. But once he has recognized and clarified the questions and the connections, perhaps the moral philosopher has done all that can reasonably be expected of him. Perhaps, for example, the external questions no more lend themselves to (restrictive) answers grounded in reflective theorizing than they do to (expansive) answers grounded in unreflective moralizing.

In this chapter I have tried among other things to show the considerable difficulties facing any attempt to ground a 'relativist' restriction of the possibilities for meaningful moral criticism between morally distinct societies upon the presumed subjective character of morality; comparable difficulties face any attempt to deduce that character from the presumed fact of agreement upon some such restriction. Aside from the intrinsic interest of these attempts, there was a particular reason for considering them here. In the first part of this essay a theory of value and valuing was developed which included a cognitive and non-subjective treatment of the members of a certain class of valuings, and it was then suggested that in intuitive terms at least some moral valuings are members of that class; it was then further suggested that (a) some of those moral valuings are understood in terms of cognitive responses to things merely worthy of desire, to things which are merely reasonable objects of desire, while (b) others of those moral valuings are understood in the stronger terms of cognitive responses to things which merit desire, which have desire owing to them, which ought to be desired (pp. 103–5). If those intuitive thoughts are correct, two things follow. First, the presence of the moral valuings mentioned in (a) brings with it under certain circumstances the possibility of moral criticism of morally distinct societies, their members and their actions: moral criticism which can arise when it is deemed that within some morally distinct society moral valuings of this kind occur which are directed to things that are *not* worthy of desire. Second, and more strikingly, the presence of the moral valuings mentioned in (b) brings with it under certain far more widespread circumstances another possibility of moral criticism of morally distinct societies, their members and their actions: moral criticism which can arise when it is deemed that within some morally distinct society there is a *difference* in the things towards which certain moral valuings of this kind are directed. In either case, when the possibility of moral criticism occurs no one need deny that any of a number of considerations might serve to obstruct the actual making of the criticism (pp. 165–6); but according to the thoughts mentioned the possibility of that moral criticism remains. It is that possibility which many 'relativists' have wished to deny.

The extreme 'relativist' position denies that possibility through the completely general denial of the possibility of meaningful moral criticism between different systems of moral thought (p. 167). But that completely general denial is so revisionary in character that acceptance of it would threaten our grasp of the very idea that the systems concerned are different systems of *moral* thought: the possibility of moral criticism between different systems of thought is partly constitutive of their being different systems of moral thought. More cautious 'relativist' positions do not have that sweeping, at least revisionary, character; indeed some even purport to deduce a 'relativist' restriction from within the terms of our moral thought itself. One of those 'relativisms', Harman's, denies the possibility of making at least some of the moral criticisms licensed by the intuitive thoughts mentioned: namely, certain criticisms directed towards particular actions of individual members of the morally distinct society, where those actions arise from the members' distinctive moral valuings (p. 168). But Harman's argument for his denial, like a familiar argument for the subjectivity of morals (p. 180), simply overlooks the possibility of the kind of cognitive and non-subjective treatment given to certain moral valuings in accordance with the intuitive thoughts mentioned. Moreover, to the extent to which it is considered that the kinds of possibilities of moral criticism invoked against Harman's denial must always be potentially in play between morally distinct societies, to the same extent it will also be considered that the intuitive thoughts mentioned must always apply to systems of moral thought.

In this chapter I also tried to illustrate the 'singularity' of morality both by giving examples of practical values which are not moral values (pp. 148–9) and through a tentative exploration of the conse-quences of that 'singularity' for questions about the internal reach of morality within normal human lives. On a more theoretical plane, that of attempted identification of central features of the theory internal to moral thought and practice, various suggestions were made:

1 The primary vocabularies of morality are those of specific vices and virtues and of yet more mundane evaluations; so the area of morality – the part of our lives which has potentially a moral dimension – is nearly 'the whole of our mode of living and the quality of our relations with the world' (p. 146).
2 Any system of moral thought will employ the concepts of justice, of harm, of well-being and perhaps of happiness; there can be varying conceptions of what those things are, but the concepts must be present if a system of thought is to be a moral one (pp. 162–3).
3 The possibility of moral criticism between different moralities is partly constitutive of moral thought itself (pp. 166–7, 183).
4 That possibility of moral criticism between different moralities is often shaped by the presence in those moralities of moral valuings understood in cognitive and non-subjective terms, and is on occasion more exactly shaped by the presence of moral valuings understood as cognitive responses to things which merit desire, which have desire owing to them; perhaps it is even the case that any morality must include moral valuings of these kinds and so must license the possibility of the corresponding forms of moral criticism (pp. 182–4).

Recognition of the truth of (1) and (4) brings with it appreciation of the importance for philosophical understanding of morality of attention to the roles potentially played by specific reasons in backing up more abstracted moral judgements, be those specific reasons what were earlier called 'desirability characterizations' or what were there called 'reasons' (p. 54; cf. pp. 146–7). The consequences of failure to pay that attention, of a completely abstract treatment of admittedly abstracted judgements, emerged time and again in the discussion in this chapter of 'moral relativisms'. It is no accident that this essay is not entitled *The Right And The Good*.

In the remaining chapter I examine the views of two philosophers who have been deemed to have criticized morality itself. I do so for three reasons. First, I think consideration of those views can help us to appreciate *what morality is not*: can help us to appreciate that certain tendentious claims are not part of the theory internal to moral thought and practice. Second, I think that consideration can lead us to appreciate certain disconcerting features of our actual *use* of moral thought, features comparatively neglected in contemporary philosophical discussions of morality. And finally, that consideration can also lead us to appreciate a problem about the character of moral motivation and its place within our moral conceptual scheme. Those last two points should serve to eliminate any impression otherwise arising that I think that all is well with our moral thought and practice.

6 Morality's critics

The Moralists have endeavour'd to rout Vice, and clear the Heart of all hurtful Appetites and Inclinations: We are beholden to them for this in the same Manner as we are to Those who destroy Vermin, and clear the Countries of all noxious Creatures. But may not a Naturalist dissect Moles, try Experiments upon them, and enquire into the Nature of their Handicraft, without offence to the Mole-catchers, whose Business is only to kill them as fast as they can?

(Mandeville)

By applying the knife vivisectionally to the chest of the very *virtues of their time*, [philosophers] betrayed what was their own secret: to know of a new greatness of man, of a new untrodden way to his enhancement. Every time they exposed how much hypocrisy, comfortableness, letting oneself go and letting oneself drop, how many lies lay hidden under the best honored type of their contemporary morality, how much virtue was *outlived*.

(Nietzsche)

TERRA INCOGNITA

As Hume had his William Warburton, so Mandeville had his William Law, according to whom the author of *The Fable of the Bees* was no more than a man 'who comes a missioner from the kingdom of darkness to do us harm'. (With worst luck of all Nietzsche had his sister; 'tis pity she were not a Wilhelmina.) And as Hume is the great ironist of philosophy, so Mandeville is one of its greatest satirists. But his satirical style should not lead us to view Mandeville as a slight figure, as a mere wag taking – and giving – delight in the parading of playful paradoxes. In historical terms he forms an important bridge between the views of Hobbes and those of Hume; more importantly for present purposes, he can be interpreted as defending claims about morality which, if true, are of importance and which, even if false, are of considerable interest.

Is man naturally good? And how is human society possible? Those questions were two of the pivots around which the debate among British moralists of the seventeenth and eighteenth centuries turned. Into that debate stepped the Dutchman Mandeville. His account of the origin of society and the social affections began, like Hobbes's, from a conception of 'natural' man as having an innate instinct of love for himself and for no other:

> Man centers everything in himself, and neither loves nor hates but for his own Sake. Every Individual is a little World by itself, and all Creatures, as far as their Understanding and Abilities will let them, endeavour to make that Self happy: This in all of them is the continual Labour, and seems to be the whole Design of Life.
>
> (Mandeville 1924: 178)

That innate instinct of self-love makes itself manifest in a large number of phenomena: the urge for self-preservation, anger, envy, love of ease, and fear, for example. (Indeed, as that 'worthy Divine' La Rochefoucauld has it, 'tho' many Discoveries have been made in the World of Self-Love, there is yet abundance of *Terra incognita* left behind' (Mandeville 1970: 240). But Mandeville also includes within his conception of 'natural' man a quite distinct innate instinct of *self-liking*:

> [W]e are all born with a Passion manifestly distinct from Self-love; that, when it is moderate and well regulated, excites in us the Love of Praise, and a Desire to be applauded and thought well of by others, and stirs us up to good Actions: but that the same Passion, when it is excessive, or ill turn'd, whatever it excites in our Selves, gives Offence to others, renders us odious, and is call'd Pride.
>
> (Mandeville 1732b: 6–7)

> All Men are partial in their judgements, when they compare themselves to others; no two Equals think so well of each other as both do of themselves. . . .
>
> (Mandeville 1924: 271)

There antecedently existing 'no Word or Expression that comprehends all the different Effects of this same Cause', Mandeville is led to coin for that cause 'the Word Self-liking', clearly understood to be a 'Term of Art'. Self-love and self-liking are distinct innate instincts, just as it is one thing to struggle most to keep in existence *one's* self, another to judge that *that* self whose existence is most struggled for is the self of most value. Moreover, self-liking can at least at times prove to be a stronger instinct than that of self-love, as in the case of one who commits suicide in order to preserve his or her honour: thus Lucretia's suicide was 'a certain sign that she valued her Virtue less than her Glory, and her Life less than either' (Mandeville 1970: 223).

> The true Object of Pride or Vain-glory is the Opinion of others; and the most superlative wish which a Man possess'd, and entirely fill'd with it can make is, that he may be well thought of, applauded, and admired by the whole World, not only in the present, but all future Ages.
>
> (Mandeville 1924: 64)

And so Mandeville's most general claim: such human behaviour as cannot be explained in terms of the operations of the innate instinct of self-love can none the less be explained in terms of the additional operations of the distinct, and at times stronger, innate instinct of self-liking.

A critical part of the behaviour concerned is the formation of human societies and the resultant social human behaviour. Men are first led to co-operate together because of their common fear of wild animals and then because of their common fear of one another. But they then, slowly, come to appreciate that 'no Species of Animals is, without the Curb of Government, less capable of agreeing long together in Multitudes than that of Man' (Mandeville 1970: 81); they come to appreciate, that is, the need for 'Laws' which

> are plainly design'd as so many Remedies, to cure and disappoint that natural Instinct of Sovereignty, which teaches Man to look upon every thing as centring in Himself, and prompts him to put in a Claim to every thing, he can lay his Hands on.
>
> (Mandeville 1924: 271)

But given the strength of man's self-love, that appreciation is insufficient for the sustained, effective realization of what is needed – and remains so even when the 'Laws' concerned are written down and backed up by institutions and practices trading upon man's fear of punishment. Fears founded upon self-love will not produce stable social formations. Sufficiency has come about – in a stumbling, unsystematic manner – through the realization on the part of 'skilful politicians' of the potential strength of the distinct instinct of self-liking. Mandeville gives concise expression to his view of this process at the beginning of 'An enquiry into the origin of moral virtue' (1970: 81ff.). The 'Law-givers and other Wise Men, that have laboured for the Establishment of Society' have tried to make people believe that it is in each person's interest to care for the public interest rather than for what seems to be his private interest. But this 'has always been a very difficult Task'. The only likely way in which it could be achieved is by giving some 'Reward' for public-spirited actions: but it is not possible 'to give so many real Rewards as would satisfy all Persons for every individual Action'. Thus the 'Wise Men' were forced to contrive an imaginary reward for 'the trouble of Self-denial', a reward which cost nobody anything but which was 'a most acceptable Recompence to the Receivers': praise and flattery. The wise men, that is, observed that 'Flattery must be the most powerful Argument that cou'd be used to Human Creatures'. And so by praising public-spirited actions as noble and rational, and condemning purely selfish ones as typical of 'Brutes', the wise men were able to persuade people to control, at least in appearance, their selfish tendencies. But only in appearance: even if people then think that they are motivated by consideration of the public interest, in reality what moves them is the prospect of a flattery which serves pleasurably to confirm their self-liking. Thus the wise men divided conceptually 'the whole Species in two Classes, vastly differing from one another': the first, 'abject, Low-minded People', always hunting after immediate enjoyment, incapable of self-denial, enslaved by voluptuousness, with no regard to the good of others; the second, 'lofty, high-spirited Creatures', free from sordid selfishness, public-spirited, valuing above all 'the Improvements of the Mind'. Given the conceptual distinction so introduced together with both the plasticity of pride and the careful direction of the wise men's flattery, people were constantly drawn to show – to give the appearance – that they belonged to the second, nobler class.

Thus we can come to see, in the best known words of Mandeville, that 'Moral Virtues are the Political Offspring which Flattery begot upon Pride' (1970: 88): a process of begetting of a kind deemed essential for the existence of the social affections which make the existence of human society possible.

As regards the role played by 'Moralists and Politicians', there is an apparent ambivalence on Mandeville's part:

> I give those Names promiscuously to All that having studied Human Nature, have endeavour'd to civilize Men, and render them more and more tractable, *either* for the Ease of Governours and Magistrates, *or else* for the Temporal Happiness of Society in general.
>
> (Mandeville 1732b: 41, emphasis added; cf. 1970: 85)

On Mandeville's philosophical psychology, however, there is no problem here: 'skilful politicians' can be as ignorant of the psychological forces which really move them as the rest of humanity. If we look into 'the Virtues of great Men' we shall find nothing 'but Dust and Cobwebs' (Mandeville 1970: 187).

POMP AND VANITY AND IMPATIENCE

For Mandeville, then, morality (in one sense of that term) is essentially a political, not just a social, phenomenon. Morality is a human contrivance prompted by the desire which arises to render men 'more and more tractable': prompted by the desire, that is, to exercise institutionalized power over other men. Thus 'it was not any Heathen Religion or other Idolatrous Superstition, that first put Man upon crossing his Appetites and subduing his dearest Inclinations, but the skilful Management of wary Politicians' (1970: 87). The 'natural instinct of Sovereignty', the 'love of Dominion and that Usurping Temper all Mankind are Born with', can, within the general circumstances of human existence, naturally give rise to a vastly heightened desire for 'sovereignty' in relation to the selves of others: within the general circumstances constituted by, say, the general benefits of living within society and the shortage of goods on which 'Hands' can be laid. That can be accounted for merely within terms of self-love; but if the desire so produced within 'wary Politicians' is to have any reasonable chance of being satisfied, then, given the facts about self-love *and* self-liking, something like the contrivance of morality is needed and will have to be propagated.

But only something like, for morality is but one of the contrivances available at this point to 'skilful politicians'. (Indeed, morality is itself a number of contrivances. One gap in Mandeville's discussion is any direct consideration of the question of why politicians and moralists foist one morality on their subjects rather than another.) Mandeville insists that men can come to feel proud of almost anything, and gives a good example of this puzzling plasticity of pride: that directed towards the achievements of one's ancestors. And it is pleasing in this context that when Buñuel tried to characterize the phenomenon of *machismo*, he did so in terms of an exaggerated sense of pride in one's masculinity: for that presupposes that a sense of pride in one's masculinity might be *unexaggerated*. And perhaps the nicest case of all: someone I know is actually *proud* of having found himself in the same lift as Marcello Mastroiani! Given this plasticity of pride, then, another possible contrivance to the same end – one which has in fact been so (stumblingly) created and which within certain societies has even existed alongside professed attachment to morality – is what might be called *the Ethics of Honour*: that set of practical values attachment to which is most clearly made manifest within the institution of duelling, codes of military honour and rules for good manners, but also perhaps in certain ideas about hunting and horsemanship and even maybe in the phenomenon now known as conspicuous consumption. This Ethics of Honour 'is of the same Origin with' what I shall call *the Morality of Virtue or Goodness*, Mandeville's own terminology not always being consistent on this point: namely, each is a contrivance of 'skilful politicians' designed to make men 'more and more tractable' by playing upon their promiscuous instinct for self-liking. But notwithstanding that similarity of origin, and even their occasional coexistence, Mandeville maintains the Ethics of Honour to be incompatible with the Morality of Virtue. Those who think otherwise in effect think 'that the strictest Attachment to the World is not inconsistent with a Man's Promise of renouncing the Pomp and Vanity of it' (1732b: 105). Nor does there seem much doubt that Mandeville's point here was not just meant as a criticism of those who are ignorant of that incompatibility: that the Ethics of Honour is incompatible with the Morality of Virtue was also clearly taken by him as constituting a criticism of that Ethics. And yet some of the very considerations which led Mandeville to maintain the thesis of incompatibility also figure in his defence of another thesis: that of the impossibility for men of their exemplifying the positive part of the Morality of Virtue! Virtue is 'inaccessible', 'a thing impracticable' (Mandeville 1970: 243).

In part, then, Mandeville is a familiar enough figure: the moralist concerned to denounce the hypocrisy and self-deception prevalent within the society in which he lives. While professing attachment to Christian values people show through their conduct that the values

really operative in their lives are quite other: materialistic, hedon-
istic, worldly. But there is also present a perhaps less familiar figure:
the philosopher concerned, as just now said, to demonstrate the
thesis of incompatibility. The really operative values are not just
distinct from but in fact incompatible with the professed values.

> The only thing of weight that can be said against modern Honour
> is, that it is directly opposite to Religion. The one bids you bear
> Injuries with Patience, the other tells you if you don't resent
> them, you are not fit to live. Religion commands you to leave
> all Revenge to God, Honour bids you trust your Revenge to
> nobody but your self, even where the law would do it for you;
> Religion plainly forbids Murther, Honour openly justifies it:
> Religion bids you not shed Blood upon any account whatever:
> Honour bids you fight for the least Trifle: Religion is built on
> Humility, and Honour upon Pride. How to reconcile them must
> be left to wiser Heads than mine.
>
> (Mandeville 1970: 232–3)

> To be at once well-bred and sincere, is no less than a Contradic-
> tion; and therefore whilst Man advances in Knowledge, and his
> Manners are polish'd, we must expect to see at the same time his
> Desires enlarg'd, his Appetites refin'd, and his Vices encreas'd.
>
> (ibid.: 202)

That this Ethics of Honour is 'diametrically opposite' (Mandeville
1732b: 77) to the Morality of Virtue is further confirmed by a variety
of other considerations. One is exemplified in the fact that good
manners, for example, are compatible with insincerity whereas virtue
is not: in general, the question of motivation – *the* question for the
Morality of Virtue – is accorded within the Ethics of Honour a
secondary status at most in relation to that of public performance.
By contrast with the Ethics of Honour, from the standpoint of the
Morality of Virtue 'it is impossible to judge of a Man's Performance,
unless we are thoroughly acquainted with the Principle and Motive
from which he acts' (Mandeville 1970: 91). And that connects, of
course, with the fact that Honour is more readily detectable by
others than is Virtue:

> A man may be just and chaste, and yet not be able to convince
> the World that he is so; but he may pick a Quarrel, and shew,
> that he dares to Fight when he pleases, especially if he converses
> with Men of the Sword. Where the Principle of Honour was in
> high Esteem, Vanity and Impatience must have always prompted

the most proud and forward to seek after Opportunities of signalizing themselves, in order to be stiled Men of Honour. This would
naturally occasion Quarrelling and Fighting.

(Mandeville 1732b: 63)

Indeed, for Men of Honour the 'Opportunities of signalizing themselves' are essential to the *point* of their practice:

A virtuous man expects no Acknowledgement from others; and
if they won't believe him to be virtuous, his Business is not to
force them to it; but a man of Honour has the Liberty openly to
proclaim himself to be such, and call to an Account Every body
who dares to doubt of it.

(ibid.: 44)

The Reward of Glory . . . consists in a superlative felicity which
a man who is conscious of having perform'd a noble Action,
enjoys in Self love, whilst he is thinking on the Applause he
expects of others.

(Mandeville 1970: 90–1)

In contrast, then, to the Morality of Virtue, the Ethics of Honour
creates for its practitioners 'Opportunities of signalizing themselves'
and then licenses the demand for 'Acknowledgement' of the selves
so signalled. And, finally, there is a practical incompatibility between
the Ethics of Honour and the Morality of Virtue: 'Good Manners
have nothing to do with Virtue or Religion; instead of extinguishing,
they rather inflame the Passions' (ibid.: 112).

A HORSE THAT DOES NOT DANCE?

From one point of view the Ethics of Honour is 'a greater Atchieve-
ment' than Morality:

Because the One is more skilfully adapted to our inward Make.
Men are better paid for their Adherence to Honour, than they
are for their Adherence to Virtue: The First requires less self-
denial, and the Rewards they receive for that Little are not
imaginary but real and palpable. . . . The Invention of Honour
has been far more beneficial to the Civil Society than that of
Virtue, and much better answer'd the End for which they were
invented. For ever since the Notion of Honour has been receiv'd
among Christians, there have always been, in the same num-

ber of people, Twenty Men of real Honour, to one of real
Virtue.

(Mandeville 1732b: 43–4)

That judgement about the contrivances concerned is explicitly relati-
vized to 'the End for which they were invented'; it is thus compatible
with Mandeville's other judgement in which the Morality of Virtue
is used to criticize the Ethics of Honour. Nor should we let ourselves
be misled by Mandeville's remark that 'The only thing of weight
that can be said against modern Honour is, that it is directly opposite
to Religion.' Maybe it is the only thing: but reading Mandeville on
duelling we must recognize that, for him, the weight of that one
thing could be considerable.

Still, the suspicion must arise that for Mandeville the odds of our
coming across a man 'of real Virtue' rather than one 'of real Honour'
are probably a good deal longer than twenty to one against – it is
not just that 'the World has yet never swarm'd' (1970: 92) with men
of virtue. Unlike 'real Honour', 'real Virtue' requires complete 'self-
denial' (according to 'The Generality of Moralists and Philosophers'
(ibid: 329)); yet for Mandeville all the natural motivations of men
arise from either 'self-love' or 'self-liking' or some combination of
them; and so passing over the supposed possibility of divine grace,
it follows that 'real Virtue' is for men an impossibility. Thus Law's
complaint against Mandeville:

1st. You consider Man, *merely* as an *Animal*, having, like other
Animals, nothing to do but follow his Appetites.
2dly. You consider Man as cheated and flattered out of his natural
State, by the Craft of Moralists, and pretend to be very sure, that
the '*moral Virtues are the political offspring which Flattery begot
upon Pride*'.
So that Man and Morality are here both destroyed together. Man
is declared to be only an *Animal*, and Morality an Imposture.
According to this Doctrine, to say that a Man is dishonest, is
making him just such a Criminal as a Horse that does not dance.

(Law 1845: 3–4)

There are, of course, terrible misunderstandings here, if not deliberate misrepresentations; but let us try to see if there is any complaint
of worth at this point, be it Law's or not.

Against those like Law who wished to see man as having been
made in God's image, Mandeville, the 'Lover of Experience' (1711:

xi), urged the need to see man in his 'Nakedness', however disagreeable that might be to endure. Ambrose Bierce once defined cynicism
as a defect of vision which compels us to see the world as it is,
instead of as it should be. Being thus 'cynical' about the nature of
man – 'One of the greatest Reasons why so few People understand
themselves, is, that most Writers are always teaching Men what they
should be, and hardly ever trouble their heads with telling them
what they really are' (Mandeville 1970: 77) – Mandeville was led to
note the prevalence in human affairs of hypocrisy and self-deception,
the strength of man's obsessive desire for praise and esteem, and
the striking general disparity between what men say and what they
do: in short, he was led to recognize 'the real Meanness and Deform-
ity' (1732a: 48) of human nature.

> WHAT *Emilia* thinks of her self is worth any man's notice. Her
> prostitution she is sure never proceeded from lust, but from
> necessity, *ergo* no sin. The mischief she does with her slander,
> she ascribes to the aversion she has to vice. When she reflects on
> the hours she spends at church, and in reading, and then thinks
> on the will she has made, she flatters her self with having per-
> form'd every christian duty, and her conscience is entirely clear.
> Is it not strange, that *Emilia*, with all her cunning, never suspected
> her self to be an ill woman, and knows not to this hour, that
> envy and vanity are her darling vices?
>
> (Mandeville 1720: 35)

> Some impose on the World, and would be thought to believe
> what they really don't; but much the greater number impose upon
> themselves, not considering nor thoroughly apprehending what it
> is to believe.
>
> (Mandeville 1970: 186)

> I am willing to pay Adoration to Virtue wherever I can meet with
> it, with a Proviso, that I shall not be oblig'd to admit any as such
> where I can see no Self-denial, or to judge of Mens Sentiments
> from their Words, where I have their Lives before me.
>
> (ibid.: 174)

Law certainly wished to complain both about the empirical, naturalistic character of this conjecture and about its content; but on both
points I think Mandeville is unassailable. But on this plausible
empirical basis Mandeville then attempts to construct an unduly
simplistic theory of human motivation. In so doing he falls into the
usual traps: ranging from that of conceiving the mind as having some

similitude to body in its operations, through that of neglecting the variety of kinds of human desire, to that of neglecting the variety of the objects of human desire. Given the theory of motivation so constructed together with his ideas about what the Morality of Virtue requires, Mandeville is then led to deny the effective possibility of 'real Virtue' for the natural human race. Further reasonable complaints arise about Mandeville's method of trying to substantiate that denial. First, his reasons in support of the denial turn upon the ill-explained 'Terms of Art' deployed within his theory of human nature, 'self-love' and 'self-liking'. And secondly, his denial also rests upon an undefended claim as to the primacy for moral evaluation of actions of a barely articulated theory of what moral motivation would be:

> Men are not to be Judg'd by the Consequences that may succeed their Actions, but the Facts themselves, and the Motives which it shall appear they acted from.
>
> (Mandeville 1970: 119)

> I see no Self denial, without which there can be no Virtue.
>
> (ibid.: 177)

> Passions may do Good by chance, but there can be no merit but in the conquest of them.
>
> (ibid.: 107)

Those are not Law's complaints. Aside from that involved in his charge that Mandeville sees Man '*merely* as an *Animal*', his main complaint seems to be that the further conclusion Mandeville wishes us to draw is that we should reject the Morality of Virtue. Morality has been supposedly 'destroyed': and that, not just in the sense that the 'institution' is in its positive part empty in relation to human actions, but also in the further sense that we are invited consciously to abandon its very terms of reference.

But the further conclusion Mandeville officially wishes us to draw is quite different:

> [S]ince it is impossible to serve God and Mammon, my choice shall be soon made: No temporal Pleasure can be worth running the Risque of being eternally miserable; and, let he who will Labour to aggrandize the Nation, I will aim at higher Ends, and take care of my own Soul.
>
> (Mandeville 1732a: 22)

Now, if asked what he thinks of 'real Virtue' it is hardly enough for

Mandeville to anticipate Gandhi's answer to the same question about 'British civilization': 'That would be a good idea.' In this passage Mandeville is gesturing at some non-moral motive for continuing deployment of the terms of reference of the Morality of Virtue: non-moral since, first, in accordance with his own, admittedly elusive, theory of moral motivation the prospect of divine rewards and punishments in interaction with a rational hedonism could not produce actions of 'real Virtue', and second, in the light of his view as to the impossibility for actual human beings of moral motivation any effective motivation for such continuing deployment must be non-moral. But the question arises as to quite what *way of deploying* the terms of reference of the Morality of Virtue Mandeville is concerned to countenance. At least three possibilities can be distinguished here. First, even if 'real Virtue' is impossible for actual human beings, it follows neither that all human actions are vicious nor that all vicious actions are equally vicious. Attachment to the Morality of Virtue cannot, *ex hypothesi*, issue in actions of 'real Virtue': but for all that such attachment could yet play some role in the selection of the morally neutral or least vicious means to some given, admittedly vicious end, and even in the selection of some morally neutral or less vicious end rather than some more vicious one. Second, even if 'real Virtue' is impossible for actual human beings, it does not follow that the project of trying to make one's self less vicious, of trying for example to strengthen one's less vicious or even morally neutral motivations, is incoherent. And third, the impossibility of 'real Virtue' does not establish the incoherence of the project of trying to make one's actions coincide externally with those which would exemplify 'real Virtue'.

One thing is clear: Mandeville's claim that 'skilful politicians' created the Morality of Virtue should not be confused with the thought that those politicians contrived to make men really virtuous. What the politicians created was *an image of an impossible ideal*, an image whose existence could be turned to their own (and others') advantage through the consequent amplification of the kinds of selfish, vainglorious action available to men. By flattering their subjects, at least at times, as instantiating that impossible ideal, these 'skilful politicians' can make their subjects 'more and more tractable': for the pleasurable pride potentially felt by the subjects about their own supposed moral virtue is strong enough a force to outweigh their other, anti-social instincts. And were the same 'skilful politicians' to come to entertain doubts about the general efficacy of the Morality of Virtue in this respect, they could have recourse to other contrivances, such as the Ethics of Honour, calculated to reinforce the same general desired effect of having men be 'more and more tractable'; if that happens, then given the presumed ends of the 'skilful politicians', any matter of the inconsistency of the Morality of Virtue with the other contrivances employed need not concern them. But none the less a double danger arises for such politicians: the first that as a result of the labours of a Mandeville the inconsistency among the various contrivances becomes generally known; and the second that as a result of the labours of a Mandeville the impossibility of 'real Virtue' becomes generally known. The first might shake the system, the second could 'destroy' it. For if 'real Virtue' is impossible, flattery of the subjects in terms of their exemplification of it is always groundless and pride felt in terms of such exemplification is never justified; and were that to become generally known it is difficult to see how the contrivance of the Morality of Virtue could continue to function for the ends of the 'skilful politicians'. So while Mandeville's labours do not threaten to 'destroy' the Morality of Virtue itself, they do threaten to destroy the *use* made of that morality by the 'skilful politicians'.

Suppose that has indeed come to pass: what are the possible reactions of 'skilful politicians'? One group of reactions, available perhaps only to the most skilful, is constituted by attempts to work with the negative dimension of the Morality of Virtue, the dimension left in reality intact by Mandeville's discussion. So one reaction would be that of continuing with flattery of the subjects, but now in terms of their being less vicious than The Others; another would be to continue with that same flattery, but now in terms of the 'true moral worth' of the subjects being made manifest in their capacity for feeling remorse and guilt about their own viciousness (so that such feelings become, paradoxically enough, further objects of the plastic pride). But there is another group of reactions more likely to occur to the less skilful politicians: this is constituted by attempts to replace the Morality of Virtue by other sets of presumed values which do not encounter the problem of impossibility. The candidates are, now, all too familiar: racism, nationalism, internal colonialism, sexism, even the very idea of 'sexual morality'. Given the plasticity of pride, each of these can enable the politician to flatter at least some of his subjects and can so give rise to acquiescence-inducing feelings of pride in their superiority in the subjects concerned. And none of these contrivances need cost the politician anything –

provided that he is of the right race, nationality, social class and caste, sex and sexual preferences. (And if he is not: *Beware!*)

EVERY BEE HAS LOST ITS STING?

Perhaps the most frequently adduced reason in support of the charge against Mandeville of 'immoralism' still remains to be considered. This is the claim, supposedly the moral of the fable of the bees, that public benefits, such as national wealth and greatness, depend for their existence upon the vicious character of private – that is, individual – behaviour, so that were men to come, *par impossible*, to lead lives of 'real Virtue' those public benefits of social living would disappear. And thus, according to Mandeville's critics, he was *recommending* that private behaviour be vicious.

The possible arguments in favour of the claim that private vices issue in public benefits will not be considered here; and I shall waste no time on more recent attempts to extend the application of the model of 'economic man' in favour among contemporary *laisser-faire* economists to 'explain' quite other areas of human behaviour. (Mandeville in fact saw part of the mistake here: 'The Mathematicks become the only valuable Study, and are made use of in every thing even where it is ridiculous' (1970: 323).) All I shall do here is to indicate some motivations which I suspect led Mandeville to devise his fable and which were they really his would come close to clearing him of the charge of 'immoralism'.

I think it clear that Mandeville's motivation for devising his fable was in part to counter an obvious objection to his account of human nature: if man were such a viciously selfish and anti-social creature as that account represents him as being, how could it come about that the phenomenon of human society exists? That countering that objection is part of Mandeville's motivation is suggested by the title page of the second of the two 1714 editions: 'The Fable of the Bees: or, Private Vices Publick Benefits. CONTAINING, several Discourses, to demonstrate, That Human Frailties, *during the degeneracy of* MANKIND, may be turn'd to the Advantage of the CIVIL SOCIETY, and made to supply the Place of *Moral Virtues*' (quoted in Monro 1975: 189). So, notwithstanding the essentially vicious, anti-social nature of man, the fact of the existence of human society can indeed be explained. Mandeville no more had to deny that fact than his critics should have denied that nature.

The same concern to be 'cynical' in Bierce's sense connects with another part of Mandeville's motivation for devising his fable. If once we face the facts, Mandeville thinks we shall be led to recognize the moral untidiness of the world we live in: for in this world good and evil are as mixed up together as the ingredients of 'a Bowl of Punch'.

> The short-sighted Vulgar in the Chain of Causes seldom can see further than one Link; but those who can enlarge their View, and will give themselves the Leisure of gazing on the Prospect of concatenated Events, may, in a hundred Places see *Good* spring up, and pullulate from *Evil*, as naturally as Chickens do from Eggs.
>
> (Mandeville 1970: 123)

> It is in Morality as it is in Nature, there is nothing so perfectly Good in Creatures that it cannot be hurtful to any one of the Society, nor any thing so entirely Evil, but it may prove beneficial to some part or other of the Creation. . . .
>
> (ibid.: 369)

> In recruiting what is lost and destroy'd by Fire, Storms, Sea-fights, Seiges, Battles a considerable part of Trade consists. . . .
>
> (ibid.: 361)

The examples can be multiplied (and Mandeville multiplies them). But if once we recognize this Manichean character of the world in which we live we shall thereby be led to accept the need for decision – decision, say, as to whether a certain price is worth paying or as to whether a certain potential benefit is to be renounced. It is the refusal to face up to the moral untidiness of this world, and the consequent refusal to face up to the need for decision, that is at least one of the primary targets of Mandeville's fable.

In perhaps one of his less acute moments, Hume asked the following: 'Is it not very inconsistent for an author to assert in one page, that moral distinctions are inventions of politicians for public interest, and in the next page maintain, that vice is advantageous to the public?' (Hume 1963a: 163). The confusion here is clear: it is the existence of an *image* of an impossible ideal that is advantageous, not the existence of behaviour exemplifying 'real Virtue'. But perhaps Hume's real complaint was another: 'It seems, upon any system of morality, little less than a contradiction in terms, to talk of a vice, which is in general beneficial to society' (ibid.).

Now, we have just seen that one of Mandeville's concerns was to emphasize the need here for decision; we have also seen (pp. 196–7) that his own decision, at least in theoretical terms, was clear: 'If I have shewn the way to worldly Greatness I have always without hesitation preferr'd the Road that leads to Virtue' (Mandeville 1970: 241). The point now is that that declaration of decision should be understood as drawing attention to the possibility that consideration of the connections between private behaviour and 'public benefits' might issue in reasonable doubts as to whether those 'public benefits' are really beneficial, are really worthwhile in the world as it is. Mandeville's determination to be 'cynical' about the evaluative untidiness of this world led him to appreciate the complexity of what has here been called 'proto-practical deliberation' (p. 20): a complexity as much overlooked by his morally optimistic contemporaries as by many of our contemporary theorists of decision.

THE SPECIOUS CLOAK OF SOCIABLENESS

To finish this discussion of our 'missioner from the kingdom of darkness' I wish to raise one general question: if Mandeville's account of the origins of moral thought were something like right, how should we expect moral thought and discourse actually to function? We have already considered the probable functioning of that discourse in the mouths of 'skilful politicians' both before and after the general recognition of the results of the labours of a Mandeville; what now of the ordinary man in society? Initially basking in the flattery of his moral virtue by the politicians, he will still wish to increase the amount of flattery: no praise is good enough. ('Few Men can be perswaded that they get too much by those they sell to, how extraordinary soever their Gains are' (Mandeville 1970: 113).) The easiest way to edge closer to the impossible limit would be through *self*-flattery. Yet, for reasons readily intelligible within the terms of Mandeville's own account, *modesty* (in one of its 'Acceptations') will be deemed one of the cardinal social virtues (ibid.: 101ff.). Our man in society might thus try to 'counterfeit' that virtue, to 'industriously conceal' (ibid: 156) his pride, this 'counterfeiting' being strictly designed to deceive others so that they fall in with his pursuit of his end: so he might hope either thereby to receive direct flattery from others for his virtuous 'modesty' or thereby to provoke flattery from others in terms of the 'real Virtue' which is hidden beneath that 'modesty'. And if such flattery is not then forthcoming from certain others, he has a further recourse available to him: that of dismissing the approval of the others concerned as not being worth having so as then to search out other others who share, or at least seem to share, his high opinion of himself. If such others prove difficult to find – or maybe even if they prove *too easy* to find – then, within the conventions of this 'modest society', our man is likely to have recourse to another device: that of trying to achieve *implicit* flattery through the criticism of the moral failings *of Others*, a criticism designed to heighten awareness, be it on his own part or on that of others, of his own comparative 'virtue' ('as well as we think of ourselves, so ill we often think of our Neighbour with equal Injustice' (Mandeville 1970: 158)). But what would be most unlikely to occur, given the dominant instincts of 'self-love' and 'self-liking', is any serious attempt at moral self-criticism and any serious attempt at his own moral improvement: and even if such phenomena *seem* to occur, they are likely to be no more than other devices designed to invite the flattering thought, in others or in himself, that he is thereby demonstrating his own moral worth, his own moral sensitivity and capacity for moral self-criticism. All this requires, of course, considerable self-deception.

If, now, the results of the labours of a Mandeville become generally known, the effective possibilities for self-deception will be at least much reduced: simple hypocrisy will generally take its place.

> Ashamed of the many Frailties they feel within, all Men endeavour to hide themselves, their Ugly Nakedness, from each other, and wrapping up the true motives of their Hearts in the Specious Cloak of Sociableness, and their concern for the publick Good, they are in hopes of concealing their filthy Appetites and the deformity of their Desires; whilst they are conscious within of the fondness for their darling Lusts, and their incapacity, barefac'd to tread the arduous, Ruggid Path of Virtue.
>
> (Mandeville 1970: 244)

Such a man in society cannot pride himself upon his 'real Virtue'. But aside from rejection of the very terms of reference of the Morality of Virtue, there still remains open to him another course: that of priding himself upon being better – i.e. less vicious – than The Others. Now the moral censure of others becomes essential for his own comparative flattery. Negative judgements upon the morality of others will become the norm: they will be the only means available of defining himself in morally acceptable terms, the very condition of his doing so. And despite his knowledge of the results of the labours of a Mandeville, his instinctive 'self-love' and 'self-liking' will continue to make minimal the likelihood of serious moral self-criticism and serious attempts at moral self-improvement; indeed, if such phenomena seem to occur they are likely to be but one more manifestation of 'self-liking' – that involved in his thought that he, *unlike others*, is at least able to recognize his own moral failings and to try to do something about them.

Alasdair MacIntyre holds that it is the fact that 'morality today is in a state of grave disorder' which explains how it is that the meaning of moral discourse can hide its use (MacIntyre 1981: 66). I have extracted from Mandeville's writings an alternative description of that use along with a possible alternative explanation of how that use has come about and so of how the meaning of moral discourse could hide *that* use. These alternatives reveal nothing, it seems to me, about the state of morality, about *its* order or disorder; the alternative description does however bring us close to ideas about the actual functioning of moral thought and discourse found in the writings of a better known thinker to consideration of whom I shall now turn.

A MORAL FIG-LEAF

For Nietzsche the worst readers 'are those who proceed like plundering soldiers: they pick up a few things they can use, soil and confuse the rest, and blaspheme the whole' (Nietzsche 1966b: 155). Here I shall consciously run the risk of finding myself at least a third of the way towards being such a reader: given my very particular purposes here I shall pick up a few things from Nietzsche's writings which I think I can use. But there might nevertheless be an incidental effect in terms of a limited *sorting out* of some of Nietzsche's thoughts about morality.

A difficulty which faces any reader of Nietzsche's writings makes them of special interest given my purposes here. The difficulty is that of knowing at various points quite what his target is. Sometimes it is clear that the intended object of his criticisms is some fairly specific moral code: most frequently certain distinctive Christian beliefs or even 'the whole Christian–European morality', but also at times various socialist beliefs and even on occasion certain elements of the moral code dominant only in his contemporary German culture. At other times it is clear that the intended object of Nietzsche's criticisms is, so to say, the priestly class: those who pretend to be authorities upon, and the enforcers of, the true morality, and even those parading moralists who renounce the world for the ways of asceticism. Again, it is clear at times that the intended object of his criticisms is some specific philosophical theory of morality: most frequently Kantian theories, but also on occasion, for example, utilitarian theories (especially in the hands of the English). But it is sometimes clear that Nietzsche has in mind a more formidable target for his criticisms – 'morality itself'. Thus he writes of 'our moral philosophers' that

> they never laid eyes on the real problems of morality; for these emerge only when we compare *many* moralities. In all 'science of morals' so far one thing was *lacking*, strange as it may sound: the problem of morality itself; what was lacking was any suspicion that there was something problematic here.
>
> (Nietzsche 1966a: 287–8)

All of that indeed seems clear enough; but two further considerations present the reader of Nietzsche with a considerable difficulty. First, at various points it remains none too clear quite what Nietzsche takes the target of his criticisms to be; and second, even when that is clear, it is often none the less none too clear that Nietzsche identifies correctly the target which is in fact hit by those criticisms. In the light of that difficulty and within the context shaped by the very particular purposes of this essay, I propose to explore the following strategy: that of considering various of Nietzsche's criticisms *as if* they were directed at the target of 'morality itself' in the hope that evaluation of those criticisms so understood will help with the task of appreciating what 'morality itself' is – or, at least, with that of appreciating *what it is not*.

'There are', Nietzsche tells us, 'no moral phenomena at all, but only a moral interpretation of phenomena – ' (1966a: 275); that claim is perhaps spelt out a little in the following passage:

> *there are no moral facts whatever*. Moral judgement has this in common with religious judgement that it believes in realities which do not exist. Morality is only an interpretation of certain phenomena, more precisely a *mis*interpretation. Moral judgement belongs, as does religious judgement, to a level of ignorance at which even the concept of the real, the distinction between the real and the imaginary, is lacking, so that at such a level 'truth' denotes nothing but things which we today call 'imaginings'.
>
> (Nietzsche 1968b: 55)

Shortly after Nietzsche says of morality that 'one must already know *what* it is about to derive profit from it'; and to know what morality is about requires, for Nietzsche, that we appreciate that, like religion, it falls entirely

> under the *psychology of error*: in every single case cause is mistaken for effect; or the effect of what is *believed* true is mistaken for the truth; or a state of consciousness is mistaken for the causation of this state.
>
> (ibid.: 52–3)

Nietzsche's theory of error is a remarkably rich manifestation of deep psychological insights. Here I shall only describe in the most schematic of terms his application of that theory to 'the problem of morality'. Man, says Nietzsche, 'would sooner have the void for his purpose than be void of purpose' (1956b: 299); that propensity interacts with a feature characteristic of certain 'small people' to produce a mistaken projection on to the world: 'He who does not know how to put his will into things at least puts a *meaning* into them: that is, he believes there is a will in them already (principle of "belief")' (1968b: 24). That mistaken projection, and its constant companions in terms of error and self-deception within agents' understandings of their own actions, can receive many further developments, can issue in '*many* moralities'. Thus Nietzsche sees Christian morality, for example, as being distinctively rooted in weakness, fear, and the peculiar kind of malice which he calls *ressentiment*. As Philippa Foot expresses Nietzsche's view,

> Those who cultivate humility and the other propitiatory virtues to cloak their weakness nourish an envious resentment against those stronger than themselves. They want revenge for their inferiority and have a deep desire to humiliate and harm. The wish to punish seems to Nietzsche one of the most evident signs of this hidden malice, and he sees the idea of free will, and accountability, as invented by those who desired to inflict punishment.
>
> (Foot 1973: 83)

Thus Nietzsche says of the doctrine 'Not to seek *one's own* advantage' that it 'is merely a moral figleaf for a quite different, namely physiological fact: "I no longer know how to *find* my advantage"' (1968b: 87). The utility of that fig-leaf depends upon the capacity of agents for self-deception, for cloaking their motivated errors from themselves; but the cost of having a Christian morality is not restricted, even for 'small people', to such motivated errors and self-deceptions:

> [Man] stretched himself upon the contradiction 'God' and 'Devil' as on a rack. He projected all his denials of self, nature, embodiment, reality, as God (the divine Judge and Executioner), as transcendence, as eternity, as endless torture, as hell, as the infinitude of guilt and punishment.
>
> (Nietzsche 1956b: 226)

Still, the prime mover in the generation of Christian morality is found also in the generation of all other moralities: 'That is your entire will, you wisest men; it is a will to power; and that is so even when you talk of good and evil and of the assessment of values' (Nietzsche 1961: 136). All moralities, with their distinctive contrast of good and evil (*böse*), are products of the will to power in interaction with various deforming factors: the products, moralities, serving precisely to *mask* that will to power. That is what morality 'is about'. And for those capable of freeing themselves from the influence of the various deforming factors, there remains but one hope: only by consciously embracing this will to power, only by consciously accepting the egoism which 'belongs to the nature of a noble soul' (Nietzsche 1966a: 405), only by experiencing himself as 'determining values' (ibid.: 395), only by knowing himself to be 'value-creating' (ibid.: 395), is there any possibility of even such a man's escaping from the errors inherent in morality. Only in this way is there any possibility of his becoming, like Zarathustra, 'a prologue to better players' (Nietzsche 1961: 226).

ENGLISH CONSISTENCY

The explanation of the supposed error is striking; but why is it supposed that there is an error here to be explained? Why, for example, does Nietzsche deny the existence of moral facts, of moral phenomena? One possibility begins to emerge with the following remarks made when discussing George Eliot:

> They have got rid of the Christian God, and now feel obliged to cling all the more firmly to Christian morality: that is *English* consistency. . . . When one gives up Christian belief one thereby deprives oneself of the *right* to Christian morality. For the latter is absolutely *not* self-evident. . . .
>
> (Nietzsche 1968b: 69)

That seems a challenge aimed at a particular family of moralities. Yet shortly after Nietzsche says this:

> If the English really do believe they know, of their own accord, 'intuitively', what is good and evil; if they consequently think they no longer have need of Christianity as a guarantee of morality; that is merely the *consequence* of the ascendancy of Christian evaluation and an expression of the *strength* and *depth* of this ascendancy: so that the highly conditional nature of its right to exist is no longer felt. For the Englishman morality is not yet a problem.
>
> (ibid.: 70)

In this somewhat ambiguous passage Nietzsche's target seems to shift to 'morality', to morality itself. His claim then is not just that there are certain elements occurring within Christian morality which cease to make sense once belief in the existence of the Christian God is lost; it must rather, it seems, be the claim that there are certain general features of Christian morality which that morality has bequeathed to all other moralities, which must be present in any other system of thought and practice if that other system is to be a *moral* system, and which *only make sense within* the context of belief in the existence of the Christian God. What might these general features be? One set of candidates would be the concepts of moral obligation, of moral duty, of what is morally right or wrong, and of the moral sense of 'ought'. And one contemporary philosopher indeed tells us that these concepts 'ought to be jettisoned if this is psychologically possible' since they are 'survivals, or derivatives from survivals, from an earlier conception of ethics which no longer generally survives' (Anscombe 1958: 1). Nor is it difficult to guess what that 'earlier conception of ethics' was: the conception which explained the concepts concerned in terms of the commands of the Christian God.

To repeat: the claim at issue is not that there are certain elements occurring within Christian morality which cease to make sense once belief in the existence of the Christian God is lost. And to concede: it is difficult to see how a system of thought and practice which jettisons *all* that Miss Anscombe says should be jettisoned could still reasonably be considered a system of *moral* thought and practice. But that concession is not yet acceptance of the claim at issue: the claim, that is, that the idea of there being moral facts cast in terms of the concepts concerned makes sense only either on the supposition that there are facts about what the Christian God commands or on some derivative analogue of that supposition.

Christian morality is not the only morality; and the claim that any other morality which employs the idea of there being facts about moral obligations and duties *must* be haunted by the ghost of the Christian God and his commands may achieve whatever attraction it has only through the influence of two 'methodological' failings. One is a fondness for an almost entirely abstract treatment of certain admittedly general moral notions (cf. Strawson 1961: 33); the other, recognized by Nietzsche himself (1956b: 209), is the failure to see the strict irrelevance of matters of origin for questions of present use or purpose. Once avoiding those failings, we can come to a quite unproblematic understanding of *certain, present* uses of the notions Miss Anscombe would have us entirely jettison:

> There is nothing in the least mysterious or metaphysical in the fact that duties and obligations go with offices, positions and relationships to others. The demands to be made on somebody in virtue of his occupation of a certain position may indeed be, and often are, quite explicitly listed in considerable detail. And when we call someone conscientious or say that he has a strong sense of his obligations or of duty, we do not ordinarily mean that he is haunted by the ghost of the idea of supernatural ordinances; we mean rather such things as this, that he can be counted on for sustained effort to do what is required of him in definite capacities, to fulfil the demand made on him as student or teacher or parent or soldier or whatever he may be.
>
> (Strawson 1961: 33)

Just so; and I suspect that the same 'methodological' failings which can blind us to those truths can also blind us to truths about a related matter.

The original Christian conception of moral facts cast in terms of the commands of the Christian God, in terms of 'supernatural ordinances', was of course accompanied by a belief in the capacity of human beings both freely to obey and freely to disobey those commands. And the general concept of 'free will' thereby introduced was then encapsulated within the conceptions of certain distinctively Christian vices and virtues. Now, at one point – when writing of Schopenhauer – Nietzsche remarks of 'the "will" ' that it is 'the greatest piece of psychological false-coinage in history, Christianity alone excepted' (1968b: 80). The coinage is false because it postulates 'imaginary *causes*' (1968a: 125), because it introduces the 'false' concept of 'spiritual causality' (ibid.: 151). In so doing it produces an immediate clash between any system of thought and practice incorporating this postulate and science: '*moral*: science is the forbidden in itself – it alone is forbidden. Science is the first sin, the germ of all sins, *original* sin. *This alone constitutes morality*' (Nietzsche 1968a: 164).

As before, Nietzsche's target seems to shift in his discussion of this theme; but at the risk of becoming the very worst of readers, we might attempt the following reconstruction of one of his thoughts here. The original Christian conception of moral facts in terms of 'supernatural ordinances' presumed the existence of 'free will', of 'spiritual causality': an anti-scientific and false presumption of the truth of what has been called 'the obscure and panicky metaphysics of libertarianism' (Strawson 1962: 25). And that presumption has been bequeathed to any system of *moral* thought and practice worthy, so to say, of the name. The content of that presumption is an essential component of the theory internal to moral thought and practice; the falsity of that presumption represents 'the problem of morality itself'.

We should make three concessions to that view of the matter. First, let us concede that Nietzsche is right about the place occupied within the original Christian conception of moral facts by some general concept of 'free will'. Second, let us also allow that there are certain elements found within that original conception which presuppose the coherence of some obscure and panicky concept of 'spiritual causality'. And, finally, let us admit too that many subscribers to moralities express attachment to this obscure and panicky metaphysics of libertarianism. The point now is that conceding all that leaves us short of conceding the conclusion Nietzsche wishes to draw.

To see that, first remember the strict irrelevance of matters of origin for questions of present use or purpose. Next, let us disregard any elements of the kind referred to within the second of the concessions made. And, finally, let us now contemplate the possible outcomes of abandonment of the almost entirely abstract level of consideration of this matter in favour of a detailed consideration of the practices of those referred to in the third of the concessions made: a consideration of their specific practices, I say, not a consideration of what at an almost entirely abstract level they say about those practices. The following possibility can now be recognized even for those subscribers who express attachment to the libertarian metaphysics:

that in their specific practices – for example, in the details of their specific *uses* of the concepts of responsibility and accountability and of related more specific concepts – the attachment so expressed is *idle*. That is to say, consideration of their specific practices reveals that attachment as playing no role in the generation of those practices. The attachment is a bequest from Christian morality and perhaps from the Kantian conception of morality but is none the less an *external* bequest in relation to their moral practice. That is the possibility which I take Strawson to have been exploring in his classic paper on the subject (Strawson 1962). I take him to have shown, moreover, that at least many of *our* practices in relation to ascriptions of responsibility or of accountability would be quite untouched were science to establish the truth of some deterministic thesis incompatible with libertarianism: 'it would not follow from that [deterministic] thesis that nobody decides to do anything; that nobody ever does anything intentionally; that it is false that people sometimes know perfectly well what they are doing' (ibid.: 3). That is: our actual ascriptions of responsibility and accountability are grounded upon conceptual considerations which are neutral in relation to the abstract debate between 'determinists' and 'libertarians', so that any stance taken within the terms of that debate is a stance external to our actual practice of making such ascriptions. I thus see no reason for thinking that 'morality itself', in virtue of its use of the concepts of responsibility and of accountability, *requires* a stance within that debate.

But let me add some disclaimers. First, it is no consequence of what has just been said that the possibility of mutual interaction between practices and participants' claims about those practices is denied. Nor is it a consequence of what has been said that participants' claims about their practices are always irrelevant when considering the matter of the theories internal to those practices. And, finally, it is no part of this present account to claim that the possibility at issue – that of 'theoretical' attachments on the part of participants which are external to their actual practices – is one which, when realized, is always easily detected. Thus a more recent remark of Strawson's:

> [T]here is a quite general ambiguity in the notion of 'our ordinary concept' of whatever it may be. Should the lineaments of such a concept be drawn exclusively from its use, from our ordinary *practice*, or should we add the reflective accretions, however

confused, which, naturally or historically, gather round it? The distinction is hardly clear-cut; but where it can be made, I prefer the first alternative.

(Strawson 1980: 265)

But this requisite caution leaves the main point untouched. There seems no more impossibility in a morality free of 'imaginary *causes*', free of 'spiritual causality', than there is in one free of 'the ghost of the idea of supernatural ordinances' – or than there is in one free of Christian morality's characteristic obsession with matters of humility, guilt and punishment; and that seems to be confirmed by the actual existence, widespread or not, of moralities free of such paraphernalia. The target actually hit by Nietzsche's criticisms is still worth aiming at; but it should not be confused with 'morality itself'.

Alasdair MacIntyre holds that Nietzsche's criticisms of morality rest upon an illegitimate generalization from a temporally particular gravely disordered condition of morality (MacIntyre 1981: 107). But if what has just been said is right the truth seems somewhat different. Some of Nietzsche's criticisms of morality can indeed be understood as resting upon an illegitimate generalization – but from the particular theories internal to certain theologically-based moralities – while others of those criticisms seem rather to rest upon the presumption that it is Kant who has supplied us with the correct philosophical description of the theory internal to 'morality itself'. Stretching the point we might say that these latter criticisms rest upon an illegitimate generalization from truly Kantian moralities. But I think the following a more useful observation: the criticisms of morality so far considered rest upon a misidentification of the theory internal to 'morality itself', a misidentification of the general institution of morality.

IF GOD IS DEAD

I want now to move away from Nietzsche's attempts at showing the theory internal to morality to be incoherent or false or senseless to consider some distinct kinds of criticisms which can be aimed at morality. The bridge for this movement has but four planks, two in my own words, two in Nietzsche's:

1 in general moralities are remarkably ineffectual in terms of their influence, 'active' and 'personal', upon subscribers to them: while facilitating all too well negative moral judgements about others

and their actions – a fact which will cause no surprise to those who appreciate Nietzsche's discussion of the conceptual primacy of evil or my Mandevillian discussion of the pragmatics of moral discourse – moralities are in general ineffectual in terms of moral influence on one's self, on one's character and motivations;

2 the exceptions to that first remark are provided in general by fanatical and repugnant moralities or parts of moralities, by immoral moralities or parts of moralities;

3 'we may set down as our chief proposition that to *make* morality one must have the unconditioned will to the contrary' (Nietzsche 1968b: 58); and

4 '*every* means hitherto employed with the intention of making mankind moral has been thoroughly *immoral*' (ibid.: 59).

There is more than one thematic difference between Nietzsche's remarks and mine. His concern is with the *moralizing* question of the means which might reasonably be adopted with an eye to the end of making more moral some *group of others* (perhaps as large as mankind itself – less oneself!). Nietzsche's thought on that question seems to be this: once we appreciate that God is not around to fix things otherwise, we might discover that the only moralizing means which could in fact work towards the stated end are themselves immoral. As Philippa Foot puts it: 'If God is dead nothing guarantees that evil may not be the condition of good' (Foot 1973: 87). As a claim about what might be the case that looks close to undeniable, but consideration of whether it is actually the case would be a complicated matter. Such consideration would need to distinguish at least three kinds of contexts: those in which the subjects to be moralized lack the pertinent moral concepts; those in which, while apparently having those concepts, the subjects concerned see no connection between judgements expressed in terms of them and reasons for acting; and those in which while the subjects see such a connection, yet the force of the resulting reasons for acting is comparatively weak. Here I prefer, however, to consider the analogue of Nietzsche's moralizing question in the individual case: the question, that is, of the means which might reasonably be adopted by an *individual* agent with the end of making *himself* more moral. But my preference for this individual question is meant as no denial of the importance of the collective question 'How might *we* make *ourselves* more moral?'; even less is that preference meant as a denial of the importance of the matter as to why the individual question arises much less frequently than Nietzsche's moralizing question within actual moral thought.

In fact my individual question still covers too wide a terrain; in what follows I shall narrow the focus a little more. Earlier (p. 82) we encountered Judith Baker's discussion of a proposal contemplated by Grice in relation to the 'internalist–externalist' debate. The proposal was this: 'if John thinks he ought to do some action *a*, then that requires that either John wants to *a* or he thinks he ought to want to *a*'. This proposal 'can be regressively applied', and that leads Judith Baker to the suggestion that for 'real people' the original judgements of obligation will be 'cashed out' in a desire *at some level*: thus John, being a real person, will either want to *a* or want to want to *a* or want to want to want to *a* or. . . . Now, suppose that in a given case the judgement of obligation is 'cashed out' in a desire of the second level: John thinks he ought to do some action *a*, does not in fact want to *a*, but does in fact want to want to *a*. Then John knows that the moral considerations are not sufficient to produce the first-level desire to act but only the second-level desire; but given that he does in fact have that second-level desire, John might hunt around for other, non-moral considerations, recognition of which would be sufficient to produce in him the lacking first-level desire. And if that hunt is successful, if such non-moral considerations are found and the corresponding first-level desire produced, John might act in a way which coincides externally with the content of his recognized obligation.

But would such an action be of moral worth? Kant held that for moral action our motives have to be pure: an action has 'genuine moral worth' only if it is performed '*only* from duty and without any inclination' (1959: 14, emphasis added). That claim is difficult to interpret: to side-step questions of textual exegesis, let us attribute to Kant, fairly or unfairly, the doctrine that for an action to have moral worth the *only* motivating considerations in favour of that action which can be contemplated within the agent's practical deliberations are moral ones. It follows on this view that, in the case just described, John's action has no moral worth. But while that consequence might seem intelligible in terms of some model of ideal moral agents, it might also seem unduly harsh in relation to 'real people'. Thus Judith Baker can be understood as defending a *modified* Kantian position which allows that John's action can indeed have 'genuine moral worth'. For on this modified Kantian position, other, non-moral motivating considerations in favour of the action concerned are allowed to enter into the agent's practical deliberations as long as they are subordinate to the moral considerations: the *primacy* of the moral motivating considerations is deemed compatible with some *secondary* or *derivative* role within the agent's practical deliberations for other, non-moral motivating considerations. And it seems that a similar possibility would be allowed upon this modified Kantian position for cases in which, while the agent does in fact have some pertinent first-level desire on the basis of moral considerations alone, yet he doubts the strength of that desire to be sufficient to issue in the corresponding action. He has a second-level desire that his first-level desire be stronger: so he will be allowed to hunt for other motivating considerations to *back up* the moral desire.

The first point to note about this modified Kantian position issues in a worry analogous to Nietzsche's complaint in the case of groups of others. For that position to give a plausible account of the circumstances in which an action has 'genuine moral worth' it is surely necessary that a further condition be incorporated within it: namely, that the secondary motivating considerations *not be immoral*. If that secondary motivation were grounded in malice or cruelty, then, notwithstanding any external coincidence with the agent's obligation, his action surely cannot be one with 'genuine moral worth'. Moreover, that condition might fail to be satisfied by a wide range of cases. Suppose, for example, that the secondary motivation concerned is grounded upon the desire for pleasure. It will prove necessary, before accepting the action concerned to have 'genuine moral worth', to consider the possibility that the production of the pleasure concerned depends upon immoral considerations – the diverse kinds of consideration involved, for example, in hypocrisy or pride or self-satisfaction or boastfulness or vanity or sanctimoniousness. Let us call the account incorporating this further condition the *modified modified* Kantian account.

Moral values are not the only practical values subscribed to by human beings; and so, within the terms of the modified modified account, the 'genuine moral worth' of an action is compatible with its being the outcome of a deliberative process in which evaluative considerations of other, non-moral kinds are invoked by the agent so as to bring about the first-level desire acted upon. But three points must be noted about this. First, any moral view which takes all other, non-moral values to be immoral will deny that possibility.

Second, certain views about *effective* motivational considerations also require denial of the possibility. For Nietzsche, 'the overriding and underlying principle of human behaviour is the will to power' (Foot 1973: 94), and that is therefore the only principle which could be operative within any effective secondary motivation. But suppose that is accepted along with the thought that such a will to power is immoral: there will then, on the modified modified Kantian position, be no possibility of secondary motivations which are both effective and morally acceptable. The result of impossibility is only forthcoming upon the assumption of the truth of Nietzsche's theory as to *the* principle determining *all* human behaviour; but, as Philippa Foot has it, 'general theories about the springs of action are traps for philosophers' (ibid.). We should therefore note as a third point that the replacement of Nietzsche's theory of human motivation by certain more cautious accounts still serves to yield a scepticism about the likelihood of actions of 'genuine moral worth'. For example,

[H]uman beings are naturally selfish. . . . [That] seems true on the evidence, whenever and wherever we look at them, in spite of a very small number of apparent exceptions. About the quality of this selfishness modern psychology has had something to tell us. The psyche is a historically determined individual relentlessly looking after itself. In some ways it resembles a machine; in order to operate it needs sources of energy, and it is predisposed to certain patterns of activity. The area of its vaunted freedom of choice is not usually very great. One of its main pastimes is daydreaming. It is reluctant to face unpleasant realities. Its consciousness is not normally a transparent glass through which it views the world, but a cloud of more or less fantastic reverie designed to protect the psyche from pain. It constantly seeks consolation, either through imagined inflation of self or through fictions of a theological nature. Even its loving is more often than not an assertion of self. I think we can probably recognize ourselves in this rather depressing description.

(Murdoch 1970: 78–9)

Thus Irish Murdoch under the influence of Freud; if anything captures the mundane counterpart of the doctrine of original sin it is surely that description of man. And one who accepts it will surely think that even on the modified modified Kantian position cases of actions of 'genuine moral worth' will be rare: for in general any *effective* secondary motivation will have to be grounded upon the 'naturally selfish' part of human beings.

A second complicating point about that position should now be noted. 'Genuine moral worth' can be conceded to an action according to that position even when the action is the outcome of some secondary motivating consideration as long as that secondary motivating consideration is morally no worse than neutral. But how exactly is this talk of secondary, or subordinate, or derivative, motivating considerations to be understood? It is not sufficient to construe such talk in merely causal–historical terms. Consider the agent John once more. He thinks he ought to do some action a, does not in fact want to a, but does in fact want to want to a; he is therefore led to hunt for other, no worse than morally neutral, motivating considerations recognition of which would in the circumstances be sufficient to produce a first-level desire whose content coincides externally with that of the presently lacking first-level desire. Suppose his hunt successful: then he has come to appreciate those other motivating considerations only because of his recognition of his moral obligation. But suppose that that recognition disappears and that he none the less comes to act upon the first-level desire he now has: could this be a case of an action of 'genuine moral worth'? Moreover, it is not sufficient just to impose the further condition that the agent's recognition of his moral obligation, together with the corresponding second-level desire, continues in existence: for that is compatible with the possibility that the fulfilling of his obligation is no more than a (foreseeable) side-effect of his acting upon his first-level desire. Some further condition seems to be needed which captures the idea that the secondary motivating considerations *remain secondary* even though they are the considerations which give rise to the action. There are a number of candidates for such a condition, but whichever be the favoured one the final account faces a further difficulty: the range of application of the consequent notion of 'genuine moral worth' is likely to be much restricted in fact in the light of the empirical difficulty of reconciling the force and vivacity of the secondary motivating considerations requisite for their issuing in the first-level desire with their *continuing* secondary status.

Perhaps over-ambitiously, the moral I wish to extract from this discussion is that *if* we accept some less harsh but still plausible variant of the Kantian account of what it is for an action to have 'genuine moral worth', there are good reasons for thinking there to be a considerable difficulty in general about the likelihood of actions of 'real people' which have that worth.

Doubtless much of what has been said for the individual case carries over to the case of moralizing some group of others; it is also doubtless true that in the latter case other considerations come into play which perhaps lend support to Nietzsche's claim that '*every means hitherto employed with the intention of making mankind moral has been thoroughly immoral*' (1968b: 59). Think, for example, of the 'social sanction' of punishment and of what passes itself off as 'moral education'; or think, more abstractly, of Mandeville's Manichean conception of the universe. Moreover, if the primary concern of our moral thought becomes that of judging and moralizing *others*, moral consideration of the means to that end – of *our* means to that end – will fall into neglect; and with that fall the risk to which Nietzsche drew attention will increase, perhaps almost to the limit.

THE MOLE AND DWARF

I wish finally to move from consideration of the means to morality to consideration of the distinct, though related, matter of morality's effects ('related' since means have effects too). But first let us note that when now talking of morality's effects the talk is unlikely to be of the effects of actions of 'genuine moral worth': such rare items are likely to have few effects. Rather, as with certain theses of Mandeville's, that talk should be understood in general in terms of the effects of the general (unspecified) deployment of moral categories of thought.

Predictably, there is a difficulty once more about the target of Nietzsche's attacks. At times it is clear that his target is some group of distinctively Christian virtues, most frequently those of pity and compassion:

> [A]s though humility, chastity, poverty, in a word *holiness*, had not hitherto done life unutterably more harm than any sort of frightfulness or vice or whatever. . . . Pure spirit is pure lie. . . .
> (Nietzsche 1968a: 119–20; cf. Hume on 'monkish virtues', see p. 134)

> With truths held back, with foolish hand and foolish-fond heart and rich in pity's little lies – that is how I used to live among men.
> (Nietzsche 1961: 204)

Pity teaches him to lie who lives among the good. Pity makes the air stifling for all free souls. For the stupidity of the good is unfathomable.

(ibid.: 204–5)

Alas, where in the world have there been greater follies than with the compassionate? And what in the world has caused more suffering than the follies of the compassionate?

(ibid.: 249)

But sometimes it seems clear that Nietzsche has a more extensive target in mind, a target tantamount to 'morality itself':

Refraining mutually from injury, violence, and exploitation and placing one's will on a par with that of someone else – this may become, in a certain rough sense, good manners among individuals if the appropriate conditions are present (namely, if those men are actually similar in strength and value standards and belong together in *one* body). But as soon as this principle is extended, and possibly even accepted as the *fundamental principle of society*, it immediately proves to be what it really is – a will to the *denial* of life, a principle of disintegration and decay.

(Nietzsche 1966a: 393)

I go among this people and keep my eyes open: they have become *smaller* and are becoming ever smaller: *and their doctrine of happiness and virtue is the cause*.

For they are modest even in virtue – for they want ease. But only a modest virtue is compatible with ease.

(Nietzsche 1961: 189)

Finally, one of the clearest passages in which Nietzsche brings cause and effect together:

The highest and strongest drives, when they break out passionately and drive the individual far above the average and the flats of the herd conscience, wreck the self-confidence of the community, its faith in itself, and it is as if its spine snapped. Hence just those drives are branded and slandered most. High and independent spirituality, the will to stand alone, even a powerful reason are experienced as dangers; everything that elevates an individual above the herd and intimidates the neighbor is henceforth called *evil*; and the fair, modest, submissive, conforming mentality, the *mediocrity* of desires attains moral designations and honors.

(Nietzsche 1966a: 303–4)

Thus morality expresses an 'absurd' expectation and demand: 'that strength will not manifest itself as strength, as the desire to overcome' (Nietzsche 1956b: 178). And the effect of its doing so is 'a form of decay, namely the diminution of man, making him mediocre and lowering his value' (1966a: 307). In the light of that fact we need to return to the question of 'what type of human being one ought to *breed*, ought to *will*, as more valuable, more worthy of life, more certain of the future' (1968a: 116); and if drawn to Nietzsche's own answer to that question – if drawn to the propagation of forerunners of the *Übermensch*, to the production of 'a prologue to better players' – we shall realize that that requires the total abandonment of morality, of 'all morality', of 'morality itself'.

A number of questions which arise in relation to this further criticism of morality and the moral drawn have been much discussed elsewhere, so I need make only brief mention of them here. One question arising relates to the *kind* of value-judgement involved in Nietzsche's talk of 'decay' and of a type of human being who is of more value. Strawson might perhaps hold such judgements to fall within the more general region of the ethical in contrast to the more specific area of the moral: to fall, that is, within the region of 'evaluations such as *can* govern choices and decisions which are of the greatest importance to men', within the region in which are found attempts to present 'some ideal image of a form of life . . . [which] may evoke a response of the liveliest sympathy from those whose own patterns of life are as remote as possible from conformity to the image expressed' (Strawson 1961: 27–8). Philippa Foot sees the matter in more detailed terms (Foot 1973: 90–3). On the one hand there is common ground between Nietzsche's system and that of 'traditional and particularly Greek morality' in virtue both of Nietzsche's insistence upon the importance of self-discipline and of his concern with the question of 'the way in which men must live in order to *live well*'. (Although we must note that much of 'Greek morality' seems to fall within the more general region which Strawson calls 'the ethical' rather than within that of 'the moral'.) But on the other hand, (i) Nietzsche at one point explicitly assimilates his value-judgements to those of aesthetics; (ii) he rejects any idea of rules of *specific* behaviour which shall be uniform throughout the community; (iii) he even rejects the idea that his kind of virtue should be preached to *all* men; and (iv) he is apparently prepared to abandon the considerations of justice in order to clear the way for the *Übermensch*. So while there is no tidy answer to the question the balance is fairly clearly in favour of denying that Nietzsche's evaluations are moral ones. Perhaps, so to say, we should see him as an *ethical immoralist*.

A second question relates to the *content* of Nietzsche's value-judgements about the *Übermensch* (and so about the prologue to them and about the effects of morality). More than one philosopher has remarked upon 'the emptiness of the Nietzschean ideal' of the *Übermensch* (MacIntyre 1966: 225), upon the absence of *determinate* values in that supposed ideal: 'Nietzsche's view is all wind-up and no pitch', if you like (Nozick 1981: 566–7n). One can be *almost anything* in a creative, self-disciplined, life-embracing way. (The most Russell could make of the ideal was this: 'very like Siegfried except that he knows Greek'; and then a characteristic aside: 'This may seem odd, but that is not my fault' (Russell 1946: 788).) But since, as Alasdair MacIntyre has noted (1966: 225), that failing was one of the features of Nietzsche's writings which permitted his misrepresentation at the hands of his sister, we might well feel that he has been posthumously punished for it more than enough.

A third question, emphasized by Mrs Foot, is the *empirical* one of whether Nietzsche is right in his claims about the historical effects of morality and the future effects of enactment of his programme for better players. But that question would require considerable sharpening before any reasonable answer to it could be given: *Morality versus Life* is not the best defined of battle lines.

To end, however, I wish to consider another question: how *could* morality have the dramatic effects which Nietzsche attributes to it? How could morality, the system of mere moral *ideas*, be historically so important and humanly so disastrous? (Compare the generally mythical claims about the importance for society, the species and the world of immorality – of immoral *actions*). It is true that Nietzsche thinks morality to have been created precisely to have such effects; but we should remember the strict irrelevance of matters of origin to questions of present use or purpose – or effects. So what features of morality *as it now exists* could enable it to have such dramatic powers? Any answer on Nietzsche's part would be a complex one; none the less, I think a large part of the explanatory burden within that answer would be carried by the following considerations:

But he has discovered himself who says: This is my good and

evil: he has silenced thereby the mole and dwarf who says: 'Good for all, evil for all'.

(Nietzsche 1961: 212)

'This – is now *my* way: where is yours?' Thus I answered those who asked me 'the way'. For *the* way – does not exist!

(ibid.: 213)

Reality shows us an enchanting wealth of types, the luxuriance of a prodigal play and change of forms: and does some pitiful journeyman moralist say at the sight of it: 'No! man ought to be different'? . . . He even knows *how* man ought to be, this bigoted wretch; he paints himself on the wall and says '*ecce homo*'!

(Nietzsche 1968b: 46)

[O]ne makes a morality, a virtue, a holiness for oneself, one unites the good conscience with seeing *falsely* – one demands that no *other* kind of perspective shall be accorded any value. . . .

(Nietzsche 1968a: 120)

Now, let us concede it to be inherent in 'morality itself' that at least some moral values are in some sense 'universal' – 'Good for all, evil for all' – and even that those values are in some sense 'fixed' – '*Over* the stream everything is firmly fixed, all the values of things, the bridges, concepts, all "Good" and "Evil": all are *firmly fixed*!' (Nietzsche 1961: 218). Those concessions should be understood in terms which render them compatible with the earlier discussions here of the subjectivity of values, of moral discrepancies and of 'moral relativisms' (Chapters 3 and 5). But so understood those concessions are far from sufficient to explain how morality could have the dramatic effects which Nietzsche attributes to it. If it is to be morality *itself* which explains the 'decay' of man, which explains the *lowering* tendency to *uniformity*, morality must also contain within itself the doctrine that moral values are 'overriding' if not the stronger doctrine that moral values are the only true values. Once again, Nietzsche seems to think it Kant who has discovered the theory internal to 'morality itself':

[Kant] designed a reason specifically for the case in which one was supposed not to have to bother about reason, namely when morality, when the sublime demand 'thou shalt' makes itself heard. If one considers that the philosopher is, in virtually all nations, only the further development of the priestly type, one is no longer surprised to discover this heirloom of the priest, *self-*

deceptive fraudulence. If one has sacred tasks, for example that of improving, saving, redeeming mankind – if one carries the divinity in one's bosom, is the mouthpiece of an other-world imperative, such a mission already places one outside all merely reasonable evaluations. . . .

(Nietzsche 1968a: 123)

But if Nietzsche were right on this, both Strawson's discussion of the complex relations between social moralities and individual ideals and my earlier discussion of questions about the reach of morality would have been incoherent; they were not, so he is not. Whatever be the historical truths about morality's companions and their effects, those truths must be distinguished from truths about the nature of morality; and the praiseworthy desire to censure some of those historical companions must be separated from the desire to criticize 'morality itself'.

Instead of worrying about the risk of finding myself among the worst of readers, I could perhaps have contented myself with reference to the remark of Nietzsche's about the history of philosophy with which the second part of this essay began (forgetting – please – the word 'better'). But while I have tried neither to soil nor to confuse nor to blaspheme, I do not think of this discussion of Nietzsche as having built so much as having dismantled and shed. In particular I have tried to show that there is no good reason for thinking that the theory internal to moral thought and practice makes sense only upon presuppositions of a theological character pp. 206–8, nor for thinking that theory to contain the obscure and panicky metaphysics of libertarianism (pp. 208–11), nor for thinking it to include some objectionably strong doctrine of the sovereignty of the moral over all other practical values (pp. 221–2). In each case the risk suggested in the introduction to this essay that a scepticism about morality be based upon a misidentification of the theory internal to moral thought and practice arises. Some of what that theory does contain has been suggested here (p. 184; see also pp. 207 and 219–21), and some important consequent scepticisms about morality have in effect been countered (Chapters 4 and 5). But I should recognize that the partial conception of morality which thus emerges is one unlikely to arouse – in either theoretical or practical terms, in subscribers or in critics – *Enthusiasm*, whose true sources are 'Hope, pride, presumption, a warm imagination, together with ignorance' (Hume

1963b: 76); but I think it far from the worse for that. Evangelism, however worthy its cause, remains distasteful.

In this closing chapter I have however also tried to indicate some features of our moral thought and practice which might constitute the starting-point for a distinctive doubt about morality. Combining either Mandeville's or Nietzsche's account of human nature with the Kantian account of what it is for an action to have genuine moral worth produces the consequence that such action is impossible for human beings (pp. 194–6, 213–15). But even just combining a more cautious but still morally pessimistic account of human nature with a weakened but plausible Kantian conception of genuine moral worth produces the consequence that there is a general unlikelihood of actual human actions with that worth (pp. 213–16). That Kantian conception represents one possible answer to the question, expressed in the terms of the first part of this essay, of whether and when moral valuings within the areas shaped by potential desires of kinds (3) and (4) morally admit of backing-up by other kinds of valuings and desirings (Chapter 3); but I must confess to being desperately unclear whether that or some other Kantian conception of what it is for an action to have genuine moral worth is indeed part of the theory internal to moral thought and practice (cf. p. 196). But even if it is just the case that that is generally *believed* to be so, that belief could combine with general acceptance of some morally pessimistic account of human nature to produce certain *morally* disagreeable features of the use of moral thought and discourse which are found, I think, in our actual use (pp. 201–3). Perhaps it is recognition of those features which is partly responsible for recent interest in the matter of 'moral relativism'; but if that is so, the consequent 'relativist' proposals restricting moral criticism fall into the error of presenting theoretical solutions to a *practical* problem – the same error found in many discussions of the internal reach of morality (p. 150). To repeat: I do not know if some Kantian conception of the genuine moral worth of actions is part of the theory internal to moral thought and practice. But if that is so, and if in consequence morality's aspirations are in general ill-fitted to our nature, to 'our inward Make', then *decision* is called for; and in this context the retort that idealization is nothing to be apologized for within an account of the nature of moral action would need to be balanced against at least moral evaluation of the actual effects of that mismatch. It might even turn out, that is, that moral considerations suggest that most of us ought to abandon the very terms of reference of the institution of morality.

Afterwords

There was a madman in Seville who hit on one of the funniest absurdities and manias that any madman in the world ever gave way to, and it was this. He made a tube of reed sharp at one end, and catching a dog in the street or wherever it might be, with his foot he held one of its legs and with his hand lifted up the other and as best he could inserted the tube where, by blowing, he made the dog round as a ball. Then, holding it in this position, he gave it a couple of slaps on the belly and let it go. 'Do your worships think, now', he said to the bystanders who were always there in abundance, 'that it is an easy thing to blow up a dog?' Does your worship think now that it is an easy thing to write a book?

(Cervantes)

The Men of Letters labouring under this Distemper discover quite different Symptoms. When they envy a Person for his Parts and Erudition, their chief Care is industriously to conceal their Frailty, which generally is attempted by denying and depreciating the good Qualities they envy: They carefully peruse his Works, and are displeas'd at every fine Passage they meet with; they look for nothing but his Errors, and wish for no greater Feast than a gross Mistake: In their Censures they are captious as well as severe, make Mountains of Molehills, and will not pardon the least Shadow of a Fault, but exaggerate the most trifling Omission into a Capital Blunder.

(Mandeville)

Bibliography of philosophical works referred to

Anscombe, G. E. M. (1958) 'Modern moral philosophy', *Philosophy*, 33.
— (1963) *Intention*, Oxford.
Baker, Judith (1986) 'Do one's motives have to be pure?', in Richard E. Grandy and Richard Warner (eds), *Philosophical Grounds of Rationality*, Oxford.
Blackburn, Simon (1984) *Spreading The Word*, Oxford.
Brentano, Franz (1969) *The Origin of our Knowledge of Right and Wrong* (trs. Roderick M. Chisholm and Elizabeth H. Schneewind), London.
Davidson, Donald (1963) 'Actions, reasons and causes', *Journal of Philosophy*, 60.
— (1967) 'Causal relations', *Journal of Philosophy*, 64; reprinted in Donald Davidson, *Essays on Actions and Events*, Oxford 1980, to which page references are made.
— (1969) 'How is weakness of the will possible?', in Joel Feinberg (ed.), *Moral Concepts*, Oxford; reprinted in Donald Davidson, *Essays on Actions and Events*, Oxford 1980, to which page references are made.
— (1976) 'Hume's cognitive theory of pride', *Journal of Philosophy*, 73; reprinted in Donald Davidson, *Essays on Actions and Events*, Oxford 1980, to which page references are made.
Dent, N. J. H. (1984) *The Moral Psychology Of The Virtues*, Cambridge.
Elster, Jon (1984) *Ulysses and the Sirens*, Cambridge.
Falk, W. D. (1947–8) ' "Ought" and Motivation', *Proceedings of the Aristotelian Society*, 48; reprinted in Wilfrid Sellars and John Hospers (eds), *Readings in Ethical Theory*, New York 1952, to which page references are made.
Foot, Philippa (1963) 'Hume on moral judgement', in D. F. Pears (ed.), *David Hume: A Symposium*, London.
— (1972a) 'Morality as a system of hypothetical imperatives', *Philosophical Review*, 81.
— (1972b) 'Reasons for actions and desires', *Proceedings of the Aristotelian Society, Supplementary Volume*; reprinted in Philippa Foot, *Virtues and Vices*, Oxford 1978, to which page references are made.
— (1973) 'Nietzsche: the revaluation of values', in R. C. Solomon (ed.), *Nietzsche*, New York; reprinted in Philippa Foot, *Virtues and Vices*, Oxford 1978, to which page references are made.
— (1978) 'Moral relativism', The Lindley Lecture at the University of

Kansas; reprinted in Jack W. Meiland and Michael Krausz (eds), *Relativism: Cognitive and Moral*, Notre Dame, Indiana, 1982, to which page references are made.

Gallie, W. B. (1955–6) 'Essentially contested concepts', *Proceedings of the Aristotelian Society*, 56.

Hampshire, Stuart (1959) *Thought and Action*, London.

Harman, Gilbert (1975) 'Moral relativism defended', *Philosophical Review*, 84; reprinted in Jack W. Meiland and Michael Krausz (eds), *Relativism: Cognitive and Moral*, Notre Dame, Indiana, 1982, to which page references are made.

Hume, David (1888) *A Treatise of Human Nature* (ed. L. A. Selby-Bigge), Oxford.

—(1902) *Enquiries Concerning Human Understanding And Concerning The Principles of Morals* (ed. L. A. Selby-Bigge), Oxford.

—(1963a) 'Of luxury', in David Hume, *Essays and Treatises on Several Subjects*, Oxford.

—(1963b) 'Of superstition and enthusiasm', in David Hume, *Essays: Moral, Political and Literary*, Oxford.

Kant, Immanuel (1959) *Foundations of the Metaphysics of Morals* (trs. Lewis White Beck), New York.

Kenny, Anthony (1963) *Action, Emotion and Will*, London.

Law, William (1845) *Remarks upon a late Book entitled The Fable of the Bees*, Cambridge.

McDowell, John (1978) 'Are moral requirements hypothetical imperatives?', *Proceedings of the Aristotelian Society, Supplementary Volume*.

—(1979) 'Virtue and reason', *The Monist*, 62.

—(1982) 'Reason and action', *Philosophical Investigations*, 5.

—(1985) 'Values and secondary qualities', in Ted Honderich (ed.), *Morality and Objectivity*, London.

McGinn, Colin (1983) *The Subjective View*, Oxford.

MacIntyre, Alasdair (1966) *A Short History of Ethics*, London.

—(1981) *After Virtue*, London.

Mackie, J. L. (1977) *Ethics*, Harmondsworth.

—(1980) *Hume's Moral Theory*, London.

Mandeville, Bernard de (1711) *A treatise of the hypochondriack and hysteric passions, vulgarly call'd the hypo in men and vapours in women . . . in three dialogues*, London.

—(1720) *Free thoughts on religion, the church, and national happiness*, London.

—(1724) *A modest defence of publick stews: or, An essay upon whoring as it is now practis'd in these kingdoms*, London.

—(1732a) *A letter to Dion, occasion'd by his book call'd Alciphron, or The minute philosopher*, London.

—(1732b) *An enquiry into the origin of honour, and the usefulness of Christianity in war*, London.

—(1924) *The Fable Of The Bees, Part II* (ed. F. B. Kaye), Oxford.

—(1970) *The Fable Of The Bees* (ed. Phillip Harth), Harmondsworth.

Mill, John Stuart (1910) *Utilitarianism, Liberty, Representative Government*, London.

Monro, Hector (1975) *The Ambivalence Of Bernard Mandeville*, Oxford.

Murdoch, Iris (1970) *The Sovereignty of Good*, London.

Nagel, Thomas (1970) *The Possibility of Altruism*, Oxford.

—(1978) 'Equality', *Crítica*, 10; reprinted in Thomas Nagel, *Mortal Questions*, Cambridge 1979, to which page references are made.

Nietzsche, Friedrich (1956) (a) *The Birth of Tragedy* and *(b) The Genealogy of Morals*, (trs. Francis Golffing), New York.

—(1961) *Thus Spoke Zarathustra* (trs. R. J. Hollingdale), Harmondsworth.

—(1966a) *Beyond Good and Evil*, in Walter Kaufman (trs. and ed.), *Basic Writings of Nietzsche*, New York.

—(1966b) *Mixed Opinions and Maxims*, in Walter Kaufman (trs. and ed.) *Basic Writings of Nietzsche*, New York.

—(1966c) *The Wanderer and His Shadow*, in Walter Kaufman (trs. and ed.), *Basic Writings of Nietzsche*, New York.

—(1968) (a) *The Anti-Christ* and (b) *Twilight of the Idols* (trs. R. J. Hollingdale), Harmondsworth.

Nozick, Robert (1981) *Philosophical Explanations*, Oxford.

O'Shaughnessy, Brian (1980) *The Will*, Cambridge.

Pears, David (1964) 'Predicting and deciding', *Proceedings of the British Academy*, 50.

Platts, Mark (1979) *Ways of Meaning*, London.

—(1980a) 'Kind words and understanding', *Crítica*, 12.

—(1980b) 'Moral reality and the end of desire', in Mark Platts (ed.), *Reference, Truth And Reality*, London.

—(1983a) 'Explanatory kinds', *British Journal for the Philosophy of Science*, 34.

—(1983b) 'La naturaleza del mundo moral', *Análisis Filosófico*, 3.

Putnam, Hilary (1981) *Reason, Truth And History*, Cambridge.

Reid, Thomas (1969) *Essays on the Active Powers of Man*, Cambridge, Mass.

Richards, David A. J. (1971) *A Theory Of Reasons For Action*, Oxford.

Russell, Bertrand (1921) *The Analysis of Mind*, London.

—(1946) *A History of Western Philosophy*, London.

Schiffer, Stephen (1976) 'The paradox of desire', *American Philosophical Quarterly*, 13.

Smith, Michael (1987) 'The Humean theory of motivation', *Mind*, 96.

Strawson, P. F. (1959) *Individuals*, London.

—(1961) 'Social morality and individual ideal', *Philosophy*, 36; reprinted in P. F. Strawson, *Freedom And Resentment And Other Essays*, London 1974, to which page references are made.

—(1962) 'Freedom and resentment', *Proceedings of the British Academy*, 48; reprinted in P. F. Strawson, *Freedom And Resentment and Other Essays*, London 1974, to which page references are made.

—(1980) 'Reply to Ayer and Bennett', in Zak Van Straaten (ed.), *Philosophical Subjects*, Oxford.

—(1985) *Skepticism And Naturalism: Some Varieties*, London.

Stroud, Barry (1977) *Hume*, London.

Taylor, Richard (1984) *Good And Evil*, Buffalo, NY.

Urmson, J. O. (1946) 'On grading', *Proceedings of the Aristotelian Society, Supplementary Volume*.

—(1958) 'Saints and heroes', in A. I. Melden (ed.), *Essays in Moral Philosophy*, Seattle.

Warnock, G. J. (1971) *The Object of Morality*, London.

Wiggins, David (1976) 'Truth, invention and the meaning of life', *Proceedings of the British Academy*, 62; reprinted in David Wiggins, *Needs, Values, Truth*, Oxford 1987, to which page references are made.

—(1980) *Sameness and Substance*, Oxford.

—(1985) 'Claims of need', in Ted Honderich (ed.), *Morality and Objectivity*, London.

—(1987) 'A sensible subjectivism?', in David Wiggins, *Needs, Values, Truth*, Oxford.

Williams, Bernard (1972) *Morality*, Harmondsworth.

—(1973) 'Egoism and altruism', in Bernard Williams, *Problems of the Self*, Cambridge.

—(1974–5) 'The truth in relativism', *Proceedings of the Aristotelian Society*, 75.

—(1981a) 'Internal and external reasons', in Bernard Williams, *Moral Luck*, Cambridge.

—(1981b) 'Practical necessity', in Bernard Williams, *Moral Luck*, Cambridge.

—(1985) *Ethics and the Limits of Philosophy*, London.

Wittgenstein, Ludwig (1953) *Philosophical Investigations* (trs. G. E. M. Anscombe), Oxford.

Wollheim, Richard (1984) *The Thread of Life*, Cambridge.

Index